How can you have a life as you prepare. You can start by reading the instructions.

_____

After the life-transforming miracle of Don Piper's ninety minutes in Heaven, he continues to share God's healing message on Earth. In *Getting to Heaven*, Piper passes on instructions for fighting life's battles and preparing for eternity in the hereafter.

_____

"Don Piper is a gifted, humorous, life-giving communicator. Don 'got' to heaven. There is no one better than him to encourage us in our process of getting there."
—Kathy Troccoli, singer, author, and speaker

"Don Piper is a master communicator and this book is a must-read for anyone who wants a future that is brighter than this world."
—Carol Kent, speaker and author of *Between a Rock and a Grace Place*

"Because of his journey, Don has a unique ability to give wonderful insight into the last words of Jesus to His disciples. Read this book and you'll get excited about your ultimate destination as well as the journey."
—Dr. Curt Dodd, senior pastor, Westside Church, Omaha, Nebraska

"Practical earthly motivation to prepare for your heavenly destination!"
—Dr. Jay Wolf, senior pastor, First Baptist Church of Montgomery, Alabama

"The book you now hold in your hands is a how-to manual for every living human being. We *arrive* in this world with no instructional guidance but that is now corrected with this *departure* manual. See you at the gate."
—Dr. Samuel R. Chand, leadership architect, change strategist, and author of *Futuring*

Berkley titles by Don Piper and Cecil Murphey

GETTING TO HEAVEN

HEAVEN IS REAL

DAILY DEVOTIONS INSPIRED BY 90 MINUTES IN HEAVEN

GETTING TO HEAVEN

Departing Instructions for Your Life Now

DON PIPER
and CECIL MURPHEY

B

BERKLEY BOOKS, NEW YORK

THE BERKLEY PUBLISHING GROUP
Published by the Penguin Group
Penguin Group (USA) LLC
375 Hudson Street, New York, New York 10014

USA • Canada • UK • Ireland • Australia • New Zealand • India • South Africa • China

penguin.com

A Penguin Random House Company

Berkley trade paperback ISBN: 978-0-425-25593-3

The Library of Congress has catalogued the Berkley hardcover edition as follows:

Piper, Don, 1950–
Getting to heaven : departing instructions for your life now / Don Piper and Cecil Murphey.
p. cm.
ISBN 978-0-425-24028-1
1. Christian life.   2. Heaven—Christianity.   3. Future life—Christianity.
I. Murphey, Cecil.   II. Title.
BV4501.3.P553 2011
248.4—dc22
2010041149

PUBLISHING HISTORY
Berkley hardcover edition / March 2011
Berkley trade paperback edition / November 2014

PRINTED IN THE UNITED STATES OF AMERICA

10   9   8   7   6   5   4   3   2   1

Cover photo by Shae Cardenas/Shutterstock.
Interior text design by Tiffany Estreicher.

Scripture references are taken from:

New King James Version (NKJV) of the *Bible*. Copyright © 1982 by Thomas Nelson, Inc., Publishers.
New International Version (NIV) of the *Holy Bible*. Copyright © 1973, 1978, 1984
International Bible Society. Used by permission of Zondervan Bible Publishers.
New Living Translation (NLT) of the *Holy Bible*. Copyright © 1996, 2004.
Used by permission of Tyndale House Publishers, Inc.,
Wheaton, Illinois 60189. All rights reserved.
Today's New International Version (TNIV) of the *Holy Bible*, Today's New International
Version®. Copyright © 2001, 2005 by Biblica®. Used by permission of Biblica®.
All rights reserved worldwide.
The Message (MSG). Copyright © 1993, 1994, 1995, 1996, 2000, 2001, 2002.
Used by permission of NavPress Publishing Group.

To David Gentiles, beloved friend
Absent from the body . . . present with the Lord

CONTENTS

CONTENTS

ACKNOWLEDGMENTS
FROM DON PIPER

You are holding the fourth book Cec Murphey and I have written together. If it's possible, I am stunned, honored, and humbled at the same time.

I'm deeply indebted to our agent, Deidre Knight, for the unflagging support she has given me in my efforts to bring my life and ministry to the printed page. Deidre, you're the best! To my editor, Denise Silvestro, and Penguin Group (USA), I appreciate your faith in our works and your efforts to get them in the hands of readers.

And to Cec Murphey: When we met at the Christian Writer's Conference in Glorieta, New Mexico, more than ten years ago, neither of us had any idea that we would now be releasing our fourth book together. That was the day we walked down the corridor of the beautiful retreat center and talked of an idea that I had for a biographical account of my death in an auto accident, my visit to Heaven, and my difficult journey to a new normal life.

After much prayer and even more work, *90 Minutes in Heaven: A True Story of Death and Life* was borne out of that meeting. Then came *Daily Devotions Inspired by 90 Minutes in Heaven* and *Heaven Is Real: Lessons on Earthly Joy.* God has blessed our work together and millions of readers around the world have reported being inspired by our books.

This book, *Getting to Heaven: Departing Instructions for Your Life Now* is our latest, and I believe most urgently relevant, collaboration. And I must say that it was Cec's idea to write this book. So I want to say thank you, Cec Murphey, for your encouragement, your boundless talent, but most of all for your friendship. Without a doubt, one of the very best benefits from our book-writing collaborations is that we have become friends. I cherish our times together. While only God can truly judge whether what we have shared in our books is meaningful to others, I know that our work together has been most meaningful to me. Thank you, Cec Murphey, a deeply valued friend and a truly gifted wordsmith.

ACKNOWLEDGMENTS
FROM CECIL ("CEC") MURPHEY

Don and I have had a long journey together that began ten years ago. I'm grateful for Deidre Knight (our agent), Twila Belk (my assistant), and Denise Silvestro (our editor), who've helped to make this book a reality. But most of all, my thanks to Shirley, whom I joined years ago on the heavenly pathway, and we continue walking together today.

1

Before the End

The murmuring of the men in the briefing room betrayed a nervousness that something pivotal was about to happen. When the lieutenant barked, "Ten-hut," it confirmed their premonitions.

War-weary pilots rose to their feet and stood at attention. In strode the commander and his entourage. "At ease, gentlemen," he said and motioned for them to sit.

As the warriors settled into their seats, the tension in the air was palpable. Officers pulled down maps while pilots grabbed their pencils and opened their notebooks.

"You have known for some time that you will soon embark on the greatest operation of your lives." He stared at the men and several pilots nodded. "That day has come. You are ready, and you will begin today."

He spoke for several minutes about the importance of their task and how much depended on them. "This mission could change the course of history. All your lives you have prepared for this day. Everything we have done has been a prelude to what you will do today."

He paused, and those who sat near the front saw the tension in his eyes and the tightness of his jaw. "Captain Simon and Major Paul will explain the details, but I want to announce personally this morning that your long-awaited mission begins within the next few hours. After this briefing concludes, you will have the information you will need to win this decisive battle and to achieve victory."

He stood in front of them and his gaze shifted from one man to the next until he had stared at every man in the room. The pilots sat in silence, waiting for further words.

"I have one more announcement. I have been called back to the headquarters, and this will be my last briefing. I want to say that it's impossible for me to express how much each of you means to me. My three years of working with you have been challenging and rewarding. You've put your lives on the line for me, and I'll never forget that. In fact, I shall prepare a special position for each of you at headquarters. After you have completed this great, final mission, you will join me there.

"As you go out today, I will not be behind the controls of your aircraft, but I assure you that I will be in each cockpit. In fact, I shall always be with you. You can depend on my influence and my presence. If I have taught you well, you will succeed in this task. Be strong. Be focused. Be vigilant. Take care of each other.

"Listen carefully to my final departing instructions . . ."

※

Most of us have read accounts or viewed such scenes on television. The patriotic background music increases, and we realize that something momentous is about to happen.

Most of those stories are fiction. But I want to tell you about a true, life-changing briefing session. It happened centuries ago in

Jerusalem. The great commander Jesus shared his final marching orders with his small but faithful band of followers. He knew he would die. But even more, he was aware of other events that would transpire, such as the betrayal by Judas, his crucifixion, and his ascent into Heaven.

On a number of previous occasions, Jesus had tried to talk about his death, but his followers had been unable to accept his words. Now they had no choice: They had to listen. Because he knew his time was short, Jesus gathered his disciples into what the Bible calls an upper room. He spent hours with them, probably most of Thursday evening before Passover.

The Bible doesn't give us a verbatim account of what transpired, but the Gospel of John devotes five chapters to show us the important words and events of those final hours together. The fact that the Lord spoke of those events before they took place shows his foreknowledge and his desire to prepare his disciples. It also reminds us that he loved them so much he didn't want them to feel alone or abandoned or to have to stumble around to know what they were supposed to do.

Try to visualize Jesus only hours before his betrayal by Judas, one of his twelve chosen disciples. He's aware that the one-time disciple has already betrayed him for money and will bring soldiers to arrest him. Not only will Jesus be arrested, but he'll be illegally condemned to death at a trial and suffer intense physical agony by being nailed to a wooden cross—a slow, painful death. Jesus also knows, of course, of the resurrection that will follow.

Despite all his careful instruction, his frightened followers will run away—but only temporarily. When they encounter the resurrected Jesus and become aware of the spiritual resources available to them, they'll be ready to accept the challenges and to put his departing instructions into practice, and they will begin to prepare for their eternal life in Heaven.

For the eleven faithful disciples, their liftoff to Heaven doesn't happen immediately. They have a mission to accomplish before they'll be ready to leave. They had listened to Jesus' teachings and observed the miracles for three years. Yet, despite being his eyewitnesses, they still hadn't grasped the most important lessons he wanted them to learn.

How could they understand the message Jesus spoke? They had no preview of the future, no realization that Jesus would die. After all, he was the Messiah. Nothing in their Jewish background prepared them to follow a Messiah who would suffer and die. They expected a triumphant, charismatic leader who would destroy the power of Rome and make them a great nation as Israel had been during the reign of Kings David and Solomon. Even after the crucifixion and the resurrection, they still hadn't absorbed what he tried to teach them. Until the moment of Jesus' ascension, they still didn't grasp his teachings. And the full implications took months for them to absorb.

As proof of what I've just written, consider the last question they asked Jesus before his ascension: "So when they met together, they asked him, 'Lord, are you at this time going to restore the kingdom to Israel?'" (Acts 1:6 [NIV]).

He didn't directly answer them except to say, "It is not for you to know the times or dates the Father has set by his own authority" (Acts 1:7 [NIV]). Jesus gave them one final word of instruction: "But you will receive power when the Holy Spirit comes on you; and you will be my witnesses in Jerusalem, and in all Judea and Samaria, and to the ends of the Earth" (verse 8 [NIV]).

Acts 1:9 records, "After he said this, he was taken up before their very eyes, and a cloud hid him from their sight" (NIV). While they stared at the empty sky, two angels told them Jesus was not there but he had gone to Heaven.

Jesus commissioned them to fulfill his plan for them. They had a promise they would receive power in order for them to be his witnesses. Jesus left, but six weeks later, they experienced the amazing coming of the Holy Spirit as well as supernatural experiences recorded in Acts 2 and 3. We would assume they had finally understood.

But not yet. The truth had only begun to seep in. They still weren't ready to comprehend the fullness of Jesus' command to go from Jerusalem to Samaria (inhabited by Jews who had intermarried with Gentiles centuries earlier) and finally to the Gentiles themselves. It took a long time for them to realize the implications of Jesus' final words. It's not until chapter 8 of the Book of Acts that Christian followers left the Jerusalem base, and then only because of persecution—and the apostles weren't among them! The scattering started the day Stephen was stoned to death because of his faithful witness to Jesus Christ.

"On that day a great persecution broke out against the church at Jerusalem, and all except the apostles were scattered throughout Judea and Samaria" (Acts 8:1 [NIV]).

We might want to shake our heads and ask, "How could you not have realized what Jesus meant?" It seems obvious to us, but we have a written record of events—something they didn't have. The disciples catch on, perhaps too slowly, but they finally grasp the messages. Once they understand, they boldly proclaim the message of Jesus' love and move out of Jerusalem until they preach and teach to the ends of the then-known world.

I don't want to sound too harsh in stating this. In many ways, we modern believers are like that first-century group. We don't absorb what we're not ready to accept. We don't want to hear instructions that aren't what we want to put into action. We may not be ready for our liftoff to Heaven. *But we can be.*

The good news is that we have the record of those early followers. We know about the crucifixion; we accept the resurrection; we believe in Jesus' ascension. We have history to show us the way. We have the words from John, chapters 13 to 17, to give us departing instructions.

We may criticize the first disciples for being such slow learners. We argue, "They had the signs and wonders and Jesus himself. Surely everything was obvious." We can see that—in retrospect—but their mind-set made them unable to take in what seems obvious to us.

It's easy to miss significant messages. For example, we can read passages in the Bible a dozen times. And perhaps we can even quote specific verses. But one day a verse comes alive and suddenly we get it. We grasp the meaning when we're ready to respond and act on what we've read.

Hearing and listening may be kissing cousins, but they can be worlds apart in their results. How often have we heard something only to discover, when that information proved quite crucial, that we hadn't been listening? Sometimes we hear the words, accept them as true, but they have no relevance for us then. If they're true and if they're from God, they'll return to our minds when we need them.

Here's a contemporary example: My co-writer, Cecil Murphey, had read the story of Job many times. On February 27, 2007, his house burned to the ground. His son-in-law died inside the house. As he watched the flames destroy everything, he thought of Job's wife who urged her husband to curse God and die. Job answered, "Shall we indeed accept good from God, and shall we not accept adversity?" (Job 2:10 [NKJV]).

Job 2:10 filled Cec's mind, and the words became alive. They were no longer Job's rebuke to his unbelieving wife, but they became an affirmation of Cec's faith as he spoke the words aloud.

Most of us have probably had such experiences when something we heard or were taught came alive to us. At the time we first heard the words, they meant little to us, but they were there, deep inside us, until the right time.

Here are two biblical examples:

First, Jesus told Peter that he would betray him three times, and the disciple promised he would never do that. Peter did deny Jesus, and Matthew records, "Immediately a rooster crowed. Then Peter remembered the word Jesus had spoken: 'Before the rooster crows, you will disown me three times.' And he went outside and wept bitterly" (Matthew 26:75 [NIV]).

Second, Peter was the first of the apostles to preach to non-Jews, and the church leaders criticized him. He told them that God had led him to the house of a Roman named Cornelius: "As I began to speak, the Holy Spirit came on them as he had come on us at the beginning. Then I remembered what the Lord had said: 'John baptized with water, but you will be baptized with the Holy Spirit.' So if God gave them the same gift as he gave us, who believed in the Lord Jesus Christ, who was I to think that I could oppose God?" (Acts 11:15–17 [NIV]).

Did you notice Peter's defense? "Then *I remembered what the Lord had said*" (italics mine). In this case, it wasn't that he remembered just the words but also the implication of those words. He meant that the first disciples had received the Holy Spirit on the day called Pentecost. They spoke in languages that none of them had ever learned. Until then, the early followers of Jesus were all Jews and preached to only their own people. Then Peter visited a Roman home, and before he could finish his message, something miraculous happened. The Gentiles began to speak in unknown languages as Jewish believers had at Pentecost.

Peter had heard Jesus' words to go into the non-Jewish world and had seemingly forgotten them. At the right moment, he remembered what Jesus said. Perhaps a better way to explain it is that Peter *comprehended* the words he had heard months earlier.

I've spent this time explaining how there is sometimes a delay between hearing (or reading) spoken (or read) words and putting them into action so that we can better understand the disciples of old and accept the truths today.

Therefore, I want to focus on those final hours Jesus spent with his disciples. Try to picture the scene in your mind as Jesus gathers with his closest followers inside a small room. He is going to leave them, and he wants to break the sad news to them. What will he say to them? What do they most need to hear? If Jesus knows the immediate future, how will he spend the last hours of freedom? What kind of legacy will he leave?

We don't have to guess at the answers. We may not have the details, but we have enough of a written record to know what he wanted them to grasp. John's Gospel devotes five chapters to describing the events of Jesus' life, beginning the night before his betrayal by Judas. In some ways, the chapters are like the death-bed legacy of a loving parent. They're the important things Jesus wants to say to his followers so he can prepare and equip them to fulfill his plan for them after he has gone.

Everything they had ever seen him do and heard him say was

about to be tested in a battle for the souls of humanity. He promises that although he will leave, they don't have to worry. He won't desert them, and they won't be left helpless and powerless. He promises to send the Holy Spirit to enable them to win the great battles that lie ahead.

Like the commander in the opening story, like the presence of Jesus in the upper room, I call you to attention. I want to give you departing instructions for the life that is still ahead.

I want to show you how to have a fulfilled and abundant life as you prepare for a blissful eternity. I want to pass on to you the important instructions you need to know now as you fight life's battles and as you prepare to depart for your eternal home.

🖋

At the end of each chapter, I have included several practical things for you to consider and to put into practice. Jesus, our great commander, provided specific, departing instructions for the small group of followers in an upper room in Jerusalem. I've taken the principles of those words to show you how they apply to your life. You can use them to fortify yourself and make yourself ready.

You're Heaven bound, and I want you to be fully prepared for the day of your own departure.

Departing Instructions

1. Believe in Jesus Christ. Believing he loves you *is* the prerequisite to receiving departing instructions.
2. Be willing to follow the teachings of Jesus Christ. In doing so, you have taken your next step toward Heaven.

3. Make sure you have a reservation in Heaven. Nobody wanders into Heaven. If you have taken the first two steps, I assure you that Jesus has already made a reservation in your name.

4. While you're waiting for the liftoff, live the rich and fulfilling life God has designed for you.

Heaven Bound?

It was just before the Passover Feast. Jesus knew that the time had come for him to leave this world and go to the Father. Having loved his own who were in the world, he now showed them the full extent of his love.

JOHN 13:1 (NIV)

For at least six months, Hal had depended on his oxygen tank, but it was becoming less and less effective. "I don't have much time left," he finally told his wife, Alicia.

Hal lived eighteen more days after he spoke those words. During that time, he tried to make amends for his wrongdoings. His son, Jim, had married an African woman he met while serving with the Peace Corps. When Jim brought her home, Hal screamed racial slurs, ending with these words: "As long as you stay married to that woman, you may never come back to this house." Twelve years later, Jim and Fibi remained happily married but the two men had never spoken.

Hal asked Jim to return home with his wife. "I was wrong," the dying man said. "I was wrong about a lot of things."

Hal had been a member of a congregation most of his life, but he had given little money to the church and bristled whenever

Alicia gave generously without consulting him or when she served on committees. He asked the pastor to visit. When he came, Hal asked for forgiveness, and Alicia presented a check for a large donation. In labored speech, he said that the amount was what he felt he owed the Lord and the church for the last twenty-five years of his life.

Hal made a list of eight people against whom he held a grudge and invited each one to come to his bedside. Despite the effort to talk, he apologized and each person forgave Hal.

One evening Hal said to Alicia, "I've done . . . everything . . . I know . . . to make . . . my life right. . . . I'm ready . . . to face . . . my Savior." For perhaps a full minute, he lay exhausted from speaking those few words. Alicia later said she had never seen such a beautiful smile on his face.

He took her hand. "Stay . . . with . . . me."

Alicia took his hand. Within minutes, Hal died.

This is a true story, although I've changed names and a few facts for the sake of privacy. Hal had the opportunity to examine his life and to undo a number of wrongs. Some people get that opportunity. They know they'll soon leave this world behind, and they can change.

Can you put yourself in Hal's place? Suppose you knew you would die within the next forty-eight hours. What would you say to the people closest to you? They might be the people who hate you (and possibly with good reason). They might be family members or friends. Whoever they are, they will be the last people you will see. What do you want to say to them? What do you want to do for yourself to prepare for that final meeting?

Of course, many people don't have the forewarning that their time in this life is nearing the end. Hundreds of sermons and printed messages exhort us to be prepared. Most of them give us the command without telling us what it means.

What do you need to do to be ready for *your* liftoff?

The answer is simple: Do the heart searching that Hal did, but do it *now*. (At the end of this chapter, I've listed several things for you to consider.)

If you believe in Jesus Christ, you know he forgives you. You have done nothing too big for him to forgive or too small for him to overlook. Your responsibility is to examine your heart. If you're aware of unconfessed sin or anger toward someone or if someone has something against you, now is the time to make things right with others. It could be as simple as malicious gossip or jealousy or as complex as questionable (or illegal) business deals. Many of us do those things, and we think the end of life seems far away. And perhaps it is.

Or perhaps it's not.

Someday you will be minutes away from death and you will have had no warning. I didn't have any warning. Maybe you know my story. Had I known that January 18, 1989, would be my last day on Earth, would I have done things differently? It's a moot question, of course, but I've wondered about it many times. But I will tell you what happened, and I had absolutely no premonition or warning.

That morning, I left the Trinity Pines Conference Center, about eighty miles north of Houston. I had been there for a spiritually uplifting conference, and I was on my way back to my church to preach that evening. In less than ten minutes after I left the conference, I drove on a bridge across Lake Livingston. Just then, an eighteen-wheel truck came from the opposite direction, smashed into my Ford Escort, and killed me.

I was dead. I opened my eyes in Heaven.

By God's grace, I returned after 90 minutes. Had I known

what lay ahead, would I have changed my route? Assessed my life? Would I have made last-minute phone calls to my loved ones? What would I have done if the Holy Spirit whispered, "Don, you have 90 minutes *before* you die?" Like many who faced certain death, would I have written some final words?

I don't know the answer. And I don't write this to frighten you and say that you might die in an accident today. But I write to urge you to take serious steps to be ready to depart from this life. You don't have to wait until you're only minutes from Heaven or facing imminent death. Instead, you can examine your life so that you'll be ready to inhabit the special place Jesus has prepared for you.

As I drove out of the gates of Trinity Pines, I had no way of knowing that I faced my last moments on Earth. I will say, however, and without bragging, I was ready. I had tried to honor Jesus Christ by the life I lived every day since I became a Christian. I wasn't a perfect Christian (and I'm still not), but I regularly examined my heart and forgave those who hurt me and asked forgiveness of those I had injured.

Because of my experience of being ready, I wrote this book. Here are two major questions I want to ask you:

- What if you seriously considered being prepared for that day—that day that will come when you will either die or remain alive to greet the return of Jesus Christ?
- If you knew you were only 90 minutes away from the end of this present life, what would you do to prepare?

The two questions aren't to make you dread the future. The purpose is for you to ponder what lies ahead so you can prepare.

Let's try it another way. Suppose Jesus walked up to you in

human form and said, "I want to help you get ready to depart for Heaven, and I don't say these things to you so you can have a dramatic death scene." How would you react if he gave you specific directions? Suppose he said, "You're Heaven bound, and I have a number of things to say to you so that you can be fully prepared for your liftoff."

If you can wrap your imagination around that thought, you can have a clearer understanding of the five significant chapters in the New Testament we are focusing on in this book. I'll guide you so you can read them as your personal list of departing instructions.

Long before his death, Jesus said to his followers, "Therefore keep watch, because you do not know on what day your Lord will come" (Matthew 24:42 [NIV]). *Be ready.* That's one part of the message.

Are you ready? What if the Holy Spirit whispered to you that you had 90 minutes left before you died? What would you do? Would you be ready to go to Heaven?

At first you may wonder why he spoke to you. You may even ask, "Why would I want to go to Heaven? Why would anyone want to go to Heaven?"

I need to answer that question before I write about Jesus' departing instructions.

My first response is a question: Why *wouldn't* everyone want to go to Heaven? It's the only place that will ultimately satisfy the deep inner longings of every human being—the needs that our Creator put there.

Even more, Heaven is the place where God is; it is also the

place where you can be. Perhaps that sounds like I'm preaching, but it's true. It's where God will satisfy every need. We'll never have to compare ourselves with anyone. We'll never feel inferior or superior. Perhaps you've longed for peace and found it in brief moments. Heaven will be a lifetime of peace.

God will satisfy your longings to be loved without reservation and without limit. You will never worry again, and you'll no longer remember even one wrong thing you did on Earth.

Heaven is a prepared place for prepared people. That's not an original statement, but it's a true one. And if you don't currently have a reservation, you can change your destiny. You, too, can be ready to live those last minutes that separate you from God's all-loving presence.

Heaven is a place lovingly arranged by a God who refused to spare Jesus from human suffering and sent him to die for our sins, failures, shortcomings, and wrongdoings. Would that same God be stingy or provide anything less than perfection?

And Heaven isn't only a permanent domicile for a few nice people. It's a place for not-so-nice people whom God has forgiven so that one day he can make them into perfect people.

Jesus transforms lives. I've listened to stories from those who have been delivered from horrifying addictions and dangerous relationships, as well as those who left lives of crime and sexual degradation. Their faces beam as they tell that placing their faith in Jesus Christ helped them leave their former lifestyle behind. Listeners often shout praises for the great miracles of redemption.

In fact, every person I was privileged to see at the gates of Heaven during my brief visit had been sinners while on Earth. As a forgiven sinner, I fit in with them. All of them had received forgiveness for their sins before they entered Heaven. All received forgiveness for every sin in their lives when they asked Jesus to become their Savior.

Through the years I've also met people who have been faithful Christians from an early age, remained faithful to their church, and encouraged others to follow the Lord. After hearing the testimony of miraculous deliverance from a reprobate life, those lifelong devoted Christians sometimes feel they must apologize for their stories as if to say, "My life has been boring by comparison because God didn't rescue me from the gutter."

Although we rejoice with those whom God has delivered from a seriously sinful life, we also rejoice with those who haven't strayed from the pathway. They have lived a longer, more fruitful Christian life. They haven't had to bottom out as they say in twelve-step programs. Believers who have walked with the Lord all their lives may not have experienced those terrible problems, but they demonstrate what it means to follow Jesus Christ faithfully all through life. Some have walked in darkness until they've seen the light of those faithful ones who have always walked on the pathway of light.

Regardless of whether you're a new believer or a cradle Christian, the pathway is the same. The path to Heaven is available to every individual on Earth—including you. I can't give answers to every question, but I can tell anyone this much: I've been there, and I can hardly wait to return.

It's a place of perfect peace: all anxieties, worries, and troubles vanish. All memories of past failures disappear. It's a place of perfect bodies: no one feels pain, nobody is flawed, and no one ages. It's a place of great reunion with those who have gone before us. It's a place of joy: Everyone is happy, and it's a joyful excitement that doesn't end and fully satisfies every human need.

Since my brief trip to Heaven, I've thought of that place many times. I can say that not a single day has passed in which I haven't felt an intense longing to be back in that celestial city where I heard the most perfect music and had total inner peace. *Why wouldn't I want to go back?*

I remain on Earth for one reason: God isn't through with me. I love being alive; I have a wonderful family and many friends. In the years since my accident I have walked my daughter, Nicole, down the aisle and given her in marriage to Scott. I have watched Nicole and her brothers, Chris and Joe, graduate from college and begin wonderful careers. My precious wife, Eva, retired after thirty-four years of being a classroom teacher. Eva and I have enjoyed the extreme joy of seeing the birth of our first grandchild, Carlee. All these things and so much more have happened since my return from the gates of Heaven.

I have a good life, a wonderful life, but I still miss the perfect one.

Yet I remain here on Earth because I have a mission. In the years since my accident I have traveled to the four corners of Earth to tell people about Heaven and how to get there; I offer assurance for a better life. After I've completed my mission—and only God knows when that will be—I expect to go to sleep and awake in Heaven, where I'll stay forever.

When I talk to audiences and to individuals on this topic, here are some of the questions I ask them, and I ask them to you, too:

- If you could be totally free from all your negative feelings, who would you be? How would you feel? How would it change the way you live each day?

- If you could choose to do the right thing and have no regrets about any of your actions, how do you think that would make you feel?
- How would you respond if I could show you a plan—a divinely given plan—on how to prepare yourself for Heaven?

In the Book of Revelation, John talks about Heaven. Here is a powerful promise and precious assurance: "[God] will wipe every tear from their eyes. There will be no more death or mourning or crying or pain. . . ." (Revelation 21:4 [NIV]).

I know those statements are true because I actually went to Heaven. There was no pain or sadness. It was a perfect place. My visit, about 90 minutes according to my time away from Earth, was enough to assure me that every promise made by Jesus Christ is true and will be fulfilled on the day when we reach our joyous and perfect destination.

I hope that such thoughts will bring peace to you. Such a knowledge and understanding of Heaven console me and others who believe in Jesus Christ as the Savior. Others tremble inwardly and fear the idea of being 90 minutes away from the ultimate destination. We need have no fear. The difference between life on Earth and new life in Heaven is only a blink. We close our eyes here and immediately open them in Heaven.

ꗠ

Preparing is important, but there's another aspect of being ready. That is to enjoy right now—today—your life on Earth, regardless of how many hours or years before you depart. I encourage you to live the rich, fruitful life that God offers you. *What if living the abundant life and enjoying the best that God has for you would be the same as living your last 90 minutes on Earth? What if your obedience to Jesus' departing instructions made you so ready you wouldn't feel anxious about dying or about what lies ahead?*

My intention is to help you focus on enjoying a peaceful, fulfilled life as you prepare for the inevitable day that you'll leave this Earth.

As you read these chapters and realize what Jesus wanted the first disciples to understand, you can also enjoy God's peace and rejoice in the goodness of the blessed life. The abundant life is for you now. *Today.* Jesus said about those who belong to him, "My purpose is to give them a rich and satisfying life" (John 10:10b [NLT]). That means you don't have to separate yourself from others and spend endless hours in isolation as you search your soul to make sure you're ready.

It also means that you don't have to do what some do: They memorize rules and wrap their thoughts around doing exactly what they're commanded. They focus on what they can do and what they can't do. They spend so much time trying to be good, they seem to have little time to enjoy the good life itself.

Instead of talking about rules of conduct, we can think of preparing for Heaven this way: All of us have a sense of what it's like to do the right thing (even when we fail), and we know that emotions such as jealousy, anger, and pride don't represent the best part of our nature. As we read the Bible, pray, and listen to God speak through sermons and lessons, we can learn what we need to know. God gives us the strength to overcome our weaknesses.

The truth is that at some future time, all of us are exactly 90 minutes away from our ultimate destiny. Will you be anxious? Scared? As a Christian, that moment is intended to bring great joy and deep inner peace. Those of us who belong to Jesus Christ are Heaven bound. We know where we're going.

"We're going home," we can say, "because Heaven is our home. We have space reserved just for us." Despite problems and hardships, peace fills our hearts. We know that our heartaches are only temporary and once we enter Heaven, God miraculously erases all painful memories.

In the two decades since my brief visit to Heaven I've encountered thousands of people who are afraid or feel horrified at the prospects of dying and facing an unknown future. Instead of anticipating joy and happiness, they cry, "What lies ahead for me? How can I know where I'm going?"

When I speak to audiences, I'm often introduced as the "minister of hope." I like that title and it states my purpose well. I want to offer hope. My role is to bring to others a joyful expectation of the future and to assure them that Heaven is real. My goal on Earth is also to urge others to prepare themselves for the endless and unlimited life in Heaven.

You may dread the dying process, and many of us do. That's a normal reaction. Experts often point out that most people aren't afraid of death itself, but of the process of dying. They think of suffering and sadness—and why wouldn't they? That's how they usually see the end of life depicted in books, films, videos, and TV.

You may have questions such as:

- Will I know anyone?
- What will I look like?
- Will I miss loved ones who don't make the journey with me?

More serious questions sound like this:

- What if I'm not good enough for Heaven?
- If I haven't lived a good life, would God still want me?
- Why doesn't a loving God allow everyone into Heaven?
- Will I know my loved ones if I get there?

These are normal questions that most people face. Many are filled with anxiety—and why not? They're going to a strange place—a place they've never been before.

I'd like to tell you the end of the famous book *Pilgrim's Progress*, written by John Bunyan in 1678. It's an allegory about a man named Christian who leaves the City of Destruction to go to the Celestial City. Near the end of the book, Bunyan tells of a dream in which Christian and Hopeful meet two men in shining clothes who point them to the city of pure gold. They can see the city, but to reach it they must cross a deep river, which Bunyan makes clear refers to death. The two angels explain that going across the deep river is the only way to the other side.

As the pilgrim named Christian starts across, he expresses deep fear. He sees the city on the other side but fears that he'll drown. In the middle of the river, Christian begins to sink and cries out to his companion, Hopeful, saying, "I sink in deep waters, the billows go over my head . . ."

Then said the other, "Be of good cheer, my brother. I feel the bottom, and it is good."[1]

Despite anxieties and fears, Christian continues forward until

1 John Bunyan, *Pilgrim's Progress* (Laurel, NY: Lightyear Press, 1984), p. 143.

he's almost to the other side and sees a heavenly host coming out to meet them and welcome them to the city.

More than four hundred years ago Bunyan captured the fear and dread of the process of dying. But he also grasped what would happen once they reached the other side. I've been to the other side, and it's even more wonderful than words can express.

Bunyan understood the problem: We want the joyful life ahead but we don't want to cross the deep river to get there. His allegory makes it clear that some of the most serious and committed believers grow fearful at the end, but that doesn't make them unready. It only makes them human. For me, Bunyan's masterpiece points out that, fearful or joyful, we can know with certainty that we have a special place in Heaven, and it's a place that's been reserved just for us.

If you want a fuller answer about Heaven and about how to prepare to enter, you need to ask the right person for the correct information. And who would know more about the pathway to Heaven than Jesus himself? After all, Heaven is his home.

✦

"How do I get to Heaven?" is a question I hear frequently. The answer is simple: Believe in Jesus Christ. That's all God requires of us. I like to explain that wonderful plan, which isn't based on my own experience, but it's an arrangement Jesus himself formulated. He left instructions on how to make ourselves ready and fulfilled while we wait for the Heaven-bound call.

I want to help you prepare for your life now and to be ready to go at any point in life, not just when you're 90 minutes away from Heaven.

Here's how one translation of the Bible states it: "This is how much God loved the world: He gave his Son, his one and only Son. And this is why: so that no one need be destroyed; by believing in him, anyone can have a whole and lasting life. God didn't go to all the trouble of sending his Son merely to point an accusing finger, telling the world how bad it was. He came to help, to put the world right again" (John 3:16–17 [MSG]).

But faith in Jesus isn't merely mental assent or passive agreement. If we truly believe, *our actions demonstrate our faith.* The Book of James challenges, "What good is it, dear brothers and sisters, if you say you have faith but don't show it by your actions? Can that kind of faith save anyone? . . . [F]aith by itself isn't enough. Unless it produces good deeds, it is dead and useless (James 2:14, 17 [NLT]).

In Matthew 25:31–46, Jesus tells a story—a parable—that shows the lifestyle of true followers. He says that at the end of the world everyone will stand before him. The people who enter into their heavenly reward will do so because of their actions toward others. He says, "Truly I tell you, whatever you did for one of the least of these brothers and sisters of mine, you did for me" (verse 40 [TNIV]).

He points out that they do such things as clothing the needy and feeding the hungry. He refers to their acts of love toward those in need.

Paul says that we Christians will face God's judgment to determine our rewards (*see* 1 Corinthians 3:10 ff.) "For we must all stand before Christ to be judged. We will each receive whatever we deserve for the good or evil we have done in this earthly body" (2 Corinthians 5:10 [NLT]).

Heaven is the ultimate destination and the perfect reward for a life well lived on Earth. No matter what the word *Heaven* means to you personally, most of us consider it as the end of suffering, of pain, and of hardship. It means we'll endure no more trials and hardships. It means there will be no regret, no guilt, no saying, "If only I had . . ." Heaven wipes away all the memories of pain, sadness, and missed opportunities.

Departing Instructions

1. If you know you will die within the next 90 minutes, who are the people you need to forgive?
2. Who are the people whom you love most? What would you want to say to them?
3. If you know you will die within the next 90 minutes, what would you want to say to those of the generation after you?
4. Because you probably don't know when you'll have your last 90 minutes on Earth, what's one thing—the first thing—you can do toward preparing for liftoff?

3

Preparation Starts
with Action

*[H]e got up from the meal, took off his outer clothing, and
wrapped a towel around his waist. After that, he poured water
into a basin and began to wash his disciples' feet, drying them
with the towel that was wrapped around him.*

JOHN 13:4–5 (NIV)

While I sat at the mall and waited for my wife, I watched a
father showing his young son how to tie his left shoe. Dad
showed him how to hold the laces, make a bow, and pull.

"Let me do it! Let me do it!" the boy cried.

Dad let the boy try—and fail. He showed him again, slowly
and patiently. I didn't count but that father must have instructed
his son at least six times. The boy excitedly untied his right shoe.
It took him three times before he got it tied right.

As I watched, I thought that the boy isn't different from the
rest of us. Isn't it strange that sometimes we have to hear instructions several times before we understand and obey?

Even a casual reading of all four Gospels makes it clear that
Jesus instructed his followers numerous times. Sometimes he said

plainly that he would leave them. "From that time on Jesus began to explain to his disciples that he must go to Jerusalem and suffer many things at the hands of the elders, the chief priests and the teachers of the law, and that he must be killed and on the third day be raised to life" (Matthew 16:21 [TNIV]).

And how did his disciples respond? "Peter took him aside and began to rebuke him. 'Never, Lord!' he said. 'This shall never happen to you!' " (Matthew 16:22 [TNIV]).

Jesus didn't stop teaching them because of Peter's rebuke or because the band of believers wasn't ready to accept what he had to say. His final instructions, the last words he would speak to them before his betrayal by Judas, appear in the Gospel of John, chapters 13 to 17. These five chapters not only show us the patient, loving heart of Jesus, but we see the significant messages he wanted them to grasp before they departed from this life.

In the recorded account, Jesus says to his followers, "You don't understand now what I am doing, but someday you will" (John 13:7b [NLT]). Jesus gently rebukes the disciples for their lack of understanding. But when we read the entire context, the words are more than a mild reprimand. His words are meant to teach them and thus push them into richer spiritual lives. Within the context of a special relationship, Jesus was also able to say many challenging things as well as to speak words of encouragement. I've often heard this described as "speaking the truth in love" or "tough love." I like both descriptions.

After my accident and during my long recovery, my closest friends and family members had to share difficult news with me and sometimes they had to speak strong words of criticism. For one thing, I didn't know how to receive gifts or accept acts of kindness from others. As a seminary-trained and experienced pastor,

I knew how to reach out to others. But I had to be rebuked—more than once—to be able to receive the acts of love that others extended to me.

I didn't always receive those rebukes in the spirit of love in which they were intended. Sometimes their rebukes hurt, but they were usually correct. Like Jesus' disciples, sometimes I had to hear messages more than once to grasp them. Now I know some of their hardest corrections and criticism made big differences in my recovery.

I share this to point out how I slowly changed my behavior. I had been used to serving and didn't know how to be served. With the disciples, they looked for a messiah who would overthrow the Romans and usher in peace on Earth. They had to get rid of their old way of thinking. They had to unlearn a few things—just as I did—and just as many others must do.

$$\mathbb{K}$$

To grasp the importance of Jesus' final instructions, we need to get into the disciples' thinking. They wanted a mighty victor, a soldier, someone who would trounce on their enemies and lead them into glorious victory.

As I pondered that, I thought of a friend who went into the army shortly after graduating from high school in 1967. I understand training methods have changed, but he went to a boot camp and learned the basics of being a soldier. He did fine until they handed him an M-16 rifle and he had to sit through a lecture on how to fire and clean a rifle.

"I've been hunting since I was a kid," he said to one of his buddies. "What can he teach me?"

My friend laughed as he recalled those days. "I thought I knew everything about a rifle, but I had to forget my hunting days and learn about using a rifle in combat."

That's the point Jesus has to make to his disciples. He has to *un*teach them before he can take them forward, and he does it in a quiet, disarming way.

We start the five-chapter account of the actions of Jesus on Thursday evening before Judas betrays him. The writer lays out an astounding account of Jesus and the twelve men meeting for the Passover meal in an upper room. Because the Jewish day begins at sunset this becomes the night of the Passover. When he sits with them, Jesus already knows this is the last meal he will eat with them before his death. He has called his loved ones to be with him and to share the sacred meal of the Jewish faith.

If we focus on this as the beginning of the last acts of a dying man, it enables us to see Jesus' purpose and desire for those first disciples. He knows his own future and anticipates the suffering he will have to undergo at the hands of the Romans. But he suspends that from his teaching. He doesn't want to distract them on what will happen to him, but to focus on what they need to know. He concentrates on the group of followers whom he loves very much.

The chapter begins with these words, "It was just before the Passover Feast. Jesus knew that the time had come for him to leave this world and go to the Father. Having loved his own who were in the world, he now showed them the full extent of his love" (John 13:1 [NIV]).

I don't claim to know what was in the mind of Jesus, but from the biblical account it seems obvious to me that he senses it's useless to try the direct approach with them. They're not open to hearing him. So he starts with action.

He shows how he wants them to live and to relate to others until they follow those final departing instructions.

He, the master, begins by demonstrating his humility. He shows his love before he uses words—which is probably the best form of expression and a good lesson for all of us. His actions show us we need to demonstrate care and affection before we throw in the words. St. Francis of Assisi is credited with commanding his followers to preach the Gospel and added, "and use words if you must."

Words can be cheap and words expressing love often are just words. I once sat in the back of a large church and at one point, the pastor shouted out, "I love you! I love all of you." I was part of "all," and he didn't know me and we hadn't met. The words meant nothing to me.

In his short letter of 1 John, the apostle writes these words, "This is the message you heard from the beginning: We should love one another" (1 John 3:11 [NIV]). He doesn't stop there but says, "We know what real love is because Jesus gave up his life for us. So we also ought to give up our lives for our brothers and sisters" (verse 16 [NLT]). He doesn't mean being a martyr and dying for other people. John shows how love *behaves*. "If someone has enough money to live well and sees a brother or sister in need but shows no compassion—how can God's love be in that person? Dear children, let's not merely say that we love each other; let us show the truth by our actions" (verses 17–18 [NLT]).

Here are two stories that show this principle in action.

A woman I remember only as Diana told me that when she was in her first year of college, someone stole her car. It was an old Ford and insured, but she had left all her college notes, handouts, and textbooks in the trunk. The next day at school, she approached the professor at the end of her first morning class. She explained her problems, and he said with sarcasm, "Do you expect me to locate your missing car?"

"No, but I—"

He waved her away.

She walked back to her desk, and a fellow student, Paul, held out his briefcase. "Here, I'd like to share my books with you."

They had three classes together—all required courses—and she was grateful to him. She had noticed him in class before, but they had said little. They began studying together regularly. One night, he said, "Do you have any idea why I offered to share my notes and material with you?"

She shook her head.

"Because I like you—a lot. I didn't have the nerve to talk to you before but it was a chance to do something for you—and to show you that I care."

She laughed. "You know I was aware of who you were and liked you a lot. The day you came to my rescue was the day I think I began to love you."

That was the story of how their romance began. Two years later they married and by now they must be married at least fifteen years. He showed his love before he spoke the words. Sometimes action before words can be the most effective way.

When my co-writer, Cecil Murphey, was a pastor, a man came to his office. "I don't know much about God and I don't care much, but I don't know where else to turn." Those were his first words.

Cec told him to sit down. The man had lost his job and his marriage had fallen apart. He was filled with anger, and even though he approached Cec for help, he was antagonistic and said he was tired of preachers trying to help just so they could get him to join their church, and "If that's your plan, you should just forget about it."

"Church membership isn't important right now," Cec said. "You need help, so let's see what we can do." Cec and an elder named Skip Cothran met with the man and connected him with other people. One time they took him to a health spa to get him into a physical exercise program. They helped him because he needed help, and neither of them said a word about God or about church membership. They decided to let their actions do the talking.

After a couple of weeks, the three of them had lunch together. The man looked at them and said, "Okay, now you can tell me about God."

This example doesn't mean we shouldn't use words. Of course we speak when it's appropriate. I insert this principle because I see too many people fill the atmosphere with words to give others the good news of the Gospel and don't express compassion and caring.

Jesus started his final teaching with actions. He demonstrated who he was by what he did. It starts when all twelve of his disciples sit together in a room to share the Passover meal. In the midst, he performs a powerful act of love and service. He could have told them what he wanted them to know, but he makes obvious his love for them before he tells them. Not many passages in the Gospels demonstrate Jesus' love more than this story.

So that readers of the Gospel won't miss the message, John writes, "Jesus knew that the time had come for him to leave this world and go to the Father. . . . [H]e now showed them the full extent of his love" (13:1 [NIV]).

Let's set the scene. John doesn't go into detail, but if the disciples' behavior were like any other time when they were together, each one wanted the place of honor, and they probably jostled and pushed to gain the best places at the table.

In another place, they argue over who will be greatest among them. James and John send their mother to the Lord and she asks, "Grant that one of these two sons of mine may sit at your right hand the other at your left in your kingdom" (Matthew 20:21 [TNIV]).

The disciples had already shown to Jesus and each other that each man wanted the prestigious places in the kingdom of God. Why wouldn't each one want to be the favored one and receive the great honors?

Apparently, none of the twelve chooses to observe the unwritten laws of courtesy or hospitality. In those days, people traveled by foot on unpaved roads. Especially in the dry seasons, the roads were dusty and their feet would be filthy. It was proper for guests to wash their feet before they entered anyone's home. Most ordinary households placed water and a basin at the door and guests could wash their own feet.

As an act of courtesy and hospitality, however, the host himself or one of his children would make guests feel welcome by doing the task so the guests wouldn't have to wash their own feet.

In the affluent homes, the lowest servant washed the feet of the guests. Washing of the feet expressed acceptance of the guest into the house. Not to wash a guest's feet was a silent way of insulting a person.

For example, Luke records a story that shows this very point. A Pharisee named Simon invites Jesus to eat at his home. The Pharisees are the most theologically conservative Jews. But more than that: They're the legalists of their time. The word *Pharisee* comes from the Hebrew *prushim*, which means "separated." That is, they see themselves as separated from others for a life of purity. They're the most careful to observe every tiny aspect of the law. Jesus rebukes them several times and calls them hypocrites, "For you are careful to tithe even the tiniest income from your herb gardens, but you ignore the more important aspects of the law— justice, mercy, and faith. You should tithe [give a tenth], yes, but do not neglect the more important things" (Matthew 23:23 [NLT]).

We assume Simon the Pharisee is such a man, and he doesn't show Jesus the courtesy of washing his feet. Later in the evening, Jesus says, "When I entered your home, you didn't offer me water to wash the dust from my feet. . . . You didn't greet me with a kiss. . . . You neglected the courtesy of olive oil to anoint my head" (Luke 7:44–46 [NLT]).

If Simon the Pharisee had truly respected Jesus and wanted to honor him by having him as a guest in his home, someone would certainly have washed his feet or at the least, he would have provided water for Jesus to wash his own feet.

In John 13, the writer says nothing about the disciples washing each other's feet as they enter. If Jesus truly is their leader, their honored one, surely one of them should have offered to wash *his* feet, but no one does. They probably thought, Let someone else do it. It's not my job. Most of us don't volunteer to perform a task that we think is beneath us.

Then Jesus does something totally unexpected. After the men have gathered, Jesus "got up from the table, took off his robe, wrapped a towel around his waist, and poured water into a basin. Then he began to wash the disciples' feet, drying them with the towel he had around him" (John 13:4–5 [NLT]).

Jesus didn't wash the disciples' feet at the beginning the way it was normally done. During the supper itself, he washed their feet. I think it was because the disciples needed the lesson of that symbolic act and the memory of it would stay with them.

He washes his disciples' feet. It's a simple story and yet in our modern culture we're apt to miss the significance of that action.

Jesus does what none of the disciples is willing to do. They must have been astonished at his actions, but I find it a bit sad that after teaching them to serve others, not one of them takes up the job. Even more astounding, none of the disciples, except Peter, object to Jesus washing their feet. They allow him, their leader and master, to come to them, kneel before them, and wash their dirty feet. They may have wondered why he did it, but no one says, "Here, let me do that."

It's a powerful story, and Jesus shows by his actions a significant lesson that his words had failed to get across. They have to see love in action and so do many of us.

To get across the point that love begins with actions, I used to do a kind of modern-day enactment of that event. For fourteen years I served several congregations as a youth pastor. When we came across this passage in John in our studies, we discussed the verses. After we finished, I brought out a basin of clear water and a towel. I walked over to one young person and knelt. I removed his or her shoes and socks. I tried to choose a youth who was not perceived as the most popular, outgoing, or even most biblically literate among the group.

The look on the face of the chosen one was nearly always a combination of surprise and unworthiness. "Why me?" the young person seemed to say. As tenderly as I could, I bathed his or her feet and dried them with a towel.

As soon as I finished with the foot-washing task, I picked up my basin and towel and returned to my seat. With no further explanation, I reread these verses. Every time I did that, silence filled the room.

The first time I did it, one teenager said to me afterward, "When I watched you get down there, I understood. It made me want to wash everyone's feet."

I stared into his blue eyes and asked, "Why didn't you?"

He dropped his head. "Embarrassed. Afraid the others would laugh at me."

"They didn't laugh at me," I said. I didn't want the boy to feel bad, so I hugged him and said, "You don't have to wash feet to demonstrate love or compassion, but you do have to do something."

And as we pondered that living Bible lesson, I'm not sure who was more humbled by the act—the young person or me. Some of those once-teens, now middle-aged, tell me they've never forgotten that particular moment. More than one has said, "For the first time I realized how important it is to help other people."

I want to add that after they've told me such things, it makes me feel good. I've learned as well. I feel better after I've done something kind or thoughtful for someone else. Instead of feeling proud, it humbled me to think that I used such a simple act and teenagers learned from it.

When Jesus washed the feet of his disciples, I hope the disciples were so shocked they never forgot the lesson. I like to believe that they forever remembered that the Lord of Glory, in the most humble fashion, not only came to Earth to save them from their sins, he also came to demonstrate his selfless, overwhelming love by washing their dirty feet.

The foot-washing story starts with the statement, "He now showed [the disciples] the full extent of his love" (John 13:1 [NIV]). It's quite obvious that they never saw the odious task as an act of love.

Let's think about this situation. Jesus sits with twelve men in the room (Judas will leave a little later). He wants to show them how deeply he cares about them. It's a small, thankless task to wash the dirty feet of a dozen men, but Jesus' action symbolizes something deeper. On his knees, Jesus demonstrates his loving relationship with these men. Jesus uses this live action as an occasion to teach them invaluable lessons.

The most obvious is that Jesus shows by his quiet action that no task is too lowly if it's motivated by love.

Cec remembers a time when he and his wife, Shirley, visited a pastor in the Williamsburg section of Brooklyn. The wife became quite ill while they were there and had to stay in bed. The husband insisted the Murpheys spend the night as they had planned.

The next morning when Cec went to the bathroom, he saw the husband on his knees, washing out his wife's soiled nightgown. He softly sang a song of thanksgiving to God as he worked.

Not once during the overnight visit did the pastor complain or speak of caregiving as a burden.

"That's love in action," Cec told his wife. He could have said, "That's Jesus' love in action."

A not-so-obvious lesson is that love sees needs and goes into action without waiting for someone to ask.

Here's one more illustration of humble love. In the 1980s, when AIDS had just made the headlines in the United States,

Cec and Shirley Murphey joined a group called AID Atlanta and signed up to work with AIDS patients who were near death, and all of them died within six months. Shirley's job was the dirty one. Because of her nurse's training, she went into their homes and bathed them.

When someone told her how disgusting that job was, Shirley just said, "I think Jesus would have done the same thing."

When the person objected, Shirley said, "In Jesus' day lepers were the untouchables. Under Jewish law, anyone who had contact with them became ceremonially unclean. But leprosy or any disease didn't prevent Jesus from reaching out and doing good."

Another lesson seems obvious: Love seeks opportunities. By that I mean that if we follow the words of Jesus to show our love by what we do, the natural outcome is that we seek opportunities to express that obedience to Jesus.

For example, in 1780, Robert Raikes owned a newspaper in Gloucester, England. With the help of a local clergyman, Thomas Stock, he started a school on Sunday in the parish church. They chose Sunday because it was the only time children were not working twelve to fourteen hours a day in the factories. They started the school in a church and taught the children to read, and the Bible was one of their main textbooks.

Although Raikes wasn't the first to see the need, he was able to report it in his newspaper, the *Gloucester Journal*. Sunday school is part of most modern-day churches, but it became accepted and popularized because love seeks opportunities. Love shows compassion where there is need. By teaching children to read, Raikes was a pioneer in the child-labor reform.

A final thing I want to point out is that when we give ourselves lovingly and without any expectation of return, that's when we're the most like Jesus himself. In those moments we are truly the most prepared for our heavenly trip.

An oft-repeated legend about St. Francis of Assisi says that he was a wealthy aristocrat but had no inner peace. He decided to follow Jesus Christ. Shortly after that decision, Francis spotted a leper who was covered with sores. Instead of recoiling, the legend says that Francis threw his arms abound the man and embraced him. When he did, the piteous figure was transformed into Jesus.

That may not be literally true, but it is spiritually true. In a previous chapter I mentioned the great judgment Jesus foretold in a parable. He says to those whom he blesses, "Come, you who are blessed by my Father, take your inheritance, the kingdom prepared for you since the creation of the world" (Matthew 25:34 [TNIV]).

But he says something else. He says that he himself was hungry and they fed him, a stranger, and they provided hospitality. He needed clothes and they provided them, he was sick and they took care of him. "I was in prison and you came to visit me" (Matthew 25:36b [TNIV]).

Those being blessed are puzzled and deny doing that for Jesus, but he says to them, "Truly I tell you, whatever you did for one of the least of these brothers and sisters of mine, you did for me" (Matthew 25:40 [TNIV]).

The lesson? When we act in love toward others, we are demonstrating our love for Jesus. When we demonstrate that selfless love, we have obeyed Jesus' first and most significant instruction preparing for the journey ahead.

Departing Instructions

1. Demonstrate love for your friends and for your family. Seek ways to show your affection for them.
2. *Show* your love. Let your actions speak more powerfully than your words. Certainly what you do speaks more powerfully than your words alone.
3. Even if others don't see your acts of love for what they are, don't let that stop you from doing them. You do them because you love, not to be appreciated.
4. Be willing to do any kind of service for Jesus Christ, regardless of how thankless the recipients may be.

4

Clean Up Your Act

*He came to Simon Peter, who said to him, "Lord, are you going
to wash my feet?" Jesus replied, "You do not realize now what I
am doing, but later you will understand. . . . Unless I wash you,
you have no part with me."*

JOHN 13:6–8b [NIV]

Tired from preaching three times that day, my battered body
was too miserable to sleep. I turned on the TV and caught
the first part of a black-and-white film. The heroine, a princess
who had temporarily escaped from the royal palace, had gone
out incognito. She met a commoner, and in three days of being
together, they fell in love.

I paid little attention to the film until the commoner, not
knowing her true identity, proposed to her.

She was shocked and obviously touched. Her eyes brightened
and she opened her mouth to say yes, but then she stopped. "I
can't," she said.

You know how those films go: The young woman explained
that she loved him and would never stop loving him, but she
couldn't marry him. She confessed who she was—the only child
of an elderly king. She finally said, "Throughout my entire life I

have been trained so that one day I shall inherit the throne and become the queen." She explained to her suitor the things she felt she must do and the reforms that only she could bring into the kingdom. Tears glistened on her cheeks, but she said her responsibility was more important than her personal life.

Long after the movie ended, I thought of her words. All her life she had been trained for one thing: to inherit the throne.

It's certainly no exact parallel, but that scene made me think about Christians and especially about my Christian experience. I had been called by the King of Kings to an eternal inheritance. Since I was a teenager, I had been trained by my king to serve and to make changes in the world—the kind of changes that only I can bring about.

The heroine in the film relied on training and duty; I relied on training and love. My love for God is so powerful that nothing can detour me or distract me from the tasks I'm called on to do.

I also realized that although God gave me a brief visit to Heaven, he hadn't allowed me to stay there. He sent me back because I had things to accomplish on Earth. I had tasks that only Don Piper could do. George Whitefield once said that our lives are immortal until our work on Earth is finished. I believe that.

God had a plan for me and had been preparing me, training me, and equipping me for what was to be the culmination of my ministry on Earth. I don't want to suggest I'm the only one with such a calling. All believers have a calling, a purpose, and a task. We're all different and we need to fulfill our tasks in our own, individual way.

After I turned off the TV, as I slowly relaxed and finally dozed, I thought of the training I received during my years since I had entered the kingdom at age sixteen. Sometimes I understood the lessons; most of the time I obeyed because they were the right things to do, even without grasping the purpose.

That's how it operates in the spiritual life. Sometimes the Lord makes the lessons obvious, sometimes we understand only in retrospect, and sometimes the reasons never become clear. What does become clear is that God loves us, is always with us, and uses every circumstance to make us more faithful for the service he has for us.

When I returned from Heaven, I couldn't physically do many of the things I had previously done, even after nearly four months in the hospital. I can say this honestly: Without the sense that I still had a purpose on Earth, I would have given up.

I had an opportunity to quit working and to receive disability payments, but I turned it down. I turned down the disability payments because I had a divine task. I didn't know what it was, and even after my crippled body went back to being a pastor, I still didn't understand why God had sent me back and what I had to do. Years passed before I finally told my story publicly and even more years passed before I agreed to work with my co-writer to get the story into a book.

But once the story came out in print my mission seemed obvious. As I've already mentioned, God sent me out, crippled and pain filled, to tell the story of divine love and a heavenly home that awaits us.

※

"Before the Passover celebration, Jesus knew that his hour had come to leave this world and return to his Father" (John 13:1 [NLT]). Verse 3 is a significant statement that sets up the powerful lesson of this story: "Jesus knew that the Father had given him authority over everything and that he had come from God and would return to God." Between those two statements we can see the entire purpose laid out: Jesus will leave Earth and return to Heaven. This is the background against the great love of Jesus. He is soon to be exalted but first he has to teach his disciples a lesson in humility and to make them realize that humility and exaltation go together.

Jesus had taught about self-humbling before, such as

- "If any of you wants to be my follower, you must turn from your selfish ways, take up your cross daily, and follow me" (Luke 9:23 [NLT]).
- "[T]ake the lowest place at the foot of the table. Then when your host sees you, he will come and say, 'Friend, we have a better place for you!' Then you will be honored in front of all the other guests" (Luke 14:10 [NLT]).
- "[T]hose who exalt themselves will be humbled, and those who humble themselves will be exalted" (Luke 18:14 [NLT]).

Although he is training them for leadership, he is first training them to serve. As I've mentioned, they had previously argued over who would be first in the kingdom or would sit at his right and left hands. We can only assume that each disciple compared himself with the others and tried to find ways to get an edge over the competition, much like people in our world do today. But the real way to greatness is to humble oneself.

That's still the principle for all true disciples. If we humble ourselves, God exalts us. If we exalt ourselves, God humbles us. "God opposes the proud but gives grace to the humble" (James 4:6 [NIV]).

The greatest example of self-humbling is that Jesus gave up all divinity to become a total human being. In Philippians 2, Paul writes:

Don't be selfish; don't try to impress others. Be humble, think-ing of others as better than yourselves. Don't look out only for your own interests, but take an interest in others, too. You must have the same attitude that Christ Jesus had. Though he was God, he did not think of equality with God as something to cling to. Instead, he gave up his divine privileges; he took the humble posi-tion of a slave and was born as a human being (verses 3–8 [NLT]).

The words of Paul, probably quoting a hymn or creed of the early church, went on to say that after Jesus humbled himself by obedience and died, "God elevated him to the place of highest honor" (Philippians 2:9 [NLT]).

Those men in the upper room didn't have the advantage of knowing the entire drama but saw it only as it took place. Many times, the Lord has tried to get across to them that the truest leader is the humblest servant.

In the past, they'd heard the words, but they didn't learn the meaning. Jesus is preparing to leave them so he instructs them in humility once again. This time, however, he doesn't use words but he demonstrates what humility means. He chooses the role of the lowest servant in a wealthy household.

The disciples have to grasp this great lesson before they can lead and carry the loving message to the world. Right now, they yearn for the glory and honor, but they aren't ready to accept the responsibility, the rejection, and the persecution that comes with them.

Jesus might have focused on the glory that lies ahead for him but as we see in John 13:4–5 (discussed in the last chapter), he washes his disciples' feet. Just when he might have proudly boasted of his glorious triumph, he shows the most supreme humility.

Isn't that how true love works? Jesus' love is so powerful that he focuses his attention on the final, most needed lessons for the disciples before his departure.

For three years he has taught them, but they never seem to grasp what he meant. It must have been frustrating to teach the same lessons repeatedly to the same men.

They still haven't fully understood that Jesus is going to entrust them with continuing his work after he is gone. They aren't ready to assume that kind of leadership, and they won't be ready until after the resurrection. Even so, he works patiently with them.

Isn't it amazing that Jesus chose men of what we'd call the lower class? He must have seen the potential in them—although hidden—because there's little outward evidence of their ability to carry on his divine mission.

They will soon be entrusted to take his message and spread it to the corners of the Earth.

Jesus chose men who showed no obvious evidence of leadership. But Jesus looks beyond the obvious and sees the hidden; he peers beyond the external and focuses on the eternal. He obviously sees what they could be and what they will accomplish.

This is the principle all through the Bible, isn't it?

For example, when God chose the second king of Israel, a man who would replace King Saul, he sent the prophet Samuel to the house of Jesse, the father of eight sons, apparently all of them robust and handsome. He saw the first one, "Eliab and thought, 'Surely this is the LORD's anointed!'" (1 Samuel 16:6 [NLT]).

Samuel was mistaken and God said, "Don't judge by his appearance or height, for I have rejected him. The LORD doesn't see things the way you see them. People judge by outward appearance, but the LORD looks at the heart" (verse 16:7).

If Jesus had been a man like Samuel and one who wasn't in vital communication with the Heavenly Father, he certainly wouldn't have chosen the men he did. There isn't much to commend them as we see when we read the accounts of their behavior. After the resurrection, however, they are changed and become strong witnesses for God.

I'm glad I didn't have to pick Jesus' disciples or I'm sure I would have moved right past all of them. That's a strong point of this story. Jesus chose *them*. He chose them because he knew what was in their hearts and he knew what he wanted to put inside their hearts. Then he molded them into the men he wanted them to become.

If Peter (or any of them) hadn't needed the lesson of humility, he would have said something like, "No, my Lord, this isn't right. Let me do it." Instead, he seems oblivious. He doesn't object to being waited on, he just objects to Jesus doing the dirty task. Not one of those twelve men has yet grasped the concept of servanthood.

But they would.

𝕂

In answer to Peter's objection, Jesus explains that their bodies are clean but their feet are dirty. He means that those who are clean belong to God and have been made clean. That is, they have been forgiven.

Jesus' actions and words are symbolic. God had declared them clean (that is, they belong to him). They need only to remove daily defilement. Jesus is saying, in effect, "Each day as you confess your failures and ask for cleansing, you are clean once again."

Jesus also says that one of them isn't clean. Right then, at the beginning of chapter 13, readers of the Gospel of John know he refers to Judas.

They seem to have understood that message about the significance of the water and their need for daily cleansing. But they didn't get the depth of his teaching because Jesus says, "You do not realize now what I am doing, but later you will understand" (John 13:7 [TNIV]). To many, this means he creates a symbol out of hospitality's tasks of washing dusty feet. Peter's heated reply makes it clear that he still doesn't get it.

"'No,' Peter protested, 'you will never ever wash my feet!'" (John 13:8a [NLT]). Peter is still an all-or-nothing person.

Jesus patiently explains, "Unless I wash you, you won't belong to me" (John 13:8b [NLT]).

True to his character, "Simon Peter exclaimed, 'Then wash my hands and head as well, Lord. Not just my feet!'" (John 13:9 [NLT]).

Peter's close but he still hasn't absorbed the meaning. Jesus patiently adds, "A person who has bathed all over does not need to wash, except for the feet, to be entirely clean" (John 13:10a [NLT]). And he adds one more statement, "And you disciples are clean" (verse 10b).

Part of the implied message is that the daily cleanings—daily forgiveness—is reserved only for true followers. It's for those who have already been forgiven or spiritually cleansed.

There is a second lesson they didn't get—or at least not clearly. It is about serving each other. After we become followers of Jesus

Christ, we have a primary responsibility to serve others. Jesus gave them an object lesson by washing their feet and said, "You ought to wash each other's feet" (John 13:14b [NLT]).

Through the centuries some groups have taken the words as a literal command and participated in foot washing. I have no quarrel with such a practice only to say that something more important lay behind the words than an ongoing ritual. It can certainly be observed as a sacrament to remind each other of our responsibility and commitment to do the lowliest of tasks for others. And the story is a constant reminder that none of us lives every day without defilement or sin of some kind.

But I like to look at the purpose behind the foot washing. Few passages in the New Testament show love so vividly. At the time when he prepares to leave them, instead of demanding honor, he demonstrates humility. He is God incarnate and he will be crucified and within three days raised from the dead. He wants not only to teach them, but to show them how love behaves.

When Jesus, their master and their teacher, kneels before each of them and washes their feet, his actions say far more eloquently than any words of explanation can communicate that he loves them. He also demonstrates how he expects them to treat each other.

If they had already learned the lesson, surely they would have all stood at the door and insisted on washing each other's feet. No one had volunteered. No one would stoop to such a common task. The lesson becomes clear later on, but as long as they see themselves as special or above doing the lowly acts, they can't learn the joy of service or the importance of self-humbling.

I think they got the message—if not then, certainly later. In the early chapters of Acts, Peter is clearly the leader, but he willingly does things for others that show he understands the principle. The first believers willingly share with each other whatever they have: "All the believers met together in one place and shared everything they had. They sold their property and possessions and shared the money with those in need" (Acts 2:44–45 [NLT]).

But a problem arises. The number of believers continues to grow and "the Hellenistic Jews among them complained against the Hebraic Jews because their widows were being overlooked in the daily distribution of food" (Acts 6:1 [TNIV]).

The twelve apostles call everyone together and announce that they need to choose people to take care of the distribution of the food. It doesn't sound like a glamorous or popular job; they need someone to serve food (Acts 6:2). But Peter must have learned from Jesus because he doesn't pick out just anybody or ask for volunteers. He tells them to "choose seven men from among you who are known to be full of the Spirit and wisdom. We will turn this responsibility over to them" (verse 3 [NIV]).

What? Elect spiritual and wise men so they can become waiters and serve tables? Here's the response of the community: "This proposal pleased the whole group" (Acts 6:5 [NIV]). But more than that, after choosing them, "They presented them to the apostles, who prayed and laid their hands on them" (verse 6 [NIV]). The meaning is obvious: Even a mundane task such as distributing food among widows is a calling from God.

But what may be surprising in the laying on of hands and prayer for seven table waiters is that's not the end of the story. Acts doesn't record the stories of all seven, but we do read more about two of those waiters. One of them is Stephen, of whom it says,

"Now Stephen, a man full of God's grace and power, performed great wonders and signs among the people" (Acts 6:8 [NLT]). Stephen becomes a powerful preacher who refuses to back down. He is stoned by the enemies of the Gospel and becomes (so far as we know) the first Christian martyr.

We also read of another food server, Philip, who later "went down to a city in Samaria and proclaimed the Messiah there. When the crowds heard Philip and saw the signs he performed, they all paid close attention to what he said" (Acts 8:5–6 [TNIV]). He was another food-distributing servant who moved on to the big things. He was apparently faithful in what he did, and God gave him a wider form of ministry.

Maybe that's how God works best. Those who are willing to take on the humble jobs are the ones God recognizes and promotes to more exalted positions.

✒

One of the most invaluable lessons I learned was after my return to Earth and the weeks I had to spend in the hospital. Others came to wash my feet—yes, literally wash my feet. I wasn't able to stand for many weeks, and the thick skin on the bottom of my feet began to crack and flake off. I could never have reached the bottom of my feet to wash them myself. I couldn't even see the bottoms of my feet for a couple of years until I could bend my knees again.

Hospital staff and friends washed my feet and applied oil to keep them from cracking. For them to do that to me was not only thoughtful and kind, but it was humbling for me. It often brought tears to my eyes that those dear souls would come to serve me and do such lowly service *out of love*.

At first I wouldn't let them. I had always been the server—the doer and giver. I was the one who knelt before others' dirty feet. It was an important lesson for me. I had to learn to accept that others were willing to act as my servants when I was in need.

That's an invaluable lesson for all of us to learn in some form—whether it's washing our feet, doing our laundry for us, or running errands. In my case I was utterly helpless and physically unable to help myself. I wish I had been able to willingly allow (and welcome) such loving acts of service. In my own way, I was as dense as those disciples in the upper room.

Often some of the most memorable sacrifices involve the most mundane activities, such as getting a haircut. When I was confined to a hospital bed for months, it wasn't a surprise, of course, to realize that my hair kept growing. It had to be washed and it had to be cut. Because I was unable to move my arms or legs, whoever washed my hair, placed my head inside a plastic halo device with a tube exiting the bottom of the halo. That tube drained water away from my wet hair into a trash can. The person who washed my hair poured water over my head, applied shampoo and lathered my hair. After that, the person poured clear water over my head and it would drain into the trash can.

Having clean hair was wonderful, but my hair still continued to grow. Word reached Carole, my hair stylist in Alvin, Texas, where I had served on the staff of South Park Baptist Church. One day she appeared at my hospital door at St. Luke's Hospital in Houston. That is a thirty-mile trip from Alvin. Her coming to the hospital involved finding a space in a paid-parking garage and probably meant canceling paying customers' appointments. But Carole came and cut my hair several times during my four-month stay. Never once would she take any money for her services. "It's my gift to you," she said. "It's the least I can do."

That simple act of giving me a haircut was deeply moving. She didn't wash my feet, but it was just as meaningful. She taught me once again how important it is to demonstrate love.

After my hospital stay, my family served me without complaining. My wife emptied the bedpan, turned the bone-stretching screws on my legs, cleaned the thirty wounds in my legs, and helped me move a body that didn't have the strength to move itself. My three children picked up for me, ran errands, or did simple things such as tie my shoes and bring my clothes to me.

None of them ever complained. My wife and my children loved me. There wasn't the slightest hint of pity. They may not have liked what they had to do for me, but they didn't hesitate. I needed help, and they did it. None of them felt too important or hinted that cleaning up after me was beneath them. Their love enabled them to care for me without hesitation.

Here is another example of love in action. My son Chris, my son-in-law, Scott, and I were invited to serve at a south Florida camp for handicapped adults called AIM (Achieve. Inspire. Motivate.). My primary responsibility was to lead two daily Bible studies.

Scott and Chris served as buddies to the campers. Some campers couldn't see, others couldn't walk, and still others had severe motor skill limitations. Some of the campers had been coming to AIM for years. That biannual camp was the only time those people were able to leave their homes during the year.

The campers were delightful. They were positive, appreciative, smiling, enthusiastic, and undaunted by any challenge. One night they even held a dance—dancing wheelchairs! All three of us fell in love with those men and women.

But the real story was the relationship between the campers and their buddies. Each camper was assigned a buddy. The volunteers came to the camp at their own expense. They dressed the campers, fed them, pushed those in wheelchairs, guided those who could not see, dried the tears of those who wept, wiped noses, and did anything else the campers couldn't do for themselves. Some of those activities included washing feet.

Seldom have I seen a more gracious display of unconditional and sacrificial love. The appreciation displayed in the final farewell between the campers and buddies was touching. The joy of service is a joy divine.

🖋

The third lesson for the disciples in the upper room was that they needed to learn to put away contention and competition. Luke 22:24 tells us that the disciples argued over who was the greatest—a natural kind of rivalry because each man wanted to be Jesus' favorite. If they knew how to serve each other, however, the argument wouldn't have taken place, because it wouldn't have mattered. Each man would have been able to say, "Jesus has a place for me and it's a special place: It's where he wants me." The same is true for us today.

The apostle Paul exhorts first-century Christians (and twenty-first-century ones as well): "Do not think of yourself more highly than you ought, but rather think of yourself with sober judgment, in accordance with the measure of faith God has given you" (Romans 12:3 [NIV]). He goes on to write about spiritual giftedness and urges them to focus on using those gifts. His point is that it's not a matter of who is greater, more gifted, or more able. It is a matter of being faithful to use the talents God has given us. "[I]f it is serving, then serve; if it is teaching, then teach; if it is to encourage, then give encouragement; if it is giving, then give generously; if it is to lead, do it diligently; if it is to show mercy, do it cheerfully" (verses 7–8 [TNIV]).

Above all, Jesus wants them to know that they are servants— servants of one another and of him. "I tell you the truth, no servant is greater than his master, nor is a messenger greater than the one who sent him. Now that you know these things, you will be blessed if you do them" (John 13:16–17 [NIV]).

Above I mentioned my new friends at the AIM camp in south Florida. The camp incident touched me deeply because it reminded me of the months I had spent in a wheelchair.

I want to tell you about another experience I'll never forget. In late summer, months after my accident, I was still in a wheelchair. It was time for the South Park Church Youth Group's annual camp trip. I had already decided to attend the camp at the East Texas Baptist University in Marshall, Texas. Against almost everybody's warnings I was determined to visit the camp when my youth group would be there. In retrospect, I should have listened to those who warned me. But I felt I had to go. I've long told people struggling with serious infirmities, "Do what your body and spirit will allow you to do. You'll know when you're in water over your head."

One of the joys of that camp was that I would be accompanied by Tony, who had once been a member of our youth group in Bossier City, Louisiana. Tony was a strapping young man who looked as if he could bench-press a truck. Each day Tony stayed in my room and helped me get into my wheelchair. He pushed me around the campus, which was quite an ordeal with no handicap ramps. In those days, few places were as handicap friendly as they now are and that included the East Texas Baptist University campus. We could enter some buildings only by climbing steps—and that included the dorm where we stayed. The main chapel where nightly services were held had dozens of steps.

That meant Tony worked hard to get me where I needed to be and often had to pick me up or at least help me climb each step. Tony didn't complain or show any sense of frustration. He had been a faithful member of my youth group at Airline Baptist Church in Bossier City. Sometimes mischievous, he had a good heart, and he struggled to find himself. I was a little surprised when he volunteered to be my helper at camp and yet, he was such a blessing to me. I couldn't have survived the campus without him.

On my final night, Tony helped me climb the dozens of steps to the chapel for the evening service. The service began with music and was to be followed by a sermon.

Just before the sermon began, someone called my name from the stage. "We have someone who has been with us this week, Don Piper from South Park Church in Alvin. He's been through an amazing ordeal and it's even more amazing that he is able to be here with us this week. Would you welcome him as he shares a little of his story?"

I stared at Tony and he looked at me. What should we do? I nodded to say, "Let's go down to the front." After we reached the front of the chapel, the hundreds of youth in attendance became quiet. All of them had seen me during my days there at camp but most of them didn't know how I came to be wheelchair bound.

Immediately I faced a new problem: Not only was there no ramp leading onto the stage, but there wasn't even a set of stairs. In order to get on stage I would have to be lifted up about six feet while seated in my wheelchair.

There was a momentary pause as my friend Tony and I pondered what to do. Almost immediately several burly boys rose from their seats. Ever so gently, they lifted me up onstage and I was able to share a testimony about my accident and miraculous trip to Heaven. After I finished my remarks, the young audience spontaneously stood and praised God for my miracles.

Just then, a tearful young preacher leaned down and whispered into my ear. "You won't believe what tonight's sermon was going to be on."

"What, my brother?" I asked.

"The crippled man whose friends brought him to Jesus for healing."

Mark 2:1–12 tells the story of a paralytic lying on a cot, which is lowered through the roof so that Jesus would heal him. Although seldom mentioned, the message of that story is as much about those who had the faith and the courage to carry the paralytic man up to the roof, as it is about the man himself.

The pastor who was to deliver the sermon was the only one in the chapel who knew the subject of his sermon. And we had never met before that night. He couldn't have possibly anticipated the supreme act of service that was performed before his very eyes.

"I'm not sure I should preach the sermon now," the pastor said. "I think your testimony just did."

"If God gave you a message for tonight, preach it."

He hugged me before the strong young hands lowered me

from the stage. That night, many young people made decisions to follow the Lord.

That experience taught me by living example what Jesus meant by serving one another.

✙

After Jesus washes the disciples' feet, he asks if they understand. He knows his hour of humiliation is near and he also knows his hour of glory will follow. John's Gospel doesn't tell us whether they answer his question but the implication is that they still haven't grasped the meaning of the message.

Jesus goes on to say, "You call me 'Teacher' and 'Lord,' and rightly so, for that is what I am. Now that I, your Lord and Teacher, have washed your feet, you also should wash one another's feet" (John 13:13–14 [NIV]).

If they had understood that part of the message, wouldn't all of them have rushed to get water and a towel? They are still too self-important to serve each other. And yet what a powerful example Jesus gives. He is Lord of the entire universe, but he washes his disciples' feet.

One more thing I love about this passage is that we sense the nearness of God by the humility of Jesus. Too often we think that those who do the big things or the preachers with the huge crowds are the ones who are closest to God. Jesus gives us a different picture.

His closeness to God shows itself by his intimacy with his disciples. He is the embodiment of a God who loves everyone so much he sent his beloved Son to save them. The Son demonstrates that love by the simple, humiliating act of washing dirty feet.

Departing Instructions

1. Become a servant. Part of learning to become a servant is to do for others, but it's also allowing others to do for you. *Which part of the lesson do you need to learn?*

2. Like the princess in the film, you've been trained for specific tasks. As you step each day closer to your departure from this life, pause and evaluate your progress. Ask yourself: Am I fulfilling my role? What must I do to fulfill my divinely appointed task in life?

3. Confess your sins daily (be cleansed). Vow to live so that you will never have any unconfessed sin in your life.

4. What do you need to do to be equipped to serve God more fully?

5. Rise above jealousy or comparing yourself with others. Humble yourself—don't seek honor or the highest places. Instead seek to serve. God exalts. If you exalt yourself, remember that God humbles the self-exalter.

5

Love Gives Another Chance

Jesus was troubled in spirit and testified, "I tell you the truth, one of you is going to betray me. . . . It is the one to whom I will give this piece of bread when I have dipped it in the dish." Then, dipping the piece of bread, he gave it to Judas Iscariot, son of Simon. As soon as Judas took the bread, Satan entered into him. "What you are about to do, do quickly," Jesus told him, but no one at the meal understood why Jesus said this to him.

JOHN 13:21, 26–28 (NIV)

He was the best friend I ever had," Bud said. "I told him my deepest thoughts and trusted him with my life. One day he betrayed me. He told someone else things that I had told him in confidence."

After Bud told me his sad story, I asked, "How did you treat him after you learned what he had done?"

"I confronted him and he didn't deny what he had done. I never spoke to him again. That was thirty-one years ago."

Bud's method isn't all that different from the way most of us act when we've been hurt, taken advantage of by friends, and especially when someone we've loved has betrayed us.

Maybe that's what makes the story of Jesus and Judas so powerful. In each of the four Gospels, the writers negatively introduce Judas Iscariot. Matthew, Mark, and Luke all call him by name and add that he was the one who betrayed Jesus. John introduces him this way: "Then Jesus replied, 'Have I not chosen you, the Twelve? Yet one of you is a devil!' (He meant Judas, the son of Simon Iscariot, who, though one of the Twelve, was later to betray him.)" (John 6:70–71 [NIV]).

In chapter 12, John tells that Judas objected because Mary of Bethany used costly perfume on Jesus' feet. He said they could use the money for the poor. "He did not say this because he cared about the poor but because he was a thief; as keeper of the money bag, he used to help himself to what was put into it" (verse 6 [NIV]). The biblical statements make it clear that Judas isn't honest or trustworthy. He is no idealist as some modern people try to make him.

Dishonesty is bad, but Judas's greater treachery is his betrayal of Jesus. For thirty pieces of silver, Judas agreed to lead soldiers to Jesus so that they could arrest him.

Jesus knows everything about Judas, including his petty thievery and his plan to betray him. And how does the Lord respond to the false disciple? *He treats Judas as lovingly as he does the others.*

After Jesus washed the disciples' feet he says that he had set them the example to wash each others' feet and that they aren't better than their master. He adds, "Now that you know these things, you will be blessed if you do them" (John 13:17 [NIV]). Immediately he adds, "I am not referring to all of you; I know those I have chosen" (verse 18a). He quotes from Psalm 41:9: "He who shares my bread has lifted up his heel against me" (verse 18b [NIV]). He goes on to make it clear that one of them will betray him. He never mentions Judas by name. Even later, when he sends Judas out to do his terrible deed, he doesn't name him (*see* John 13:26–30).

What is going on here? Why doesn't Jesus rebuke Judas? Renounce him? Throw him out? No one can definitely answer that, but the most obvious answer is that Jesus loves the man. By speaking of Judas's deeds before he does them, Jesus offers his betrayer a chance to repent and no one else in the room would have realized what he did. It also seems clear that if at any point Judas had said, "Forgive me," Jesus would immediately have done so.

I also want to point out something else that's significant. While all the disciples are in attendance that last night, Jesus speaks quietly to Judas so that no one overhears. For him to be able to speak privately in that small upper room, Jesus would likely have had to put Judas in the special place of honor, which is to his left. John's head is at Jesus' breast (the right side), so Jesus' head would have been at Judas's breast—Judas on the left, the most prominent position. Some scholars say it was the place for the most intimate friend. Jesus sets his betrayer in the place reserved for someone special. Isn't that a glorious example of Jesus giving his betrayer another chance?

Isn't that the way God operates? As long as we are alive, God constantly holds out grace and the opportunity to change. This story also sets the example for us on our journey to Heaven. The question never ends with God pointing out our sins. The question ends with, "Will you come to me?"

For me, this is what makes the Christian faith unique. It is a religion of new beginnings. If we turn to God, we're forgiven.

God wipes the past clean. We may have to pay the penalty for our wrongdoing, but the Bible assures us that we have been forgiven.

From this account of Jesus' treatment of Judas, we see the heart of God as it reaches out to us. God is love and love always gives others another chance. And another. And another.

Jesus surely knew Judas's heart from the beginning, but he offers him the opportunity to change. The man had heard Jesus' deeply spiritual and insightful teaching, seen the miracles, had observed Jesus embarrass the religious leaders, and watched the Lord draw people to himself. That man had the same opportunities as the other eleven. As I've said, Jesus treated Judas as one of them, but in fact, he treated him even more specially than the others.

After the Lord announces that one of them will betray him, the other disciples want to know which one. The only answer the Lord gives is, "It is the one to whom I will give this piece of bread when I have dipped it in the dish" (John 13:26 [NIV]). He dips the bread into the dish and hands it to Judas and says, "What you are about to do, do quickly" (John 13:27b [NIV]). None of them understand, but Judas does.

Many scholars believe that Jesus handed Judas a special piece of bread, perhaps the first one. Some have called it a *sop*. In some cultures this is significant because it's a way to honor the guest. Jesus, the host, dips a piece of bread into the dish and hands it to one of the twelve. He chooses Judas.

Perhaps this modern-day story will make the significance of the action clearer. My co-writer told me of a time when he was a missionary in Kenya, in east Africa. After he had been there for nearly four years, a church prepared a big feast called *siku kuu* (a big day). The highlight of the event was the presentation of the *sawo*—the roasted tail of a sheep. The *sawo* is an offering of great respect and honor, and at that *siku kuu*, they chose to give it to Cecil Murphey to show their appreciation for all his work.

In Africa, the *sawo* was the sign of special recognition and friendship. Isn't it possible that Jesus offered Judas more than a mere piece of bread? The fact that John makes such a point of Jesus dipping the bread and handing it to Judas might indicate Jesus was presenting Judas with a great honor. Isn't it quite likely that Jesus is saying, "Here's one final chance. Turn from your evil ways"?

Judas's response is amazing. He does nothing. I envision the locking of their gaze. Judas knows that the Lord is aware of his betrayal but he won't accept grace and forgiveness.

We know Judas is a thief. The Bible may also be implying more than the fact that he stole. It may also speak of a covetous heart—one that never has enough and always grasps for more. It may mean that Judas focuses so much on money and possessions that he sees no value in anything else. His greed blinds him and he is unable to see the grace that Jesus offers.

John 13:27a says: "As soon as Judas took the bread, Satan entered into him" (NIV). That is one of the saddest statements in the Bible. It's a way of saying that Judas has run so far from God he can't accept Jesus' love. Another powerful statement by John reads, "As soon as Judas had taken the bread, he went out. And it was night" (verse 30 [NIV]). *And it was night.*

Throughout John's Gospel the writer uses the contrast of light and dark, daytime and night. Night means more than evening; it also paints the blackest, saddest pictures. Someone said, "It's always night when people turn away from Jesus."

By contrast, if we follow Jesus, we walk in the light. And we constantly have the choice of walking in light or following the darkness.

God wants us to enjoy the best life possible and he will always offer us the chance to walk in his light. He is a loving and forgiving God and constantly gives another chance—a second, third, or fourth chance. Not only is this a great gift for us, it is also a great example. The more we love and show compassion, the better people we become.

Jesus' treatment of Judas is another lesson for us. We are to love others, even when we recognize the weaknesses in them. We need to love them and forgive them and be willing to forgive them again.

The most dramatic and poignant example of giving a second chance I have ever seen portrayed was in a movie titled *The Mission*. In that 1986 movie, Robert De Niro is a slave trader named Mendoza from Paraguay. He seems to be a conscienceless man, who goes into the jungles of South America, traps helpless nationals, and takes them to public markets where he sells them like cattle. While Mendoza captures humans to turn them into slaves, his brother begins a relationship with Mendoza's girlfriend. Mendoza returns to discover the relationship and in heated anger draws his sword. In an act of passion, Mendoza kills his brother. Realizing what he has done, he goes to the Jesuit priests to see if there is any penance he could do to remove such a shocking sin from his life.

As penance, the priest assigns Mendoza the task of going back into the jungles where he kidnapped many natives. His mission (hence the title of the movie) is to become a priest to them. The people have known him as a killer, but his forgiveness revolves around caring for them and ministering to their needs.

As further penance, he must carry the armor he wore when he ventured out on the slave-trapping trips. Accompanied by other priests, Mendoza drags his heavy armor behind him on a rope across raging rivers, valleys, and sheer cliffs. Several times his armor, the vestige of his horrible past, almost drags him down.

After many hardships and much suffering, Mendoza reaches the land where he had captured the nationals to make them slaves. The other priests arrive first because Mendoza still struggles to haul his armor up a sheer bluff. When he finally reaches the top of the cliff the locals recognize their mortal enemy and his armor. They draw knives to stab him.

One young man places the edge of his knife against Mendoza's neck. Anyone seeing that frightening scene could certainly understand if the tribesman slit Mendoza's throat. After all, Mendoza had sent many of the tribe's members to horrifying slavery or painful death.

Mendoza begins to weep uncontrollably. He makes no effort to get away or to explain his former actions. Still tied to his armor, he resigns himself to a justified death. The young tribesman takes the knife and cuts the rope that holds the armor. With one swift motion Mendoza's armor clambers down the escarpment and frees the penitent from his burden.

The tribesmen embrace Mendoza as his tears of remorse turn to tears of joy and acceptance of forgiveness. Their compassion and forgiveness have set him free.

That film—now more than twenty years old—has stayed with me because it helps me understand that love gives another chance—especially when the person doesn't deserve it.

Here's another illustration: I heard a man speak at an AA meeting where I went as a guest. The speaker, who said his name was

Tom, told of a life of debauchery and dependence on alcohol, which he started in college. One time he phoned his parents, told them that he was an alcoholic, and they brought him back and accepted him and let him live with them. Within months he was out drinking again and stole some of their property to pay for his drinking.

He told us he came home four times because there was no other place to go. All four times his parents accepted him. They put restrictions on him such as that he couldn't drink inside the house. If he did, he would have to leave. He promised, but soon fell. Yet they always took him back. Eventually, he left home and didn't come back.

When he was forty-three, his mother notified him that she was dying of cancer and begged him to come home. "I know you are powerless to help yourself," she said but she also told him that she prayed every day that he would let God help him. Her last words were: "I'll wait for you in Heaven."

"Those words, 'I'll wait for you in Heaven,' changed my life," Tom said. "I didn't know enough about the Bible to know what that meant, but I realized that no matter what I did or how badly I had behaved, my mother had never stopped loving me." He went on to tell us that he had gotten sober, cleaned up his life, and had married. He and his wife had taken care of his father for the past two years.

As I listened I was struck by the way real love works. It holds no conditions and makes no demands. Love hopes and yearns for the best and it always holds on.

🖋

As I think about love giving another chance, it reminds me of one of the most frequently asked questions since my accident of twenty years ago. "Did you ever meet the man who drove the truck that killed you?"

I regret to say that the answer is no. I tried to connect with him several times. The man was a prison inmate driving a prison truck. By the time I was sufficiently physically able to travel, he was no longer incarcerated. I did read a transcript of his deposition regarding the accident. There is no doubt in my mind that he had no intention of hurting anyone that day. Regardless of his intentions, he killed me.

But I have long ago forgiven him. Some find it difficult to fathom that I bear him no grudge or ill feelings. To harbor such feelings would only hurt me, not him. But if I could connect with him, here's the statement I would like to make:

"Raymond, wherever you are, I forgive you. I know you didn't mean to hurt me. And I'm doing all right. I was knocked down, but not knocked out, beaten up, but not defeated. I may not meet you this side of Heaven. If that is not meant to be, and you have not already done so, please place your faith in Jesus. He is able to forgive all sins, including yours and mine. Accept him as your Lord and Savior. If I don't meet you here on Earth, I would like to meet you there at Heaven's gates. Our accident won't even be a memory there. Neither will prison. We'll walk the streets of gold where there are never any accidents."

Departing Instructions

1. Remind yourself today that God loves you. An awareness of that love will strengthen you as you face the hardships of life.

2. You have a sure hope—an expectation—that lies ahead of you. You will one day inherit the perfect life. Until then, live the best life possible with divine help.

3. Love the unlovable. Reach out to those who don't deserve love. Treat them as you would your close friends.

4. Forgive those who have wronged you. You can do that. God forgave you for your wrongdoing; you can forgive others—even without being asked.

6

Love Each Other

A new command I give you: Love one another. As I have loved you, so you must love one another. By this everyone will know that you are my disciples, if you love one another.

JOHN 13:34–35 (TNIV)

One of the annual youth Bible studies I used to teach when I was the minister of youth revolved around an imaginary court room. We set it up with a judge, jury, the evidence, and opposing attorneys. As the young people filed into the meeting room, I assigned them their roles. Some were jurors; one was the judge and got to wear a robe. I tried to select one young person from the group to be the defendant—someone I felt everyone would know reasonably well. I played the role of the prosecutor. I really chewed up some scenery with my overacting. My character called for slimy sarcasm because the prosecutor was the devil.

As the accused sat in the witness box, I challenged him or her with an ever-increasing tirade of charges.

- "Is it or is it not true that you have been a member of this church for five years?"

- "Is it or is it not true that you were actually baptized in the baptistery of this church?"
- "Is it or is it not true that you were seen actually helping out with the children's church services just a few weeks ago?"
- "And were you seen singing in the church youth choir?"

My prosecutor's voice rose to a crescendo and I turned from the accused. "Ladies and gentlemen of the jury, I submit to you that I have evidence that the defendant has not only invited others to this church but, dare I say, has actually contributed to others becoming Christians as a direct result of sharing his faith with other young people.

"Your honor, I move that you charge the jury to find this defendant guilty as charged beyond any reasonable doubt. Can there be any question that the defendant is guilty of being a Christian? The prosecution rests."

"Thank you, Mr. Prosecutor," the judge said.

I turned to the youth group and said, "But the real question of the hour for everyone present in this courtroom is this: "If *you* were on trial and accused of being a Christian, would there be enough evidence to convict you?"

I did that little play because I once saw a poster on the wall of a church. It went something like this: If being a Christian were a crime, would there be enough evidence to convict you?

When I think about the evidence that people would hold up, I can envision them saying things such as:

- "She gave to people in need."
- "He was a preacher and a teacher."
- "She tried to be a good person."

As I've thought about that little play-trial, I've also thought of myself and what it would be like if I were on trial. If they talked about me, I hope they'd find an abundance of evidence. Beneath the actions and acts of service, I hope they would sense that I acted with the right motivation. I hope they would see me as a person who cared. Or to put it biblically, I hoped they would see me as a man who loved.

As many others have pointed out in hundreds of books, the Greek has four words for *love* and two of them appear in the New Testament. The two that don't appear are *storge* (which refers to familial love) and *eros* (sexual love). The two that the biblical writers use are *phileo* (friendship) and *agape*.

The noun *agape* is a word that doesn't involve emotions. It's an attitude or a commitment. I like to define *agape* as "caring in action." It means that we do our best for others and that our actions are what count. We may or may not have warm emotions in doing our deeds.

The apostle Paul devotes an entire chapter (1 Corinthians 13) to describing fifteen characteristics of *agape*. And they're all descriptions of action. For example, he writes that love shows itself in patience, isn't jealous, doesn't brag, doesn't insist on its own rights, or fly into a temper (*compare* 1 Corinthians 13:4–7).

In John 13, we learn that once Judas leaves the upper room, Jesus faces his loyal followers and gives them his final words. He begins by calling them *children*—a term of affection that is used several times in the letters of John (*see* 1 John 2:1, 12, 18, 28, 3:7; and 3 John 3). This is a moment of tenderness from the teacher to his children (or learners).

Jesus knows that the time is short. If they are to heed his final words, they need to hear them now. He will go on a journey on which none of them can go. He will take a road where he must walk alone. Before he goes, however, he says a powerful and profound thing, but he states it not as a teaching, but as a command— *a new command.*

Jesus announces that the time has come for him to be glorified. He has said words like that before, but this time he must have spoken with such solemnity that none of them interrupts or asks what he means.

After he says that he is going away to a place where they can't come, he follows that up with a powerful statement. "So now I am giving you a new commandment: Love each other. Just as I have loved you, you should love each other. Your love for one another will prove to the world that you are my disciples" (John 13:34–35 [NLT]).

Jesus calls it a new command, but it's probably just new to them—or at least new in emphasis—because Leviticus 19:18 says essentially the same thing. Apparently that was one of the verses from the Old Testament that people passed over or chose to ignore.

It's remarkable just how many times we find *new* in the Bible. New Testament Greek has two words for *new.* One is *neos,* which means "new in existence," and we use it in such terms as neonatal. The other, used here, is *kainos,* and it appears more than forty times in the New Testament. It carried the idea of being "fresh or recent." It can mean recently made or fresh, but it also means unused, unworn, unprecedented, or uncommon. *Kainos* is used when it speaks of the new covenant (Luke 22:20), becoming a new creation (2 Corinthians 5:17), or the new Jerusalem (Revelation 21:2).

What was new in John 13:34–35 was that Jesus' love was to be demonstrated among his followers and would become the standard for judging their relationship to him. Their commitment to the good of each other was to become the *standard of behavior* for them and for all followers. Even us today. They were to show love with the same intensity and quality that he had shown them throughout his ministry. That mutual Christlike love would be the proof to the world that they were his disciples.

As I've thought about that scene in the upper room, it reminds me that Jesus knew what lay ahead. For example, he knew the betrayal before it happened; he knew the disciples would run away after the soldiers came; he knew he would be tortured before he died. But there is no rebuke in his words. There is only compassion and a powerful exhortation for them to love.

If they had a question about exactly what he expected them to do, he cleared that up with these words: "Just as I have loved you, you should love each other" (John 13:34b [NLT]). He set the standard. As his disciples, they were to follow the behavior he had demonstrated.

He not only commanded, but he gave them an example: His own actions and behavior. Not many people could talk that way—perhaps none. Too many say, "Do as I say and not as I do." They realize how imperfectly they follow their own values and principles. But Jesus could hold himself up as the supreme example. He loved them. He had been with them, taught them, and provided for their needs. They would soon be without him, but they must stop their bickering and infighting and give freely and compassionately to each other.

He pointed out not only that they would become better people and be more faithful disciples, but their commitment to each other would become a powerful witness to the world around them. If people observed their love to each other, they could more easily point those people to Jesus.

How faithfully did those eleven men follow the command? No one knows, but in the early chapters of the Acts of the Apostles, the implication is that they followed it closely enough that everyone seemed to know they were Jesus' disciples. The first followers gave up their possessions and lived in a community. That made them a distinct minority, even though they faced some persecution. Yet people continued to join them. There had to have been good reason for that.

At first believers were called followers of the way, probably after Jesus' statement that he was *the way*. Acts 9:2 in the New International Version translates this clearly. Saul/Paul went to the high priest "and asked him for letters to the synagogues in Damascus, so that if he found any there who belonged to the Way, whether men or women, he might take them as prisoners to Jerusalem."

But the name of Jesus' followers changed, and I believe their obedience to the command to love was a major reason. Acts 11:26 says that they were first called Christians in the city of Antioch. That term means *little Christs*. It may have been intended as a derisive term, but it stuck. What would persuade people to call them little Christs—which probably meant Christlike or followers of Christ? Surely it was more than the words they preached and was because of the demonstration of following *the* Christ. Is it possible that their love for each other and for people around them was so apparent that even their enemies had to say, "They're little Christs in their behavior."

They loved in the same way Jesus loved.

One of the most gratifying and yet stunning responses to my first book, *90 Minutes in Heaven: A True Story of Death and Life,* came from Scandinavia. I traveled across Sweden with Joel Sjöberg, a second-generation preacher and Christian publisher. Joel demonstrated the servanthood aspect of love so many times.

Twice he loaded his van with books and drove over the miles of fiords, mountains, and valleys of Sweden. We preached in a five-hundred-year-old cathedral in Stockholm. We preached in a tent to thousands in Lapland. Joel is a bright young husband and father who deeply loves his country and its people. In the post-Christian world that is Europe and Scandinavia, Joel remains a "little Christ." He would willingly charge the gates of hell with a water pistol if that were his only weapon.

I have stood beside him as we preached to churches where so many people came that the buildings were packed and many faces pressed against windows from outside. Shapeless forms stood outside in the dark trying to get close enough to hear the service.

Some statistics report that only 2 percent of the Swedish population is evangelical Christians. But Joel is there and certainly one of the little Christs in the country.

In Stockholm we were to speak in a beautiful old cathedral at two o'clock on a Saturday afternoon. After Joel and I arrived, the head priest apologetically told us he didn't know who scheduled our appearance, but that no one was likely to show up at that time of day except local prostitutes and drug addicts in search of a handout.

"That's wonderful," Joel said. "That is just our kind of audience."

As the time for the service drew near we went into the priest's office to pray. We left the office not knowing what we would face. To the priest's surprise, nearly twelve hundred people had filled every seat and some had to stand in the back. Joel and I preached, and although it's not the tradition of that church, at the priest's request we offered an altar call—an invitation for them to turn to Jesus Christ.

I'm sure there were many factors, but certainly one of the reasons for the success was Joel himself. He had given himself to others. That is, in the biblical sense he had loved. He treated others well and made no distinction between those who believe and those who don't.

After hours of counseling respondents, Joel left to perform a previously scheduled wedding and I was the dinner guest of the priest and his wife.

As we sat down to dine, the kindly old priest put his head on the dinner table and began to weep. Not sure what to do, I placed my hand on his shoulder.

After a few minutes, he looked up with a brilliant smile on his face. "Pastor Piper, fourteen years ago our parish planned to sell the church where you preached today to the city of Stockholm. The city would tear it down and build an Olympic swimming pool.

"Fourteen years ago the bishop gave me six weeks to increase the size of the Sunday attendance or else we would sell the building. Twelve old women came that first Sunday. The outlook was dismal. Slowly I began to convince more people to attend. We stayed just a little ahead of the wrecking ball. But we have survived.

"On that bleak Sunday fourteen years ago I prayed that God would let me live long enough to see my church filled just once."

The priest began to weep again. "Today, the Lord answered my prayer. Now, I can die a happy man."

As I listened to him tell his story, I understood. He had loved the people. It was more than just preserving a building; it was a deep compassion for people. He had loved them and God honored that love and commitment.

Here's another example. When the Murpheys were missionaries in Kenya, Shirley worked with women. She taught them the Bible along with classes on hygiene and other practical topics. Then the time came for them to move from that part of the country. Another woman, who had previously worked with the women, would return soon and take over Shirley's work.

At the conclusion of the last conference where Shirley was scheduled to speak, an African woman named Margaret threw her arms around Shirley and told her how much the women loved her.

Shirley thanked them and said that the other missionary would be with them soon. "She speaks the language better than I do and she's been with you before."

"But it is not the same," Margaret said. "You have loved us."

"But she—"

"No, you do not understand. Many things she taught us, but you have loved us."

※

If there is one parting instruction that stands above all else, it is to love others. It means we love those who are different, those who are indifferent, and those who don't want to be different but continue in their old ways.

Jesus said it to the disciples in the upper room and says it just as strongly today: "Love one another. As I have loved you, so you must love one another" (John 13:34 [NIV]).

If we are to be true disciples who prepare for liftoff, loving isn't a choice. It's a joyful responsibility that shows our readiness to be Heaven bound.

Departing Instructions

1. Love others because that is your calling. The greatest testimony you can give of your faith in Jesus Christ and show that we are preparing for Heaven is that you love others.
2. Show your love by the way you treat people. Make them know you care, even if you do not use words.
3. Treat all people lovingly. By your behavior, others will know who you are and they will know whom you follow.
4. Remember these words: "This is how we know what love is: Jesus Christ laid down his life for us. And we ought to lay down our lives for one another. If any of you has material possessions and sees a brother or sister in need but has no pity on them, how can the love of God be in you?" (1 John 3:16–17 [TNIV]).

7

Follow Jesus

Simon Peter asked him, "Lord, where are you going?" Jesus replied, "Where I am going, you cannot follow now, but you will follow later." Peter asked, "Lord, why can't I follow you now? I will lay down my life for you."

JOHN 13:36–37 (NIV)

The story of Judas is a strange contrast to that of Peter. Judas willingly betrayed Jesus. He sold information to the Roman soldiers so they could locate the Lord and arrest him. Later that night, Peter also proves faithless but his intentions and his reaction to his actions are markedly different from those of Judas.

When Jesus tells his disciples that he will be leaving soon, Peter, always the quick one, asks, "'Lord, where are you going?'

"Jesus replied, 'Where I am going, you cannot follow now, but you will follow later'" (John 13:36 [NIV]).

The tenacious Peter isn't satisfied and he presses Jesus by asking, "Lord, why can't I follow you now? I will lay down my life for you" (John 13:37 [NIV]).

That's a powerful commitment from Peter. Does he mean it? I have no doubt that he did. At least he did at that moment. He was in the presence of his teacher and leader and the small band of men hasn't experienced serious opposition. Even though the religious leaders detest them, the common people follow them.

Peter loves Jesus, and the four Gospels make that clear. His boast—and it was a boast—is also a powerful statement of his faith. "I'm ready to die for you" (John 13:37b [NLT]).

Jesus stops him. I can envision the Lord holding up his hand or perhaps shaking his head slowly as he responds, "Will you really lay down your life for me? I tell you the truth, before the rooster crows, you will disown me three times!" (John 13:38 [NIV]).

Most people know the story. Later, when the high priest interrogates Jesus, the boastful disciple warms himself at the fire as he stands outside the gate along with other onlookers. When asked, twice he denies any relationship to Jesus.

Luke records the poignant third time like this: "About an hour later another asserted, 'Certainly this fellow was with him, for he is a Galilean.' Peter replied, 'Man, I don't know what you're talking about!' Just as he was speaking, the rooster crowed. The Lord turned and looked straight at Peter. Then Peter remembered the word the Lord had spoken to him: 'Before the rooster crows today, you will disown me three times'" (Luke 22:59–61 [NIV]).

For me, that's a strong emotional picture, and I can visualize the sadness on Jesus' face as he sees his words fulfilled.

The next verse, however, enables us to glimpse Peter's heart: "And Peter left the courtyard, weeping bitterly" (Luke 22:62 [NLT]).

Peter had been sure he wouldn't fail, but he did. In a moment of great testing he failed. I want to insert here that he didn't fail deliberately, but only out of human weakness.

I understand that story. I've been a preacher and a pastor for three decades, and I've met many people who make such rash statements. Sometimes they come out as promises of what they'll do for God, for the church, or for people in disaster-torn countries. When they promise, I usually believe them. I don't think they're lying.

Many of these promises come during moments of crisis. At other times, people make rash promises in the midst of a high emotional level. For example, many times I've preached and asked people to turn totally to God. Many respond and I've watched tears stream down their cheeks. I've heard confession of countless sins.

Some people keep their promises; others don't. Yet at the time they make them, both groups seem sincere and committed. The writer James of the New Testament must have encountered some of those same people because he wrote, "[D]on't just listen to God's word. You must do what it says. Otherwise, you are only fooling yourselves. For if you listen to the word and don't obey, it is like glancing at your face in a mirror. You see yourself, walk away, and forget what you look like. But if you look carefully into the perfect law that sets you free, and if you do what it says and don't forget what you heard, then God will bless you for doing it" (James 1:22–25 [NLT]).

James refers to people who glance at their reflected images in a mirror—and they see their imperfections. But they go away without taking action—that's the same thing as forgetting what they saw as soon as they turn away. If they looked deeply at themselves they would have seen things they need to do and would have made changes. Who would look at their own uncombed hair and not at least try to pat it down?

By contrast, Christians stare at the truth ("the perfect law that sets you free," James 1:25 [NLT]) as their mirror. For those who see the truth and prepare to obey what they learn, James says, "if you do what it says and don't forget what you heard, then God will bless you for doing it" (verses 25–26).

✒

It's easy to raise an eyebrow over Peter's denial of Jesus, but maybe we'd do better to think about it a little more.

First, Peter was the only disciple who boldly promises to lay his life down for Jesus. Where are the voices of the other ten men? Peter was also the first of the disciples to recognize that Jesus was the Messiah (*see* Matthew 16:13–20). We've sometimes said that Peter had foot-in-the-mouth disease, but he's a man who is quick to respond. We have to admire him for that.

Second, we also need to compare Peter with Judas. Judas *betrays;* Peter *denies.* The first is a calculated and cruel action; the second is an unplanned, emotional experience. Judas has carefully planned his betrayal; Peter never plans to deny Jesus but he gets swept away in a moment of weakness, perhaps fear for his own life.

Third, we need to think of the results of the two courses of action. Judas eventually realizes the horror of his actions. Here's what Matthew says: "When Judas . . . saw that Jesus was condemned, he was seized with remorse and returned the thirty silver coins to the chief priests and the elders. 'I have sinned,' he said, 'for I have betrayed innocent blood.' . . . Judas threw the money into the temple and left. Then he went away and hanged himself" (Matthew 27:3–5 [NIV]).

The question arises over Judas's suicide. Did he repent before he killed himself? The Bible offers no statement or hint that he did. Throughout the history of the church, the teaching has been that Judas realized the enormity of his sin, but didn't reach out for grace and forgiveness.

We know from other passages that he was a thief and greed was probably the reason for the betrayal. Once he saw his sin, Judas could have cried out for forgiveness, but there is no indication that he did. He must have been overwhelmed by his sinful act, but there is no indication that he ever repented.

Jesus said these words to Peter on the night of Judas's betrayal: "Simon, Simon, Satan has asked to sift you as wheat. But I have prayed for you, Simon, that your faith may not fail. And when you have turned back, strengthen your brothers" (Luke 22:31–32 [NIV]).

In the garden, before the betrayal, Jesus prays for his disciples, "While I was with them, I protected them. . . . None has been lost except the one doomed to destruction so that the Scripture would be fulfilled" (John 17:12 [NIV]).

Here's the difference: Judas chose to betray Jesus; Peter denied Jesus out of weakness. And Peter repented. When Peter realizes he has denied Jesus, he shows immediate remorse.

I feel for poor Peter. Yes he denied Jesus, but he had the right heart. At the time he just didn't have the right fortitude. How could we not love Peter? How could we not resonate with that transparent disciple? He denied Jesus, but he paid for it with his tears and his obvious repentance. That's the mark of true discipleship. Peter sets the example for us as we prepare for our heavenly liftoff. We need to make things right with everyone—especially in our relationship with our loving Savior.

I've been a believer for more than forty years, and I've been a bit like Peter at times. I've failed—not because I planned to do so.

I failed out of weakness, sometimes out of ignorance, occasionally out of fear of ridicule. But when I've been made aware of my sin—and it is sin—I can say that I have confessed to God. I admit my wrongdoing and know that, like Jesus forgiving Peter, God has forgiven me.

The New Testament contains no words that speak of Jesus pronouncing words of forgiveness over Peter. But when we read the Book of Acts, Peter dominates the first twelve chapters. He's the obvious leader. He could never have held that position if Jesus hadn't forgiven him.

One more thing, I wonder if Peter *needed* to fail. In my years of ministry, I've realized that the most tender, most forgiving, and the most understanding saints of God are those who have failed in countless ways, but they know they've been forgiven.

To say it another way: They have understood grace. They know what it's like to be weak and to stumble along. Paul sets a wonderful example for us by a personal testimony in Romans 7. Before he writes of the powerful grace and victory we have available in Jesus Christ, he writes, "I don't really understand myself, for I want to do what is right, but I don't do it. Instead, I do what I hate" (Romans 7:15 [NLT]).

I've had people tell me about knowing the right thing and doing the bad. We all do that at times but the true disciple not only says, "Forgive me," but also says, "Help me not to do it again."

Perhaps the most important mark of true disciples is that we love the Lord and don't want to fail. We don't want to displease the Savior who died for us. But alas, we fail. However, failure isn't the end, but the opportunity to repent, change, and, like Peter, become stronger in our preparation for our homebound journey.

Departing Instructions

1. Follow Jesus—regardless of the obstacles and the fears.
2. Don't plan to fail, but if you do, remind yourself that even the great apostle failed and Jesus forgave him.
3. Follow Jesus. You may not understand what you'll face and you don't know what's ahead. But he knows and that's enough.
4. Ask for and expect divine help. Because Jesus is with you, he wants you to be fully prepared.

8

Trust God, Trust Me

[Jesus said,] "Do not let your hearts be troubled. Trust in God; trust also in me. In my Father's house are many rooms; if it were not so, I would have told you. I am going there to prepare a place for you. And if I go to prepare a place for you, I will come back and take you to be with me that you also may be where I am."

JOHN 14:1–3 (NIV)

John 14 starts with these words from Jesus: "Do not let your hearts be troubled. Trust in God; trust also in me" (verse 1 [NIV]).

In a few hours, life will turn upside down for the eleven disciples who are with Jesus in the upper room. Roman soldiers will arrest Jesus and the men will run away in fear. Knowing that, Jesus tries to prepare the eleven men who are with him, and he doesn't want them to worry about what will happen.

They have known the ire of the Jewish leaders and must have sensed the growing anger from them. But they have had no run-ins with the Romans. In fact, all references to the Romans in the Gospels are positive, and John even tells the story of a nobleman who wanted Jesus to heal his son.

That situation will change. The Romans will arrest Jesus, beat him, and crucify him. Jesus knows all that is to happen and yet he says to his small group of followers, "Do not let your hearts be troubled."

It's strange to read those words. Most of us probably get agitated or angry when anyone says such mundane words to us. People say, "Don't be nervous or anxious or upset," as if we only had to dial a number or punch a key and all would be well. They seem to dismiss our concern over a troubling situation.

When I was in the hospital, a number of well-meaning people said, "Don't worry. Everything is going to work out all right."

I didn't answer them, but a few times I wondered: How would you know? Those words came from people who cared and they weren't trying to be glib. What they meant was that they didn't want me to worry and they also wanted to assure me that God would take care of it.

The difference is that Jesus has the right to make such statements. We can even label them commands; they're certainly more than suggestions.

He could say such things because he is also the one who can take away our fears, anxieties, and uncertainties. He provides a means to enable these disciples *and us* to stay free from anxiety. In effect he says, "If you commit yourself fully to God in a relationship of loving trust, you can do the same by trusting in me. The pains of life don't last forever. You'll have problems, but if you know the end and what follows this life, you can endure."

I've realized that the more experiences we have in trusting God, the more we can trust. Those disciples should have been experienced enough. Didn't they see Jesus multiply food in the presence of five thousand men plus women and children? Didn't Peter start to walk on water? They saw healings take place and demons cast out. Didn't they watch Jesus perform miracles? They were around when Lazarus was resuscitated after four days.

Here's an example that helps explain what I mean. Years ago I attended a Kristallnacht service and three elderly Jews told their story of that night in 1938 when Nazi storm troopers began their violence against Jews.

When Nazi storm troopers destroyed stores in Germany and Austria, they killed hundreds of Jews and left the streets covered with smashed glass. That became the origin of the name—"Night of the Broken Glass." It became the most widely reported atrocity of Nazi Germany at the time. One man, with a heavy accent, told us that he had been a young boy in the Warsaw ghetto. His family was starving, so he would slip outside the walls that had been built to cordon off the Jews, to get them food. Each night he crept out in the midst of darkness. He dodged patrols and soldiers and went into the Aryan part of the city. He returned with provisions to help his starving family. He escaped the final Nazi roundup of the Jews and survived the war.

In the Kristallnacht service, someone asked him if he wasn't afraid. He said something like this: "The first time I was very much afraid. I was less afraid the second time. Each time I slipped through the wall, it was easier. Finally, I went out with absolute calm. I remained vigilant so that I did not get caught, but I did not worry about the Nazis. I knew I would survive."

He went on to say that he felt he had a mission—to help his starving family. "I would say to myself, 'I am in God's hands,' and that gave me peace."

That's a message that can inspire many believers. If we are in God's hands (and we are) why should we worry about anything?

The disciples had ample evidence of God's loving and protective hand. They had good reason to listen and obey the command not to be anxious. But they still had not been tested in their faith. When life collapses, Jesus wants them to know they have one thing to do: hold on and trust that the God who has preserved them and provided for them in the past is the same God who is with them now.

I've received hundreds of e-mails, letters, and phone calls from people over the past few years that recount their dark moments. They tell me of the horrible situations such as the death of someone they love, an unexpected divorce, or the loss of a supposedly secure job. Yet each of them say that something held them together. Even if there was initial panic, fear, or worry, they realized that everything would be all right or that an inner peace filled their hearts. Their expressions are all different but they seem to have one commonality: Their faith pays off when life caves in on them. Because they know with utter certainty that God is with them, they can go through the worst situations.

By telling his disciples to believe in God and in him, Jesus declares his divinity—his oneness with the Father. He also wants to assure them of the promises he has already made to them, such as those in John 10. He calls himself the good shepherd. "The good shepherd sacrifices his life for the sheep" (verse 11). In verse 14 he repeats that he is the good shepherd and says, "I know my own sheep, and they know me" (NLT).

Because of their culture, they would have understood those words—even if they weren't ready to accept them. The good shepherd protects his sheep, even if it means giving his life for them. He makes the point that hirelings run away in times of trouble, but the good shepherd stays because he loves those under his care.

In the same chapter, Jesus says, "My sheep listen to my voice; I know them, and they follow me. I give them eternal life, and they will never perish. No one can snatch them away from me" (verses 27–28).

Jesus constantly gives them assurances of his presence, but (as we see after the betrayal) they don't grasp the reality. Many of us today are like them: We hear the words, sing them in worship, and perhaps we've memorized them from the Bible. The real test of our faith, however, is when we're called to stand firm in the midst of chaos.

Jesus pleaded with his disciples not to worry or to be anxious. "Do not let your hearts be troubled" (John 14:1 [NIV]). He went on to speak about trusting God and trusting him as well. If we trust, we don't worry.

I heard the following story, which shows this in action. A woman's husband died when he was barely into his thirties. She had to bring up six children on her own. She not only raised them, but all turned out to be fine, godly people.

One day a local reporter interviewed her and asked, "How did you raise six children on your own and do such an excellent job?"

"I entered into a partnership with God."

"What do you mean by a partnership?" he asked.

"I made a deal with God Almighty. I said that I would do all the work if He would do all the worrying. And he did."

As we look toward Heaven we have Jesus' promise to be with us. Although doubts may assail us at times, we're exhorted to trust.

Jesus says he is going to Heaven to prepare for his followers. He makes it clear that the road to Heaven holds pain as well as reward. When Jesus urges them not to be anxious, he obviously refers to situations that would produce such a response. If there were no such situations, they would not feel tense, worried, or concerned. He never misleads them (or us), but assures us that he's present with us all the way.

The way to a worry-free life isn't easy. I want to offer you five suggestions to help you combat worry.

1. Your life is more important than things. We probably all know that but it's easy to get distracted. Jesus told his listeners, "[D]o not worry about your life, what you will eat or drink; or about your body, what you will wear" (Matthew 6:25 [NIV]).

Some people stand at the door of their overflowing closet and agonize over what they'll wear. Or they stare at their overstocked pantry and wonder what they'll eat or worry that they might eat too much and gain weight. Jesus wants us to enjoy life and not be upset or distracted over things that aren't that important. Life is more important than worrying about acquiring or holding on to the material things. Don't allow things to become an end in themselves, but a means to the end of serving God.

2. God cares about you. If God cares, God also acts on your behalf. Jesus said, "Look at the birds of the air, for they neither sow nor reap, nor gather into barns; yet your Heavenly Father feeds them. Are you not of more value than they?" (Matthew 6:26 [NKJV]).

3. Pause and consider how good life really is. We tend to get tied up with problems and concerns and forget that life can be good. We also forget that worrying drains us of energy but nothing improves through our worry. "Which of you by worrying can add one cubit to his stature?" (Matthew 6:27 [NKJV]).

4. When you're tempted to worry, remember God's promises to you. Or as someone put it, "Do your best and trust God for the rest." Jesus said it this way, "Seek first the kingdom of God and His righteousness, and all these things shall be added to you" (Matthew 6:33 [NKJV]).

5. The good life is taking everything one day at a time. Jesus said, "Therefore do not worry about tomorrow, for tomorrow will worry about its own things. Sufficient for the day is its own trouble" (Matthew 6:34 [NKJV]).

"One day at a time" has become a cliché in our culture. But we'd be wise to heed that advice. What it means is that we should focus on now and not try to anticipate all the problems and difficulties that could lie ahead.

A friend named Dave bought a television set. After he got it home, he was unhappy and felt the salesman had misrepresented the features. The company's customer service department was closed and he had to wait until eight o'clock the next morning to call. Dave obsessed about it. He was sure he'd have to explain the problem, get switched from department to department, have to explain to each person, get angry, demand to talk to supervisors, and would have to make strong demands to get satisfaction.

He couldn't relax that night. Whenever he tried to sleep, he'd think of more obstacles he'd probably have to face before he could get satisfaction. He marshaled all his arguments and wrote the facts on a piece of paper.

The next morning he called and forced himself to be calm. The customer service representative said, "I'm sorry for your trouble. Would you like to bring the set back for a refund or would you like a different television?"

When Dave told me the story, he laughed self-consciously. "I worried for nothing."

He did. He had forgotten to live one day at a time. He was trying to live tomorrow's problems before they occurred.

I think many of us are like Dave.

Jesus' words mean "Don't worry."

Cec said that when his oldest child, Wanda, was five years old, she traveled with him for two weeks to visit several churches before they left for Africa. They stayed with a pastor near Des Moines, Iowa.

The pastor's wife worried about everything. She constantly rushed behind Wanda, fearing she would knock over something or spill her milk. She kept asking her if she was warm enough or had enough to eat.

On the third morning, the wife asked Wanda how much she liked being there. "Well, it's all right," she said, "but I don't think you're a Christian. Are you?"

The horrified woman said, "Of course I am!"

Wanda looked at her father and said, "But she worries all the time. If you believe Jesus, you're not supposed to worry, are you?"

Wanda was a child, but in her sweet childish way she spoke a powerful truth. The woman worried. If she worried, she wasn't trusting.

The end of that story is that months later the woman wrote Cec a brief note and thanked him for the words of his daughter and here are her final words: "Jesus said a child would lead them. That's what happened to me."

Whether you get the message from a child, the Bible, or directly from Heaven, the command remains the same: Don't worry. Prepare for that blissful eternity. If you trust now, you're already equipped.

Departing Instructions

1. Don't worry. If you are a believer, Jesus is with you. The Bible assures you of his presence even in the darkest of times.
2. Accept God's peace. God promises that if you focus on him and get your minds off circumstances, you'll have peace (*see* Isaiah 26:3).
3. Handle today's problems today. When you start to worry, remind yourself that you are trying to do God's job. God takes care of tomorrow.
4. When you doubt, talk to the one who takes away doubts. Ask him to help you to live in peace and be ready for Heaven.

9

Believe Jesus' Promise

[Jesus said] "There is more than enough room in my Father's home. If this were not so, would I have told you that I am going to prepare a place for you? When everything is ready, I will come and get you, so that you will always be with me where I am."

JOHN 14:2–3 (NLT)

One cold winter day I saw a neighbor boy standing on a curb about a mile from home. I pulled over, rolled down my window, and asked if he wanted a ride.

He shook his head.

"Are you sure?" I asked.

He was about nine years old and he nodded vigorously. "I'm waiting for my daddy. He told me to wait here, not talk to strangers, and not to move."

Intending it as a joke, I asked, "Are you sure he won't forget you?"

"He's my daddy," the boy said emphatically. Just those words, but the conviction in his voice said all I needed to hear. I waved, rolled up my windows, and drove away.

That's faith in action. He had it right. His daddy would come because he knew that if his father had given his word, he would fulfill that promise.

That's also how the Christian life works. When we're tempted to get discouraged, give up, or get fearful, we only have to remind ourselves that our daddy—God himself—has promised to help us. We don't have to worry or fear.

Jesus always speaks with candor. He never promises an easy time or a lack of problems. No one who reads the New Testament could ever claim to have been seduced into Christianity by false promises of a soft or prosperous life. Even though Jesus promises rewards and honor in Heaven, he also explains the other side of discipleship. For example, here are a few of the promises Jesus made to his disciples:

"I am sending you out like sheep among wolves. . . . Be on your guard against men; they will hand you over to the local councils and flog you in their synagogues. . . . But when they arrest you, do not worry about what to say or how to say it" (Matthew 10:16–19 [NIV]).

"Everyone will hate you because of me, but those who stand firm to the end will be saved" (Matthew 10:22).

"Whoever wants to be my disciple must deny themselves and take up their cross daily and follow me. For whoever wants to save their life will lose it, but whoever loses their life for me will save it" (Luke 9:23–24).

"I have told you these things, so that in me you may have peace. In this world you will have trouble" (John 16:33 [TNIV]).

Jesus never bribes his disciples, but he promises that if they are faithful and obey him in every way, they will achieve greatness. Jesus not only told his disciples not to be anxious, but also went on to say, "In my Father's house are many rooms; if it were not so, I would have told you" (John 14:2 [NIV]).

When I was a young Christian I used to puzzle over those words. First, Jesus says not to be anxious and then he speaks about the many rooms in Heaven. I didn't get the connection. He obviously refers to Heaven—no one disputes that. The only way I could make sense of it was to add implied words between the two statements, such as these: "Life will be difficult, but don't worry. At the end, you have a reservation in Heaven. You have it because I'm going there to prepare the place for you."

The other thing that bothered me was the phrase *many rooms.* Why would there be many rooms? I used to envision Heaven as a place where we had everything and never needed a place to be alone. Why would we want or need separate rooms?

I've come to the conclusion that was Jesus' way of saying there is space for all of us—for everyone who chooses to go to Heaven. Someone once said to me, "Heaven is as wide as the heart of God and there's plenty of room for whoever wants to come."

Jesus may also have been saying to the disciples, who would face their own forms of rejection and persecution, "Don't be afraid. In this world, people may shut their doors or refuse to allow you into their homes, but in Heaven you'll never be shut out. You'll always have a place."

Some ancient manuscripts show John 14:2 as a question rather than a statement. "If this were not so, would I have told you that I am going to prepare a place for you?" (*see* NLT). Jesus wouldn't have told them anything false. He implies that he had already told them that at his death he would go straight to the Father so he could prepare a place for them.

Jesus blazes the trail for us. Hebrews reads, "[A]nd let us run with perseverance the race marked out for us. Let us fix our eyes on Jesus, the author and perfecter of our faith" (12:1b–2a [NIV]). That verse reminds us that Jesus is our companion along the way and the goal of our journey.

Hebrews 6:20 speaks of Jesus going behind the curtain in the temple into the holy of holies (by which is symbolically meant Heaven) "where our forerunner, Jesus, has entered on our behalf" (TNIV). The word translated as "forerunner" (Greek *prodromos*) was a term used to refer to reconnaissance troops that went ahead to make sure the area was safe. They would mark the trail for the rest of the army to follow. That is what Jesus was saying to them.

He also promises, "I will come back and take you to be with me" (John 14:3 [NIV]). It's like the story I mentioned at the beginning of the chapter of the boy who waited on the corner for his dad. He had no doubts that his father would come back for him. "He's my daddy." Those words make clear the level of the boy's trust. They also help remind us that Jesus' promise is absolutely sacred. It's also a powerful word of encouragement to each of us.

The word he uses in John 14:3 is *paralambano*, which means "to take or to join with." When will Jesus come to take them? Those first disciples surely must have wondered. Will it be immediately after his own resurrection? No, because they have tasks to fulfill. One thing we can assume is that at the death of each of them, Jesus waits at the gate of Heaven. Until then, he also promises his presence with them and his ongoing help as long as they survive on Earth.

Jesus is called the author or "pioneer" of our faith (Hebrews 12:2 [TNIV]), which says that by his death he shows the way to eternal glory. But his promise makes a strong statement that death isn't the final word. He will return at the end of the world, or he will meet us when we depart from this life. Either way, we meet Jesus at the end of our journey.

I have no doubt about those words because I was there—in Heaven. The one regret I have about my brief stay in Heaven is that I didn't get to see Jesus face-to-face. I did see his glory "high and lifted up" as I looked through the gates. Just as I drew close to the entrance, my brief sojourn ended. Of course Jesus is there. Heaven isn't Heaven without him. If I had seen him face-to-face, I'm positive that nothing—absolutely nothing—could have called me back to Earth.

❦

When Jesus speaks, the disciples seem to have no understanding of his impending death (even though he has repeatedly told them), but he wants them not to fear death or anything else that might happen. He wants them to know that he will wait for them in Heaven.

For Christians, Heaven is where Jesus is. That's all we really need to know, isn't it? If we follow him on Earth, we'll have everything we need or want when we reach Heaven.

I don't have to speculate on what Heaven will be. I *know*. Heaven has its own language and we'll all speak it—a language of pure joy and unmitigated peace. Unlike on Earth, there is nothing there to divide us and only Christ to unite us. We'll dine at the Lord's table not for sustenance but in order for fellowship with Jesus. In stark contrast to my earthly journey, in Heaven I experienced no pain, no tears, no death, and no loss. God is the audience of the heavenly praise but we are privileged to hear it. Angels hover around the holy throne praising him, but we will be ministered to by them.

Heaven is a place, a city, a kingdom, a realm. It is, quite simply, the most real thing I have ever experienced.

We don't have Jesus physically present now, but we have the Holy Spirit to guide us and we have his promises. True faith means that we hang on to the promises, or as Hebrews 11:1 puts it, "Faith is the confidence that what we hope for will actually happen; it gives us assurance about things we cannot see" (NLT).

Jesus waits for us and he is the one who ultimately calls us home. As we think of our personal liftoff, we can prepare by believing.

If doubts trouble us, we can ask his help. He wanted his first disciples to be ready; he also wants to help us to be ready.

Departing Instructions

1. Confirm your reservation for one of the rooms in Heaven. You do that if you believe in Jesus Christ.
2. Trust God. When you doubt or worry, you imply that your problem is too big for God to handle. Because you know your final destiny, you can trust God through all the heartaches and pains of life on Earth.

3. Live in such a way that everything you do honors your country, and your country is Heaven. "But our citizenship is in Heaven. And we eagerly await a Savior from there, the Lord Jesus Christ, who, by the power that enables him to bring everything under his control, will transform our lowly bodies so that they will be like his glorious body" (Philippians 3:20–21 [NIV]).

10

Believe—Even If You Don't Understand

[Jesus said] "You know the way to the place where I am going."
Thomas said to him, "Lord, we don't know where you are going,
so how can we know the way?" Jesus answered, "I am the way
and the truth and the life. No one comes to the Father except
through me. If you really knew me, you would know my Father
as well. From now on, you do know him and have seen him."

John 14:4–7 (NIV)

Years ago I read a short story about a young man who passed a number of college entrance tests with such high scores that the university gave him credit for undergraduate classes and he signed up for a class on logic theory.

The professor walked into the classroom, nodded to the more than fifty students present. He laid his notes on the podium and began to read. The new student listened for about five minutes and didn't understand a word. He picked up his books and started to walk out.

"Where are you going?" the professor asked.

"I don't understand anything you've said," he answered. "Even when you use words I recognize, it doesn't make sense to me."

"You think you're too stupid to understand?"

He shrugged. "Guess so. The others nod or take notes, so—"

"Sit down. You have just learned the first principle of logic. Language must make sense. I used many common words, but nothing I said had any meaning. You're obviously going to be a top student: You recognize nonsense when you hear it. You have every right to question what I say."

Although there was more to the story, that's all I remember, and it reminds us that we don't always understand, and when we don't, we have the right to ask questions. As I studied John 14:4–7, I thought of that story. In this case, when Jesus tells his disciples his intention to leave them, only one man says, "I don't get it." Probably none of them understands his words. But then, Jesus had spoken many things they hadn't understood.

For example, in John 7:33–34, Jesus said similar words: "I am with you for only a short time, and then I go to the one who sent me. You will look for me, but you will not find me; and where I am, you cannot come" (NIV). Those words were spoken in front of a crowd that included a number of Pharisees. Those leaders of the people asked, "Where does this man intend to go that we cannot find him? Will he go where our people live scattered among the Greeks, and teach the Greeks?" (verse 35).

If they had listened carefully to the teachings of Jesus, they wouldn't have had to ask. Or maybe they weren't able to take in information that they couldn't handle. A therapist once told me, "People don't hear what they're not ready to accept." As I wrote earlier, sometimes the words come to us, but they don't sink in because we're not ready to act on them. At other times, however, those words fall into some slot in the back of our memories and stay there until we're ready for them.

And sometimes people hear what they want to hear. For example, years ago, when I was in the broadcasting industry, we often received viewer complaints about TV commercials. We'd air a commercial about an item being on sale. The ad would clearly state the product, the price, and the length of days for which the sale would last. Invariably irate customers would call the station and tell us the store wouldn't sell that product for the advertised sale price. Most of the time it had been several days after the particular sale ended, but these people insisted that there was no expiration date mentioned during the commercial or that the sale was still going on. Every instance I recall was a matter of the consumer not paying very close attention to the ad. They heard what they wanted to hear and they didn't want to be confused with the truth.

When Jesus speaks to the Jewish crowds, they take his words literally and he doesn't explain to them. But this is a different situation. Jesus is with his disciples, his chosen few. He knows he will soon leave them and they must carry on the work he started. These are his departing words and, as much as they are able, he wants to be certain they comprehend. Jesus says he is going away and while he's gone, he'll prepare a place for them. "You know the way to the place where I am going" (John 14:4 [NIV]).

Thomas interrupts before Jesus gets any further. We've often referred to that disciple as the doubter. I think that's unfair. My sense is that Thomas is a questioner. And he asks questions that you and I might ask. "Lord, we don't know where you are going, so how can we know the way?" (John 14:5 [NIV]).

Jesus answers, "I am the way and the truth and the life. No one comes to the Father except through me" (John 14:6 [NIV]).

Why does Jesus use those three terms, saying he was the way, the truth, and the life? The answer is that he used words any Jew would probably have understood. Those terms would have had significant relevance to his people; it's remarkable that they retain that relevance to us in the twenty-first century.

First, the concept of the way (or the path) occurs throughout the Old Testament. Here are a few examples:

- "Teach me your way, O LORD; lead me in a straight path" (Psalm 27:11 [NIV]).
- "So be careful to do what the LORD your God has commanded you; do not turn aside to the right or the left. Walk in all the way that the LORD your God has commanded you" (Deuteronomy 5:32–33 [NIV]).
- "Observe the commands of the LORD your God, walking in his ways and revering him" (Deuteronomy 8:6 [NIV]).
- "In all your ways acknowledge him, and he will make your paths straight" (Proverbs 3:6 [NIV]).

My son Chris and I travel all over the United States sharing with those who want to hear my testimony in person. We go to places such as Tampa, Los Angeles, and Chicago. But we've also been to Bumpass, Virginia; Burlingame, Kansas; Durant, Iowa; and Wasilla, Alaska. We purchased a global positioning device (GPS) that gives us directions as we travel along. We want to arrive at the right place at the right time. We want to know the way and not get lost.

If we are in an unfamiliar area and don't have a GPS, Map-Quest, or a cell phone, we could easily get lost. But if a friend says, "I'll show you the way," I can relax. Jesus is the friend who always shows us the way. However, when Jesus says these words and points the way, he also means that he, himself, *is* the way—he is the path to God. Jesus promises to be with us at all times, and part of that being with us is to lead us down the right way until we reach our destination. It's not that Jesus only points out a road for others to follow, but he *is* the road itself. And he is the only road.

As an itinerant evangelist, I travel thousands of miles each year and often I travel by air. Not once in all my trips have I approached an airline ticket counter, placed a pile of cash on the counter, and said to the agent, "Just give me a ticket, please."

"A ticket to where?" I can imagine the agent would say. "What is your destination?"

"Oh, I don't know. Anywhere, just as long as I get to where I want to be."

Growing increasingly impatient the agent might ask, "And where would that be, sir?"

You know such a strange request on my part would never get me off the ground. To buy a ticket, the agent requires a destination. A specific destination requires a specific ticket. If I want to go to Atlanta, I will need a ticket to Atlanta. All flights don't go to Atlanta. Likewise, if I want to go to Heaven, all paths don't lead to Heaven. That's why Jesus made such a strong statement to make clear that he, and only he, is the way.

Second, Jesus also says he is truth. Again, that's a term any good Jew would have understood.

- "Teach me your way, O LORD, and I will walk in your truth" (Psalm 86:11 [NIV]).
- "Guide me in your truth and teach me, for you are God my Savior" (Psalm 25:5 [NIV]).
- "For your love is ever before me, and I walk continually in your truth" (Psalm 26:3 [NIV]).

Jesus speaks the truth and he embodies the truth. Others may speak truth at times, but only Jesus embodies it. Not only does he proclaim the right way to live, but he epitomizes it by his actions.

In my travels, I've been invited to speak to many groups of students. They range in age from middle school to graduate school. I constantly encourage them to get a good education. In doing that, I also exhort them to always seek the truth. But I don't leave them without pointedly saying, "If you really seek the truth, you'll find Jesus *is* the truth."

Third, Jesus says he is life. Consider that choice of words when you realize that his earthly life is about to end and after that, he will be resurrected. The significance of his choosing the word *life* is borne out in these references.

- "He who heeds discipline shows the way to life, but whoever ignores correction leads others astray" (Proverbs 10:17 [NIV]).
- "You have made known to me the path of life; you will fill me with joy in your presence, with eternal pleasures at your right hand" (Psalm 16:11 [NIV]).
- "For these commands are a lamp, this teaching is a light, and the corrections of discipline are the way to life" (Proverbs 6:23 [NIV]).

His words say more than his being the one who enlightens; he is life, that is, he is the giver of life. John says that Jesus is "full of grace and truth" (John 1:14, 17 [NIV]). It's not merely for the sake of knowledge that we seek truth, but we seek truth because that makes life worth living.

Jesus says, perhaps as a mild rebuke: "If you really knew me, you would know my Father as well. From now on, you do know him and have seen him" (John 14:7). This is a powerful statement. The Jews often said that no one had seen God and lived. So the disciples must have been taken aback by Jesus' statement.

Was that a challenge? A test? I don't know. Jesus had just said that by knowing him, the disciples also know the Father, and by seeing him they also see God. I suppose Philip, another of the eleven men, doesn't know what to make of his words. I bet he could hardly take in the staggering possibility of the Lord's words. Philip realized that to know the Father is all-important, so he asks Jesus, "Lord, show us the Father and that will be enough for us" (verse 8).

We can almost hear the sadness in Jesus' response to Philip: "Don't you know me, Philip, even after I have been among you such a long time? Anyone who has seen me has seen the Father. How can you say, 'Show us the Father?'" (verse 9).

I can envision Jesus staring directly at them as he asks, "Don't you believe that I am in the Father, and that the Father is in me?" (verse 10). Before they have a chance to answer, Jesus hits them with this statement: "The words I say to you are not just my own. Rather, it is the Father, living in me, who is doing his work. Believe me when I say that I am in the Father and the Father is in me; or at least believe on the evidence of the miracles themselves" (verses 10b–11).

His point is obvious: To see Jesus—that is, to perceive who he truly is and what his words and his deeds mean—is to see the Father actively at work. The Father and the Son are so closely linked that to see and to be in touch with one is to see and be in touch with the other. All through his ministry, Jesus makes it clear that he never teaches or acts independently of the Father or behaves as though he alone is the final authority. The Father dwelling within Jesus does the work—both the teaching and the miracles—through Jesus. He's now trying to explain to the eleven disciples that between the Father and Jesus the Son there is total and absolute unity and purpose. If the disciples comprehend that idea, they will understand that to know either the Father or the Son would be to know both.

I don't understand exactly what Jesus meant, but I believe and that's all Jesus requires. I truly believe there is a harmony or a unity between the Father and the Son. That's enough for me.

Who says we have to understand everything? Who says we need to comprehend before we can experience? If we waited until we grasped the full truth about everything, we'd hardly venture outside our own homes. I don't understand many of the items and machines I use every day, but I have faith that they will perform the tasks for which they were designed.

Most of us don't want suspense or surprises. We want explanations, and if they meet our approval, we'll agree to them. That's not Jesus' way. He talks to his followers and says, in effect, "Believe me. That's all you need."

Those men had been with him for three years. They listened to his words of wisdom; they heard him talk about his unity with God; they saw the miraculous deeds he had done. Where did they think he got that power and the insight he evidenced?

Thomas is honest enough to say that he can't grasp Jesus' words. Probably none of them do. Aren't we like that? We don't understand a thousand things that happen to us or in the world around us. Philip wants assurances and explanations, but Jesus reminds them that he had been with them and taught them. He has manifested God's love and presence.

Don't we sound a little like Philip? We may not understand many things we read in the Bible. God doesn't ask us to understand, but he does ask us to obey.

After Philip's question, we read no more interruptions. Maybe the disciples are shocked into silence; maybe they remain confused; or perhaps they begin to comprehend the powerful, mystical union between the Father and the Son. Possibly they need to stop talking and start listening.

Perhaps we need to listen to the real significance and gravity of the Lord's words.

Jesus is really saying to Thomas, Philip, and the others, "If you can't believe the words, look beyond the words. Look at the works I've done among you. See what I did in your presence. Believe the actions because they also tell you who I am."

That's where we have to place our final verdict: His words and his works are the evidence. When we read the words of Jesus two thousand years later, they still speak to us. They appeal to us in ways we can't explain, but we know they are there for us to obey— even if we don't comprehend everything.

Months before Jesus gave his departing instructions, John the Baptist had been in prison and began to doubt that Jesus was the Messiah. He sent messengers to ask. Here's Jesus' response: "Go back and report to John what you hear and see" (Matthew 11:4 [NIV]). He told of miracles of healing the blind, the lame, the deaf, raising others from the dead. That was enough, and apparently John's doubts ended.

✍

Doubt seems to be a large part of modern living. We're skeptical about almost everything we hear or read. It's probably no surprise that many people have contacted me and expressed genuine skepticism about my being killed in a car crash and that I lived again to tell about it. Some question my visit to Heaven and subsequent return. Despite what I say or how much I try to explain, some still insist I had a near-death experience.

I understand and I don't want to argue. My experience *is* an incredible story. I'm not the least bit bothered by those who express doubts about my heavenly journey. I *know* I experienced it even if they don't believe it. What does disturb me, however, is when I talk to people who doubt the reality of Heaven, or say that they can't believe that a loved one could go there. Or they question the ability of Jesus to take us there.

Having doubts is part of the human experience. We're not perfect beings, so doubt may creep into our minds every now and then. Doubts can be negative, but they can also lead to an even stronger faith. That is, they can if we deal with our doubts and don't allow them to become a way of life. Doubts are not always bad guests, but they are awful residents.

The oft-told story of a father who brought his son to Jesus for healing states the dilemma well.

"Have mercy on us and help us if you can."

"What do you mean, 'If I can'?" Jesus asked. "Anything is possible if a person believes."

The father instantly cried out, "I do believe, but help me overcome my unbelief!" (Mark 9:22–24 [NLT]).

I can't give anyone an instant way to overcome doubts. I do know I've learned that the longer I follow Jesus and see his guidance in my life, the less I doubt. Because he has proven himself faithful in the past, I know I can trust him in the present.

Here's a prayer that I've found to be very effective over the years: "Lord, please give me the ability to doubt my doubts."

Regardless of *our* doubts, regardless of the doubts of those who first heard Jesus (but later believed), those doubts do nothing to diminish the truth. Jesus said clearly that he is the way, the truth, and the life. His life and his actions are all the proof we need.

As you think of your future, focus on obeying. And for us, most of his commands are easy to comprehend. There are things about Heaven you don't understand, but why should you? If you're prepared, you'll receive the answers at the right time.

Departing Instructions

1. Believe, although you haven't seen Jesus. Even if you don't understand Jesus' integral union with the Father, you can still believe it.
2. Know your Heavenly Father. If you know Jesus, that also means that you know the Father.
3. Examine the evidence that Jesus was who he said he was. Study the way he lived and his actions. Learn more about Jesus to strengthen your own life.

11

Act as a Representative of God

[Jesus said] "I tell you the truth, anyone who has faith in me will do what I have been doing. He will do even greater things than these, because I am going to the Father. And I will do whatever you ask in my name, so that the Son may bring glory to the Father. You may ask me for anything in my name, and I will do it."

JOHN 14:12–14 (NIV)

As incapacitated as I am now, it probably seems difficult for people to believe that I once ran on a track team. These days, my legs can barely carry me across a room, but there was a time when I ran very well. In fact, my orthopedic surgeon tells me that one of the reasons they were able to save my left leg after my accident was because I had strong legs.

I wasn't a fast runner, but I had the stamina for long-distance running. I could also run a decent 440 yards. Occasionally, I ran relays. In relay races the execution is almost as important as the speed. Each runner has to take off at exactly the right moment and get in sync for the passing of the baton. The runner next in line must extend his hand backward just as the runner finishing the leg extends his hand forward. He must hand off the baton and place it securely in the next runner's hand. To drop the baton is an automatic disqualification. It won't matter how fast each person runs if the baton isn't efficiently and carefully passed.

The idea of a relay race helps me understand the passage that opens this chapter. What Jesus is talking about is not a game, but the principle still applies. Jesus passes the baton to his faithful followers. He spends a lot of time with them teaching them, training them, so that they will be ready to receive the baton. He didn't want them to drop it or to fail him.

And when he does hand over the baton, he makes what may seem like startling statements about what would happen after he leaves them. He gives two significant promises to his disciples.

First, he promises, "I tell you the truth, anyone who has faith in me will do what I have been doing. He will do even greater things than these, because I am going to the Father" (John 14:12 [NIV]).

If we read the Acts of the Apostles we see that they did the deeds that Jesus did and in a few instances, even greater deeds. Here are two examples:

- "[P]eople brought the sick into the streets and laid them on beds and mats so that at least Peter's shadow might fall on some of them as he passed by. Crowds gathered also from the towns around Jerusalem, bringing their sick and those tormented by evil spirits, and all of them were healed" (Acts 5:15–16 [NIV]).

- "God did extraordinary miracles through Paul, so that even handkerchiefs and aprons that had touched him were taken to the sick, and their illnesses were cured and the evil spirits left them" (Acts 19:11–12 [NIV]).

Chapters 12 to 14 of 1 Corinthians suggest that the spiritual gifts were in wide operation during the days of the early church. Apparently having these gifts had puffed up some people and made others feel inferior, because Paul wrote two chapters (12 and 14) of admonition about the gifts. He placed the love chapter (13) in the middle as the way to say, "No matter how gifted you are, if you don't love, your gifts are nothing." But it is important to note that although Jesus doesn't say it, the disciples don't have the power to do those greater works alone. Only after the coming of the Holy Spirit as recorded in Acts 2 is there a change. Immediately after the Spirit comes, Peter heals a lame man and thousands of people flock to join the church.

Throughout the Book of Acts we read of miracles and healings as the word spreads westward to Rome. Even though Jesus is no longer on Earth among men, his work goes on because he has many disciples to carry it on.

Jesus uses the words *greater works* and some have taken it to mean that the disciples spread the Gospel to the ends of the Earth. That's a possible meaning because Jesus never left Palestine, and tradition says that Thomas went to South India and Andrew reached Scotland. Within three centuries, the Gospel had penetrated North Africa and Europe, and Christianity became the official religion of the Roman Empire. But I doubt that Jesus meant geographic greatness.

The promise may also include the gathering of great numbers of believers into one flock, something that Jesus looked forward to (*see* John 10:16). In John 17, as I'll point out later, Jesus prayed for the oneness of his disciples.

I'd like to remind you that we are one with all believers, even when we're divided by time, diversity, and theology. As long as Jesus Christ is the center of our faith, we can accept others and they can accept us. One of the great joys of my ministry is that I get to visit a great variety of those who are authentic followers of Christ. Whether speaking under a tent in Scandinavia, an ancient cathedral in Stockholm, a small country church in South Carolina, an inner-city church in Mexico City, a lovely chapel in Eastbourne, England, or to those of a dozen denominations, each believer is still part of the family of God.

One Sunday morning as I approached the platform to speak I was preceded by a hymn performed to a hula in Hawaii. On other days in other places, I heard drums and chants on an American Indian reservation, listened to robed choirs sing anthems, and watched barefoot women dance while holding flags. Those are expressions of genuine faith.

Sometimes I speak in civic centers where the parking lots are filled with church vans. Emblazoned on the side of those vans are the names of an amazing variety of church affiliations.

I have discovered what I always knew but sometimes forget: God isn't an Anglo-Saxon Protestant who speaks only English. I've prayed in churches where I was the only person who spoke English. The others prayed anyway and the songs they sang had familiar tunes but the words they passionately offered were foreign to me, but not to God. Hope is not a gender, a nationality, a denomination, or a worship style.

🖋

Jesus' second promise is even more startling. Jesus says that he will answer any prayer offered in his name.

It's sad but too many people believe the phrase "in his name" or "in Jesus' name" are a kind of magic formula. The implication is that if people repeat those three enchanted words, they'll have their prayers answered. But Jesus means far more than repeating a few special words. We miss much of the significance of what Jesus is saying because we don't ordinarily think of what it means to pray *in his name.*

In the Bible, and especially in the Old Testament, names are important. They tell others about the person and his personality. God changes the name Abram (a father) to Abraham (a father of a multitude); Jacob, the deceiver, became Israel, the prince of God. Naomi (pleasant) asked to be called Mara (bitter) after the death of her husband and two sons. In the New Testament, the early Christians recognized the generosity of a man and changed his name from Joseph (may God increase) to Barnabas (son of encouragement or an encourager) (*see* Acts 4:36–37).

A name was more than a pleasing sound, it described or declared who a person was. When my co-writer lived in Kenya, the people called him *Haraka*, a Swahili word that means "fast or quick." That accurately describes him because he moves quickly.

One of the most hilarious introductions I have ever received went something like this: "We're so glad to have Don Piper here with us tonight. He is the man about whom Billy Graham asked, 'Who?'"

As humorous as that occasion was for me, it is also a powerful truth. Billy Graham may not know my name, but God does. And he knows yours, too, even if you don't know his. God knows each of us by name.

In ancient times to know someone's *name* meant to have a relationship with that person. It also meant one could have influence or sometimes even have power over the person. When Jacob wrestled with the angel, he said, "Please tell me your name" (Genesis 32:29 [NIV]). Jacob never received an answer, but he did receive a blessing. However, if Jacob had known the name of the one with whom he wrestled, he could have overpowered him and controlled him.

It's not just about speaking a name; it's about relationship. Jesus made a statement about true and false disciples: "Not everyone who says to me, 'Lord, Lord,' will enter the kingdom of Heaven, but only those who do the will of my Father who is in Heaven. Many will say to me on that day, 'Lord, Lord, did we not prophesy in your name and in your name drive out demons and in your name perform many miracles?' Then I will tell them plainly, 'I never knew you. Away from me, you evildoers!'" (Matthew 7:21–23 [TNIV]).

Jesus makes it clear that just because people use his name (and that certainly implies they evoked his name in prayer) doesn't mean they have a relationship with him. He says he doesn't know them. That is, he doesn't acknowledge them as being his disciples. Those who use his name properly are those who "do the will of my Father who is in Heaven" (verse 21).

Here's another example. My son Chris travels with me and helps me with my schedule. When he tells people that I'll be at a particular place, it is as good as if I had said it. He is speaking *in my name*. He represents me. When he represents me, that is the true use of my name. It's the same as when the secretary of state offers foreign policy statements. He or she speaks for the United States.

Another biblical example is when Mary goes to Jesus' tomb on Sunday morning. Jesus has already been resurrected, but she doesn't recognize him. She isn't expecting to see him outside the tomb. She mistakes him for a gardener. Jesus speaks to her. Still she doesn't recognize him. Then he speaks her name. Instantly, she knows it is him. He calls her Mary. No one says *Mary* the way he does.

If we know Christ as Lord, he knows our names. That's the importance of relationships. That's when knowing a name carries significance. That's when praying in the name of Jesus has true meaning.

Doesn't it then seem obvious what Jesus meant? To pray in his name means to pray in a manner worthy of Jesus' representative. If I pray for punishment and judgment on someone that hardly seems like the way Jesus would react. Our prayers are to reflect the one we represent. To ask "anything in my name" doesn't mean that we can ask selfish, petty, and unworthy requests and they'll be granted. He promises he will answer all worthy prayers—those that appeal to Jesus and his work with a loyal commitment to God's will as Jesus has made it known.

John 14:14 repeats the promise of verse 13, and the New Living Translation reads: "You can ask for anything in my name, and I will do it, so that the Son can bring glory to the Father. Yes, ask me for anything in my name, and I will do it!"

Jesus himself lays out the one condition that makes the prayer answerable and certain: "so that the Son can bring glory to the Father." It's not that we always know those requests that fit into that category, but we have a strong sense of the things that *don't fit*.

The secret of praying in Jesus' name is to ask ourselves if our requests are the kind of things that honor God, that do good to others, and that aren't based on our selfish desires or prejudices. We can't always know for sure, but perhaps learning that is part of our spiritual growth and acting on our departing instructions from Jesus.

If Jesus had wanted to state it any stronger, he would have done so. Maybe that's part of the walk of faith. We ask and wait to see if our petitions please God. If they do, we have the answer for which we ask.

Here's how I see the way this promise works: The more intimate my connection with God, the more I sense the kind of things that honor God. As I grasp more fully who he is and what he wants in my life and in the world around me, I become better at praying. It also means I pray with the same sense of John 13:34–35, where he exhorts them, "Love each other. Just as I have loved you, you should love each other. Your love for one another will prove to the world that you are my disciples" (NLT). When we love as Jesus commanded, we also pray on the same level. If we know we're praying from motives of love and compassion, we know we're praying rightly.

Here's an example of what I mean. The story of the destruction of Sodom and Gomorrah is one of the most compelling in the Bible. Because of the rampant wickedness and profligate evil of the people of Sodom, God decided to destroy the city. Abraham sensed that there might be some among the citizenry of Sodom that were righteous—and his own nephew lived there—so he pleaded that God would spare the city (*see* Genesis 18:16–33[NIV]).

When God had told Abraham of his plans, the patriarch prays, "What if there are fifty righteous people in the city? Will you really sweep it away and not spare the place for the sake of the fifty righteous people in it?" (verse 24).

God listens and responds that he will spare the city if there are fifty righteous.

"What if the number of the righteous is five less than fifty? Will you destroy the whole city because of five people?" (verse 28).

After God accedes, Abraham pleads in decreasing increments of five, and then ten, until he finally asks, "May the LORD not be angry, but let me speak just once more. What if only ten can be found there?" (verse 32).

Each time God agrees to spare the city.

What makes this story powerful for me is because it points out that God hears and responds to the prayers of his people when they pray with the compassion and fervor that honors him.

Another thing I see from this is that even though God has a plan, he is sometimes willing to change it. James reminds us that we don't have the things we want because we don't ask for them (see James 4:2). Prayer is never futile unless we believe that it is.

I've been approached many times by people who have prayed for their hurting loved ones, just as my church and family prayed for me after my accident. They're confused and sometimes feel devastated because they prayed but their loved ones died.

"Why did God answer the prayers of your loved ones and failed to answer ours?" We must know that sometimes the answer to our prayers is no. At other times, the answer is later, or as the Bible expresses it, "in the fullness of time" (see Galatians 4:4).

God often answers prayers beyond anything we could ever

think to ask and exceeds our requests. Paul writes, "Now to him who is able to do immeasurably more than all we ask or imagine, according to his power that is at work within us, to him be glory in the church and in Christ Jesus throughout all generations, for ever and ever! Amen" (Ephesians 3:20–21 [NIV]).

I've lived long enough that I am glad God has answered some of my prayers in the negative. If I had always gotten what I asked for, my life would have been a disaster. God knows best, and he always answers correctly, but not always affirmatively.

I want to pray with a heart filled with compassion—with the kind of love Jesus demonstrated and spoke about in his departing instructions. If I pray in anger or a yearning to get even, how could that be a prayer in the name of Jesus? To pray in his name is to invoke the character of God. It is to *identify* with Jesus and to pray in a manner worthy of Jesus.

🖋

We need to realize one more significant lesson from these words. Why did Jesus promise they would do greater works? Why does he promise to answer their prayers? It's because he is preparing them to go out and to continue the work he started.

We may be only 90 minutes away from Heaven at this minute or any minute, but even in that last hour-and-a-half of life, we can serve Jesus Christ. In fact, Jesus' command answers the cries from our hearts so we can serve him and serve others by praying for them and doing good for them. We serve God best when we serve other people as his representatives on Earth. We serve God best when we pray petitions that honor God. That is, when we pray in Jesus' name.

It may help if we continually remind ourselves that as we study these five chapters in John's Gospel, they are more than Jesus' final words and the notice of his departure. They are the words of the divine commission for the eleven as well as the divine instructions for us today.

Jesus promises great things, but he never promises to make us inactive. He promises to those who are willing to serve that even greater things than occurred during his time on Earth will happen. These are powerful words of encouragement to us.

Departing Instructions

1. Know Jesus' name. That's important, but more important, Jesus knows your name.
2. Heed Jesus' instructions. As he taught the eleven disciples, if you work for him, you will have the power to do what he did and perhaps even greater things than he did.
3. Pray so that your petitions and desires bring honor to God (in the name of Jesus). Then God will answer your prayers.
4. Look for answered prayer in your life. Be open to experience God's blessings.

12

Live in Complete Obedience

[Jesus said] "If you love me, you will obey what I command. And I will ask the Father, and he will give you another Counselor to be with you forever—the Spirit of truth. The world cannot accept him, because it neither sees him nor knows him. But you know him, for he lives with you and will be in you."

JOHN 14:15–17 (NIV)

Years ago I visited a friend's home, and during our conversation, we spoke about grace and the people who call themselves believers but get entangled in what he referred to as "the excesses of grace." I shook my head at first, because I couldn't understand how grace could ever be excessive.

For several minutes he went on and on and I still wasn't sure what he meant. Finally he said that he had recently left his church because of what he called "greasy grace."

"What do you mean by that?" I asked.

"They acted as if it didn't matter what they did, God would forgive them," he said. "'It's all grace,' was their favorite saying."

"That is true, you know," I said.

He nodded and added, "But is it also true that you can

knowingly do something wrong because you know God will for-give you?"

I got his point.

He told me that the pastor of his former church had been involved with two women members and one of them had become pregnant. The board confronted the pastor and he, in turn, spoke to the entire congregation. He said, "I have sinned, but I also know God has forgiven me."

My friend said he raised his hand. "Did you think of that before you sinned?"

The pastor stared at him for several seconds before he said, "Yes. You see, at the cross, Jesus forgave all my sins—past, present, and those I'll commit in the future."

"That's not grace," my friend said. "That's presumption."

My friend got up and walked out.

I don't know the entire story (or care to know) but the pastor stayed and so did about half of the congregation. As my friend said, "The rest of the sheep scattered."

I tell this story because it's so easy to take grace and forgive-ness for granted. My friend said the pastor had *presumed* on the grace of God. If the story is true, I agree. Grace is what we receive when we try to honor God in everything we do. Grace is never a prepaid license to do wrong.

My friend Jeff Adams says it this way: "Demand perfection; settle for excellence." If we truly love in the biblical sense, we'll never plan to sin. We'll run as far away from it as we can.

Our goal—our intention—should always be to honor God in everything we do. We intend to overcome obstacles, to rise above temptations, and to do the things that honor God. Grace is there as a kind of safety net to catch us when we fail.

As serious Christians, our goal is to live in complete dedication and full obedience to Jesus Christ. John 14:15 makes that abundantly clear: "If you love me, you will obey what I command" (NIV). Those who love him express their love and their faith by obedience. And Jesus exhorted his disciples to keep his command after he goes to the Father. In fact, with Jesus gone, those men will have to become even more faithful. They won't have a physically present Jesus to rebuke them when they're wrong. They will become his witnesses on Earth. People will judge Jesus by the actions of his disciples.

At first it sounds impossible; Jesus has always been there beside them to encourage them and to correct them. Jesus now expects more from them—but he always wants them to know that he hasn't left them without help. He won't be physically present, but he will send someone who will be with them.

They will have a helper—the Holy Spirit. Jesus promises, "And I will ask the Father, and he will give you another Counselor to be with you forever—the Spirit of truth" (John 14:16–17a [NIV]). The relationship will be different, but the Helper will be with them constantly.

Here is the implication of Jesus' departing instructions: "I'll send you on a difficult mission, but you don't have to worry. I'll send you someone with the same power as I have. He will guide you, you'll know what to do, and he will enable you to do it."

Jesus promised the gift of the Holy Spirit in John 14:17, 14:26, 15:26, and 16:7–15. Those are words the original disciples probably didn't understand. That may also explain why he has to say it three times. The Spirit of God is mentioned in the Old Testament, but it's rare. It is an external force that moves over the face of Earth like a great wind, or it can refer to the spirit of God. The Hebrew word for the Spirit is *ruach*, which means "breath or wind." Some-times the Spirit comes on individuals and they prophesy or fight great battles. But the Holy Spirit isn't clearly defined.

In the New Testament, the Holy Spirit comes as the gift of the exalted Jesus. Beginning on the day called Pentecost (fifty days after the resurrection), the Holy Spirit becomes an internal mani-festation of God. Now the Holy Spirit dwells within us, comforts us, and guides us. The New Testament word is *pneuma*. That's a Greek noun that also means "wind or breath." God's Spirit dwells within all believers. The idea of an indwelling Spirit can also remind us that every *breath* we take is a gift of God.

The Spirit interprets what the Bible says, speaks to us, and con-tinues to guide us. The Spirit teaches and empowers us to serve. The Holy Spirit helps us keep Jesus' commands because they are the condition of enjoying the Father's love and abiding presence.

✍

John 14:16–17 refers to the Holy Spirit in two ways. The first is the Greek word, *parakletos*, often translated as "counselor." It means a legal helper or an advocate or someone called in to help in times of need. I like to think of the Holy Spirit as our defense attorney because he stands up for us and defends us against our sins. God wants the best for us and wants us to realize that we have been set free from our failures, sins, or transgressions. The *parakletos* reminds us that Jesus' death paid the penalty for all our sins. Paul writes, "The Spirit helps us in our weakness. We do not know what we ought to pray for, but the Spirit himself intercedes for us. . . . And he who searches our hearts knows the mind of the Spirit, because the Spirit intercedes for God's people in accor-dance with the will of God" (Romans 8:26–27 [TNIV]).

In his first letter, John also shows Jesus Christ as our *parakletos:* "My dear children, I am writing this to you so that you will not sin. But if anyone does sin, we have an advocate who pleads our case before the Father. He is Jesus Christ, the one who is truly righteous" (1 John 2:1 [NLT]).

The "Spirit of Truth" is the second way Jesus refers to the Holy Spirit (*see also* John 16:13). The Spirit isn't merely true and honest but also *teaches us* the truth and guides us to know, witness to, and express in life the truth about God and about Jesus Christ.

🖋

In referring to the Holy Spirit, Jesus says, "The world cannot accept him, because it neither sees him nor knows him. But you know him, for he lives with you and will be in you" (John 14:17 [NIV]). The Spirit will dwell with those who obey and will remain within them as someone they know in a way that the world can't understand. A hostile world doesn't understand or receive the Spirit because God's Spirit is a gift only for believers.

I find it interesting that he says the world can't recognize the Spirit. As I point out in another chapter, we don't recognize what we're not open to see. The people who have refused to turn to God live as if there were no God. But we see the Spirit because we're open to God and have been fitted to see. We see through the eyes of faith. "Faith is the confidence that what we hope for will actually happen; it gives us assurance about things we cannot see," reads Hebrews 11:1 (NLT) and in verse 6 of the same chapter, we read these words: "And it is impossible to please God without faith. Anyone who wants to come to him must believe that God exists and that he rewards those who sincerely seek him" (NLT).

Given the choice, I'm sure all of us would prefer to have a

human Jesus walk beside us, teach us, and show us what to do and what to avoid. But we don't have that choice. Jesus lived a life without sin. He showed the first disciples how to live in total obedience to God's will.

Jesus is gone but his gift to us is the Holy Spirit. We might call it our inner voice or our spiritual conscience; one friend refers to it as the "Holy Whisperer." Although not biblical terms, I like them because they help us to grasp that the Spirit speaks softly and we have to learn to listen.

The closest parallel I can suggest is the family. Good parents try to teach their children how to behave in public and in private. When the children leave home they have choices. They can listen to the parental voices or they can shut them off. That's how God's Spirit works in us.

Jesus said the Spirit would come to them. The purpose was to enable them to live in fuller obedience to the will of God. That hasn't changed: The Spirit is just as active—if we listen.

🖎

As a child, my understanding of God was limited because my family was seldom involved in church. My dad was a career army soldier and we moved often because of his transfers. We didn't put down roots physically or spiritually until he retired and came home from Vietnam. Prior to that, my contact with the church and Jesus was limited to my grandmother taking me to church, Vacation Bible Schools, or Mrs. Norris, my next-door neighbor, rounding up children who wanted to go to church.

It wasn't until I was sixteen that I began to actually ponder eternal things and my reason for being alive on this planet. An invitation to a church by three thoughtful and devoted teens afforded me the opportunity to see God for the first time—I saw him through their zeal and commitment and through the warmth of the people at that church, First Baptist Church of Bossier City, Louisiana. When I speak to youth groups today, I unfailingly exhort them to share their faith with their peers. Had it not been for those three teenagers, Jan, Barry, and Carmen, reaching out to me, I might not be a follower of Christ today.

By contrast, my co-writer had been to church maybe a total of six months during his childhood, but as an adult in his early twenties he decided to read the New Testament. He read the words each day for several weeks and one day he said to himself, I believe this.

Both Cecil and I couldn't stop with saying we believed. We had to move on. What happened next? We had to learn what God wanted us to do and how we might serve more effectively.

Although our backgrounds differ, both of us sought to live in obedience to the Holy Spirit. Here are a few obvious-but-simple things we did so that we could become more sensitive and obedient:

- We listened to pastors and teachers.
- We read the Bible daily.
- We made prayer a daily priority.
- We read other books about God.
- We asked questions of other Christians.
- We obeyed and did the things we knew to do.

On that last point, the more faithful we became in obeying what we knew, the more the Holy Spirit took us into more depth and understanding.

✑

Many have marveled, as I do, at the remarkable display of obedience by my friend, the late Dick Onarecker. He was the man who climbed into the wreckage of my car on that day in 1989 and prayed over my dead body because the Holy Spirit told him to do that.

As Dick himself would later tell people, he had never prayed for a dead man before or since; however, that day he felt compelled by the Holy Spirit to pray for me. Although four paramedics were present, Dick talked to the police officer who was handling the accident. He then asked permission of two EMTs to get under the tarp that was covering my wrecked car and pray.

"I'd like to pray for that man," he said. They laughed at Dick, but he persisted. "I feel compelled to pray for him."

"He's dead and he's been that way a long time," one of the paramedics said.

No one would give him permission. When the final ambulance was about to leave without me, he threatened to lie down on the bridge and force the ambulance to run over his body.

Dick said the Holy Spirit wouldn't let him back away. Finally he said, "If you don't let me pray for him, I'm going to lie down in the middle of this road. You'll have to run over me to drive out."

They gave in. Because I've told the story in my earlier books, I won't go into details. But it's a true story of miracles and answered prayer.

Defying logic and accepting ridicule from the EMTs at the scene of my death, Dick didn't question God; instead he obeyed. Nothing in his theology told him that praying over a dead man was the sensible thing to do. His insistence forced them to allow him to get under the tarp covering my Ford and pray.

That's exactly how God works, by using those who are willing. God rewards obedience. Dick didn't have to understand, he only had to obey the leading of God's Holy Spirit to pray for me. Because Dick heard and obeyed the Spirit, I am alive today.

Sometimes we're not sure what to do or what God wants from us. The real issue for me and for many of us is this: How do we hear Jesus (or the Holy Spirit) speak to us today? How do we know when God wants us to do something or to refrain from doing something?

No one can really answer that question for anyone else. We hear God speak in different ways. Some individuals are more spiritually perceptive and intuitive. Others need something specific and concrete before they can believe God has guided them.

I've heard God speak in many ways. I've read a verse in the Bible that suddenly takes on life. As I read it, it's as if the Spirit of God whispers, "Obey this." Sometimes it's purely a sense of *inner knowing*. We pray to God and know that he answers us.

Six days after my 1989 accident, I developed double pneumonia. Because both legs were broken and one was in traction, it wasn't possible to elevate me to receive breathing treatments. Complicating matters further was my horribly mangled left arm. Following the great joy associated with my initial survival, spirits in my ICU cubicle began to plummet. Drastic action was required. Time was running out.

The doctors summoned my wife, Eva, to a conference in

which she was presented with a choice. My left leg was missing four inches of femur, which had been devastated by the collapsing dashboard of my car. There are no replacement bones for the largest bone in the human body, so doctors explained to her that because of my critical condition, amputation was an immediate option. If that were done I would be able to be elevated or raised up. That meant I could receive breathing treatments to overcome the pneumonia.

"There may be one other option," the doctors said. "It's experimental. We've never done a surgery like this before here. The technology was just patented here in the U.S. last month. If we did that, it would involve an external fixator of stainless steel that would encapsulate your husband's leg. As many as thirty pins or wires would be placed through your husband's leg. The fixator would be anchored firmly in his hip by large rods. Steel halos would encircle the leg from the hip to just below the knee."

While Eva digested those words, he added, "If we go this route, your husband may have to wear the fixator for a year or perhaps longer. Infections are a distinct possibility, and they can be fatal. Screws have to be turned several times a day to replace the missing bone. Normally candidates for this type of surgery receive months of presurgery counseling to psychologically prepare them for the pain and hardship."

Eva listened without asking questions. She wanted to absorb what she heard.

"There is no time for counseling for your husband. If we do not do something tonight, he might not be alive in the morning. What do you want us to do?"

Many have heard me say, in the years since that harrowing

night, that my wife is the hero of my story. I survived, but she endured. That night she passionately and confidently prayed. As she began to pray, she realized that her decision would affect all our lives. I was the father of her three children, the son of Ralph and Billie, the minister and friend to many. Her thirty-eight-year-old husband's life was in her hands. As she prayed, she felt a strong conviction and certainty and knew the answer. She had no doubts that the Holy Spirit guided her to make the right decision.

She told the doctor to install the fixator.

Eleven hours later I awakened with the monstrosity embedded into my thigh. Eleven months later, I was finally freed from it. Years of therapy and rehabilitation followed. Her faithful prayer and the diligent acts of many allowed me to walk—and I continue to walk.

Eva prayed, the Spirit whispered to her, and she believed God would answer. When she sensed the answer, she obeyed. And God responded.

Inner knowing is the method my co-writer, Cecil, relies on most. He says he prays for guidance and continues to pray daily. He doesn't hear God speak audibly, but he has an inner assurance—a certainty—that makes him know the right thing to do.

He was a missionary for almost six years in Kenya, East Africa. He said he was called to service one Saturday as he stood on a street corner in Chicago's loop. He wasn't praying for guidance, yet, in an instant, he knew God had a mission for him. He never questioned the calling, although two years passed before he left the United States.

The missionary service was to have been for four years, and he passed up the furlough because he felt no nudge from the Holy Spirit. The fifth year passed and he stayed. "I was ready to remain in Kenya for the rest of my life," he says. But one evening when he was praying for guidance, he *knew* it was time to return to the United States.

Some people speak of dreams in which God speaks as God spoke to the wise men and to Joseph in the birth stories of Jesus. Or the Old Testament stories of the young man Joseph. Or when king Nebuchadnezzar had Daniel interpret his dreams. Some of Scripture's greatest revelations came in dreams. I wonder if it's because God has our undivided attention when we're asleep.

I find that the more crucial the guidance I am seeking and the more important the decision I need to make, the more I ask God to be direct and forceful in his revelation. Sometimes I ask God to give me a holy billboard as I travel down life's road. I feel it takes a lot of attention grabbing for me to grasp what God wants me to know. I've prayed, "Dear Lord, please write with your fingertips in the sky. I need to hear from you."

The heavenly billboard can come in the form of an earthly messenger. On more than one occasion, individuals will tell of powerful experiences but they had no awareness that the Spirit spoke to them.

A friend drove west across Texas on I-20. On a drizzly, late afternoon he followed a red sports car because it was easy to see and traveled at the same speed he wanted. About two hours before they reached the state line, my friend became thirsty. "I don't think I'd ever felt so thirsty in my life." He pulled off at an exit and drank two cans of Coke. He got back on the Interstate. About ten minutes later, blue lights stopped the traffic and all cars pulled into the far left lane. They crept along for at least half an hour.

It was a four-car accident. The second and third vehicles were crushed and two ambulances were removing the injured people. The second car was the red sports vehicle.

"If I hadn't stopped, I would have been the third car," he said. He insists, "It was the Holy Spirit and I didn't know it. I simply obeyed."

That's another way the Spirit works in us: We recognize God's guidance only in retrospect. In the Book of Genesis, for example, Jacob ran away from home. He slept in a field and dreamed about angels ascending and descending from Heaven. God spoke to him in the dream and promised many descendants and that he would bless everyone on Earth through Jacob's offspring. "I will not leave you until I have done what I have promised you" (Genesis 28:15 [TNIV]).

"When Jacob awoke from his sleep, he thought, 'Surely the LORD is in this place, and I was not aware of it'" (Genesis 28:16 [TNIV]).

As with my friend and as with Jacob, we're often aware only afterward.

We sometimes perceive divine guidance by looking out the rear window as we drive along. We see where we've been and how far the Lord has led us. That enables us to be more trustful in the present because of the blessings of the past.

Sometimes God makes the way obvious and clear and it's easy to obey. Sometimes I seem able only to put my right foot in front of my left and then the left in front of the right and keep going. In taking one step after another I have to trust God's promise, "The

LORD directs the steps of the godly. He delights in every detail of their lives. Though they stumble, they will never fall, for the LORD holds them by the hand" (Psalm 37:23–24 [NLT]).

As a general guideline, however, we can be sure that the Spirit of truth won't lead us into anything that's a lie or deceptive or that will intentionally hurt others. Guidance may be to say *no* to certain things because God has a bigger, better *yes* ahead for us.

This brings us to another significant departing instruction: If Heaven is your home, you need to prepare for it. You prepare by obeying the instructions Jesus gave. No matter who we are, we always remain learners, followers, and servants. "Whoever has my commands and keeps them is the one who loves me" (John 14:21 [TNIV]). The Holy Spirit will guide us. That's a promise.

Today, it works this way for us: Jesus is in Heaven waiting for us. On Earth we listen for the Holy Spirit to speak, to prepare us for our final days on Earth and our liftoff to Heaven.

Our love for Jesus Christ enables us to listen more carefully to the Spirit. As we seek divine guidance, we're living in obedience and following the departing instructions.

Departing Instructions

1. Make your actions glorify Jesus Christ. You can easily say, "I love God," but your actions make more noise than your words.
2. Let people judge your relationship to God by your behavior and not only your words.
3. Listen to the voice of your *paraclete*—the helper or the Holy Spirit—to speak and to show you the right way to live.

4. "Heaven is my home." Say those words to yourself as often as you need to hear them. No matter how difficult life becomes, Heaven is your home. If you want to prepare and be ready to depart for Heaven, you do so by obeying Jesus' departing instructions.

13

Remember: Jesus Is with You—Always

[Jesus said] "No, I will not abandon you as orphans—I will come to you."

JOHN 14:18 (NLT)

Almost every day I receive hundreds of e-mails. Most of them concern people enduring great losses or asking eternity questions and many of them are poignant. One came in recently from a man named Jared and it deeply touched me.

In his e-mail he said that he is a freshman at a western university. He is an only child, from a small midwestern town, and a devout Christian. He wrote to tell me how utterly lonely and isolated he felt. He indicated that he had considered dropping out of college and returning home.

Jared wrote:

I had no idea when I left home that I would feel so alone. I knew college would be a dramatic change from the way I had lived before. I knew that I would be so far away from home that it was highly unlikely I would know anybody on campus when I arrived. My parents and I are close but I didn't know I would end up missing them so much. There were times in my first few weeks at college that I felt as if I were the only person left on Earth and yet I was surrounded by a sea of people. I thought, This is what it must be like to live in an orphanage.

My heart went out to Jared. I remember my parent's taking me to Louisiana State University as a freshman; I still remember that first night alone in my dorm room after they returned home.

I knew I was about to begin a new chapter in my life and I was excited. Yet it was frightening and I felt lonely. I realized I had to make friends. I also realized that all of us freshmen were in the same situation. All of us had to start to adjust. A few left, but most of us eventually made it across the stage to receive our diplomas at graduation time.

After Jared's e-mail triggered memories of my own adjustment to university life, I wrote him an encouraging e-mail about the new friends he would make at college and that his parents would be at home waiting for him when he could return. Mostly I reminded that young man on the threshold of life that with Jesus Christ he would never be truly alone. Even though he might feel like a spiritual orphan, he wasn't.

✒

As I read chapter 14 of John's Gospel, I wondered how long the disciples had to listen to news of the impending departure of Jesus before they grew discouraged. We have no way to know how much they grasped—and they seemed not to understand a great deal of what the Lord said. But even they must have had some sense that tragedy was about to take place.

My assumption is that when Jesus detects their sadness, he wants to assure them that they won't be left desolate and alone, so he says, "I will not leave you as orphans; I will come to you" (John 14:18 [NIV]).

Jesus used the word *orphanos*, and in the patriarchal society it meant literally "without a father." But the word was also used of students or disciples who had lost their beloved teacher. That's the case here. Jesus is leaving them, but he won't leave them *orphanos* because the Spirit will come to them while he is away.

"I will come to you," Jesus says. The return is obviously the resurrection, although he doesn't use that word. He also doesn't explain his betrayal, beating, crucifixion, and being raised from the dead.

He wants them to look ahead, and he speaks in words they'll comprehend. Jesus knows they won't understand until the resurrection. His point is simple: They will see him again because he will be alive. They will touch him and eat with him. They'll spend time together.

That's exactly what happened when Jesus rose from the dead. Paul records that Jesus "was seen by Peter and then by the Twelve. After that, he was seen by more than five hundred of his followers . . . by James and later by all the apostles" (1 Corinthians 15:5–7 [NLT]).

A short time after Jesus returns to Heaven they will receive his power in the form of the Holy Spirit—a power available to all true believers through the centuries.

He points to the resurrection because that will be the most difficult for their minds to comprehend. He will be crucified, soldiers will place his dead body in a tomb, and on the third day Jesus will appear again. They have nothing in their personal experience or their history to prepare them for that powerful event.

They will gain new understanding—not immediately, but after Jesus' triumph over death. And part of what they will grasp is that Jesus lives in an unbreakable union with his Father. They will also realize that they live in an intimate, loving fellowship with Jesus. That intimacy will make them loyal and aware that they are not *orphanos*. Jesus' Spirit will be with them to guide them.

But more than that, Jesus wants them to understand where he will be. Although he had said it earlier the same evening (verses 1–6), they were unable to "hear" everything. Patiently Jesus said, "On that day you will realize that I am in my Father, and you are in me, and I am in you" (John 14:20 [NIV]).

That's mystical language, which is the way Jesus often speaks, but it is more than using symbolic words. He wants them to know about his unity with the Father. He and the Father are one in purpose.

In the modern world, we seem to have little trouble with that concept because we know the entire story and we've read the Bible, but it had to have been mind boggling to them. Jesus would leave them but he wouldn't totally leave. He was going to Heaven where he and the Father were one.

Jesus had previously spoken of his unity with the Father although not quite so strongly: "While Jesus was teaching in the Temple, he called out, 'Yes, you know me and you know where I come from. But I'm not here on my own. The one who sent me is true, and you don't know him. But I know him because I come from him, and he sent me to you" (John 7:28–29 [NLT]).

A little later on the night of his betrayal Jesus prays alone and asks the Father's protection. He says, "I have given them the glory you gave me, so they may be one as we are one. I am in them and you are in me. May they experience such perfect unity that the world will know that you sent me and that you love them as much as you love me" (John 17:22–23 [NLT]).

Jesus became a total human being (incarnate) as well as God's revelation of the divine nature to the world. This is basic to Christian understanding. Paul quotes a hymn of the early church (Philippians 2:6–11 [NLT]) that tells us that Jesus, being equal with God (verse 6) "gave up his divine privileges . . . and was born as a human being" (verse 7). Jesus demonstrated everything about God's character that he could convey in human terms.

Jesus had used that language before but, slow learners that they were, they obviously still didn't get it. In John 10, Jesus refers to himself as the good shepherd. He also speaks about his relationship with the Father. "I am the good shepherd; I know my own sheep, and they know me, just as my Father knows me and I know the Father. So I sacrifice my life for the sheep" (John 10:14–15 [NLT]).

When the religious leaders challenge Jesus, he speaks again of his sheep and says, "No one can snatch them away from me, for my Father has given them to me, and he is more powerful than anyone else. No one can snatch them from the Father's hand. The Father and I are one" (verses 28b–30).

The leaders wanted to stone him because, in their eyes, he blasphemed by making himself equal with God. Jewish law stated, "Anyone who blasphemes the Name of the Lord must be stoned to death by the whole community of Israel" (Leviticus 24:16 [NLT]).

Jesus doesn't back down. He knows who he is and allows his words to stand.

He doesn't change when he gives his departing instructions. He isn't using metaphysical language or abstractions. He refers to a personal relationship.

Jesus' oneness or unity with the Father is based on his perfect obedience and total love. His mission on Earth is to make us what he already is.

Although the language may seem strange, even to us today, Jesus' desire is that we who believe will live in unity with each other and in unity with Christ. If we so live, we won't be *orphanos*, because the Spirit of Jesus will be with us.

This isn't the only place Jesus promises to be with us. His final words, according to Matthew's Gospel are, "And surely I am with you always, to the very end of the age" (Matthew 28:20b [NIV]). Hebrews 13:5 quotes Deuteronomy 31:6 with the promise, "Never will I leave you; never will I forsake you" (NIV).

To be aware of his presence, especially in times of struggle or hardship, isn't easy, but he *is* with us. He shows that by guiding us in the painful, difficult times.

Although it's been twenty years since my brief trip to Heaven and I'm constantly in pain, I know Jesus Christ is with me. If I didn't know that, I couldn't possibly be on the road, traveling and speaking as much as I do.

🖋

It has been years since I graduated from college, got married, had my own family and career, but Jared's e-mail reminds me once again of preparing to leave home. I knew that my parents loved me, that they cared about me, and that they thought about me every day. No matter what happened in my life, they would resolutely stand by me.

Years after my parents drove me to the university the first time, I learned that my mother cried most of the 250 miles back to our home. Her firstborn had left the nest. As a parent, and even now as a grandparent, I understand. I experienced the same apprehension and sense of loss after my own children left our home. I wanted my three children to know that as long as they need us our doors are open. In the same way, as long as my parents are alive, I know that I can go to their house and I'll always be welcomed. And yet I carry them in my heart whether I am physically with them or not. I always will. Likewise, Jesus is preparing us a home where his followers will be welcomed always. In the interim, he is with us always.

Always.

Departing Instructions

1. You can stand strong in the face of any hardships that come your way. Remind yourself in the difficult times, "God loves me and is always with me. The Holy Spirit is with me."
2. Think back to a particularly difficult time in your life. Did you feel despair? Were there moments you didn't know if you could survive or endure? Obviously you survived. Reflect on that time. Can you now see that Jesus was with you during that ordeal?
3. How does recognizing the faithfulness of Jesus in your past enable you to be aware of his presence in your present circumstances?
4. Every situation isn't difficult and sometimes Jesus' presence and guidance is obvious. Ponder a time when you had

to make a decision, so you prayed and clearly knew what to do. Think of that experience as part of your departing instructions. The more clearly you're aware of Jesus Christ in your life, the more you grasp the meaning of his words, "I will not abandon you as orphans—I will come to you" (John 14:18 [NLT]).

14

Let the Holy Spirit Guide You

[Jesus said] "I am leaving you with a gift—peace of mind and heart. And the peace I give is a gift the world cannot give. So don't be troubled or afraid."

JOHN 14:27 (NLT)

I wish Jesus had sat down with his faithful disciples and read from a carefully thought-out list of things he wanted them to know. He could have gone down the list from the most important to the least or started with the least and gone to the highest. It would have made life much easier for us—something like giving us the Ten New Commandments.

In that sense, he wasn't systematic. He repeated himself several times. I can only assume it's because those things were important and he did it for emphasis. In John 14, for instance, he starts out by telling them not to be anxious or worried. Near the end of the chapter he says again, "Do not let your hearts be troubled and do not be afraid" (verse 27 [NIV]).

Jesus must have sensed the anxiety and confusion of his followers and repeated what they needed to have reaffirmed.

He also makes the point in verse 24, "These words you hear are not my own; they belong to the Father who sent me." To the Jews, such words were blasphemy; to his disciples they were assurances. He had lived the perfect life among them and constantly pointed to the Father. Now he says plainly that he speaks the words of the Father. He emphasizes his unity with God—and the unbelieving would surely have called that blasphemy.

He goes on to make it clear that after the resurrection he will be with them and so will the Father, but then it is primarily through the Holy Spirit that he will guide them. He has taught them, but the Counselor whom the Father would send in Jesus' place will continue and complete his ministry: "But the Counselor, the Holy Spirit, whom the Father will send in my name, will teach you all things and will remind you of everything I have said to you" (verse 26).

The Book of Acts shows this clearly. Here are three instances of the divine direction that comes through the Holy Spirit.

First, in Acts 5 is a sad story of a man and woman named Ananias and Sapphira who tried to deceive Peter in the amount of their giving. Peter's rebuke makes it clear that it's the Holy Spirit who has revealed the truth to him: "Ananias, how is it that Satan has so filled your heart that you have lied to the Holy Spirit?" (Acts 5:3 [NIV]). The man dies and later Peter confronts the wife and says to her, "How could you agree to test the Spirit of the Lord?" (verse 9a).

Second, in Acts 13, Barnabas and Saul [Paul] go to Jerusalem and meet with the elders. We read a list of the primary leaders followed by these words: "While they were worshiping the Lord and fasting, the Holy Spirit said, 'Set apart for me

Barnabas and Saul for the work to which I have called them'"
(verse 2).

Later, Paul and Silas established and strengthened many
churches. "Paul and his companions traveled throughout the
region of Phrygia and Galatia, having been kept by the Holy
Spirit from preaching the word in the province of Asia" (Acts
16:6 [NIV]). They decided to enter a place called Bithynia "but
the Spirit of Jesus would not allow them to" (verse 7).

These three examples show us how clearly Jesus meant for his
followers to turn to the Holy Spirit and rely on his guidance.

The Spirit would also enable them to recall what Jesus had
taught them, and it helps them understand the meaning of the
words Jesus had spoken.

For example, the first followers believed that they were God's
chosen people—which was part of their Jewish heritage—but they
didn't grasp that God loves and welcomes Gentiles (non-Jews).
Acts 10 records a remarkable story of the Holy Spirit preparing a
Gentile and awakening Peter to reach out to him.

When Cornelius, a Roman military officer, prayed one
afternoon, he had a vision in which an angel said that God had
answered his prayers. He was to send men to Joppa to summon
Peter (*see* Acts 10:1–7).

The next day, before Cornelius's messengers arrived, Peter
prayed. The Bible says he "fell into a trance" (verse 10 [NIV]). He
saw a vision of unclean animals, reptiles, and birds, and three times
"a voice" (obviously the Holy Spirit) told him to eat them. All three
times Peter refused. "I have never eaten anything that our Jewish
laws have declared impure or unclean" (verse 14 [NLT]).

When the vision or trance ended, "The Holy Spirit said to [Peter], 'Three men have come looking for you. Get up, go downstairs, and go with them, without hesitation. Don't worry, for I have sent them'" (Acts 10:19–20 [NLT]).

Peter obeyed the Spirit of God, even though he later tells Cornelius, "You know it is against our laws for a Jewish man to enter a Gentile home like this or to associate with you. But God has shown me that I should no longer think of anyone as impure or unclean" (verse 28).

Here and all throughout the New Testament, we watch as truth unfolds in the lives of members of the early church. As we read of them, we realize that we are always learners. The point for us to remember is that we're always disciples. None of us reaches the place where we have all the truth. We can experience the divine lessons the Holy Spirit imparts. Although the Spirit won't lead us to believe or do anything contrary to biblical teaching, we need to be open. For example, what we call social justice wasn't an issue among most conservative Christians two decades ago. Isn't it possible that the Holy Spirit has led us into awareness of the need for justice and mercy in the world?

The Holy Spirit will lead us into deeper truth, but we have to be teachable and open to learning. I've never met people who boast that they know everything there is to know about God, but I've met a few who acted as if they had plumbed the depths of spiritual understanding. In reality, no matter how much we know, we have only begun to understand. We can't let arrogance or a presumed knowledge of everything in the Bible keep us from grasping the meaning of all the Word has to offer. We need to let the Holy Spirit guide us.

Jesus said to his disciples, "But when he, the Spirit of truth, comes, he will guide you into all truth" (John 16:13 [NIV]). That same Holy Spirit seeks to guide us into all truth because his job isn't finished.

🖋

For many years I served in the broadcast television business. I left that business in 1984 and sought God's will for the next phase of my life. I had known since I was twenty-one years old that God wanted me to serve him in what I call a vocational capacity. In 1984, at the age of thirty-four, I knew the time had come but I didn't know exactly what God wanted me to do.

During that time, I prayed for guidance and talked to several close friends. I also drove to Natchitoches, Louisiana, to visit my father in the faith, Dr. Damon Vaughn, the pastor who had baptized me, and the minister to whom I had originally shared my decision to serve the Lord.

It was touching and humbling when Dr. Vaughn confirmed, "I know God has a call on your life." He also said that the sooner I moved on that call, the better it would be for me. He sensed I wouldn't be truly happy unless I served as a full-time Gospel minister.

I took temporary secular jobs as I sought God's direction. At that time we lived in the Shreveport, Louisiana, area. I worked in New Orleans, 320 miles away, and spent much time away from home living in a hotel. One particularly anxious night I was in my hotel room praying that God would reveal his exact will with all deliberate speed.

The yearning for God's will became so intense I lay on the floor, face down, and prayed. I don't know how long I prayed but peace finally came. Nothing seemed outwardly different, but I had peace.

A few minutes later I called Eva to ask how things were going with her and our kids. Eva told me, "You had a phone call and when I said you weren't here, the caller wouldn't leave a message."

It was only a phone call, but I wondered if that might have been God speaking to someone to phone me. I was somewhat frustrated because I knew—I absolutely knew—God would soon give me directions.

I returned home a few days later and no one called, no one wrote, and no one visited. I had been so certain God was going to open exactly the right door, and my frustration level intensified.

What does God want me to do?

One Sunday afternoon Eva took our kids and visited her mother. She left me alone to pray (and, yes, to fret). I prayed but felt nothing was happening.

A few minutes later, the doorbell rang. When I opened it, a woman whom I knew from an area church was at the door. She told me she represented that church. "I wonder if I could talk to you about coming to our church and serving as youth pastor."

"Of course we can talk." I opened the door and we began to talk. "Come inside."

No sooner had our conversation begun than the phone rang. I excused myself to answer. It was a pastor from Baton Rouge inquiring whether I might be interested in coming to be his assistant.

I told both the person on the phone and the woman from the local church that I felt honored to be considered, that I would pray and let them know. I felt the Holy Spirit was at work but I still didn't have that perfect peace that the Bible speaks about.

Two days later, Dr. Vaughn phoned to say that he had accepted a call to become the senior pastor of a church in the area where I lived. "Would you consider being my assistant?" he asked.

I gave Dr. Vaughn the same answer: I felt honored to be asked, and I would pray.

After I hung up the phone, I realized I suddenly had an embarrassment of riches.

I was even more astounded when I learned about that mysterious phone call and the person who wouldn't leave his name. I learned that while I was on my face on the floor in a hotel room in New Orleans, the pastor from Baton Rouge called our house and Eva answered. That experience amazed me. At the very moment I cried out for guidance, God was already in the process of answering me.

I faced a strong dilemma, but Dr. Vaughn's plea was too important to turn down, and he had been my spiritual mentor. To work with someone who meant so much to me would be a great joy. At that pivotal moment in my life God's plan was clear. And like he often does, he not only provided an opportunity for me, he supplied a host of them. I knew he would come through. I knew God had called me when I was twenty-one years old. When I surrendered, he delivered. He told me he would. He did.

Here's a second story about guidance. When Cecil Murphey felt a call to Africa, he was startled. He had never thought seriously about serving God overseas. But he believed in the call. He and Shirley started to do what they could to follow up, and for almost two years everything they tried slammed against a closed steel door. In desperation, Cecil prayed one night for guidance. "If you really want me there, you'll have to show me clearly and positively."

That night he had a dream. He was sitting across the table from a missionary named Arthur Dodzweit (whom he knew). "I'm so glad you've come to Kenya," Arthur said. "I've looked forward to it."

The table was clear except for a bowl filled with what looked like peaches. That seemed strange because Cec knew peaches weren't native to Africa.

Cec went ahead with his efforts to serve overseas, feeling that was divine guidance. A few months later (and long after he had forgotten about the dream), he sat at a table in Nairobi with Arthur. "I'm so glad you've come to Kenya," the older missionary said. "I've looked forward to it."

Just then Cec remembered the dream. In the center of the table was the fruit bowl. It contained mangoes—a fruit Cec had never seen before. That dream gave him a strong assurance of being in the will of God. It also encouraged him greatly two years later when he was beaten and several Africans tried to kill him. He said, "God made it clear this is where I belong. So this is where I stay until God shows me it's time to leave."

God graciously does such things for us at times. Such occurrences aren't usual, but the Holy Spirit is always free to intervene in our lives.

Here's another example. In the fall of 2004, I felt the Spirit lead me to begin searching for a new ministry. I had served at the First Baptist Church of Pasadena, Texas, for eight years, but I knew it was time for something new. Several churches contacted me about serving as their senior pastor. That seemed like the natural next step, and it's always flattering to be wanted by a congregation. I assumed that was probably the direction the Lord wanted me to follow for the next phase of my life and ministry. One Houston-area church in particular interested me. I began a dialogue with their pastor-search committee. Before long we had several meetings. Everything seemed positive. It was obviously a fine church with potential for more growth. The fact that they invited my wife, Eva, to meet with them as well was a thoughtful gesture. It seemed like the natural move for me.

In September 2004, *90 Minutes in Heaven* was released. I wanted the book to do well. Because I was between pastorates, I had already accepted a few invitations to talk about the book. I enjoyed speaking at different churches, but I saw it as a temporary thing while Eva and I prayed about whether to accept the call to serve as the senior pastor of the Houston church.

To my amazement, invitations began to pour in from other churches who wanted me to share my testimony in person. At first there were half a dozen, but then the number of invitations increased. In fact, one week after the book was released I received thirty-two speaking invitations.

Meanwhile the Houston-area church, having heard me preach several times, extended an invitation to come to their church to "preach in view of a call." That's Baptist parlance for "come to our church and preach to our congregation, and after you preach, we'll vote on whether to invite you to become our pastor."

There are no statistics, but to be asked to come in view of a call generally leads to being called to the church; it indicates the congregation's interest in that person becoming their pastor. To accept the invitation to preach in view of a call is significant, because it indicates the candidate's sincere interest in serving as pastor of that church.

The week I received the call was the same week I received the thirty-two invitations to speak in other churches about my testimony and book. The pressure to be in two places at the same time doing two different ministries was immense. Eva proposed the only wise solution: "Let's pray that the Holy Spirit will guide us."

Part of the dilemma was that I wanted to be a pastor but I also wanted to accept those thirty-two speaking invitations. To turn down the pastorate and to become a full-time speaker meant I would have no guaranteed income. It would be a big step of faith for us.

We asked many of our family members and friends to covenant together to pray about the crucial moment in our lives. After much prayer, Eva looked at me and said, "I think you need to answer the invitations for you to speak now rather than go to the church and preach in view of a call. I really believe that the Spirit is saying, 'This is what I want you to do now.' The overwhelming number of invitations is an indication of how important the Lord feels this is."

I listened and she said one other thing that assured me that the Holy Spirit had spoken to her. "If God wants you to pastor a church again, he will give you one later." I turned down the invitation to preach at the church toward a call. It was the right thing to do. It was the leading of God's Spirit.

Aside from the money, Eva made that statement knowing full well what it would mean. I would travel a great deal. She was a classroom teacher and would have to run the household by herself while I traveled.

Eva had already been with me many times when I shared my story and knew the response it often brought. She knew that my sharing the message of hope and healing through books and preaching around the world was what I needed to do.

I informed the Houston church of my decision. While I regretted the time and effort they had put into my consideration, it's better to do the right thing than force the wrong thing just because it is inconvenient or disappointing to someone.

I agreed to speak on the road for six months. More books followed, and seven years later, I'm still on the road.

That's the Holy Spirit at work.

Here's one more example.

It is quite amazing the number of e-mails, letters, and phone calls I receive in response to the books Cec and I have written. The overwhelming majority of them are very positive, some even gushing. Occasionally, I will receive a message not quite so nice. Sometimes these words can be hurtful because they are so harsh.

Shortly after our first book came out, I received a mean-spirited message from a woman. I won't bother to go into details, but apparently she felt I had been harsh, thoughtless, and didn't consider her feelings.

She didn't consider my feelings either and the words hurt. I was ready to fire off an angry reply. I typed a few sentences and stopped. I prayed for guidance. I wasn't aware of the Holy Spirit speaking to me, yet in retrospect, I believe that the Spirit did speak. I sensed that if I wrote in anger, the other person would be even angrier and the harsh words would escalate.

I prayed and decided to do nothing at the moment. Perhaps there was some therapy in just typing the response, even though I thought several times of sending her a harsh reply. Yet each time I prayed, I felt I wasn't ready to answer her.

The next morning I received an e-mail from that same woman. It was a heartfelt apology. The woman had shown the e-mail she had sent to me to her daughter, who was appalled by its content, and even more important, by its tone. The daughter asked, "Should Christians say those kinds of things to each other?"

Her mother reread the e-mail she had sent me. "No, you're

right," she said. "That's not the way Christians should behave." Immediately she wrote and asked me to forgive her.

I praise God that I didn't send my harsh message to her. I believe the Holy Spirit guided me and kept me from writing an equally harsh note—or perhaps one even harsher—in retaliation.

It doesn't always work that way, of course, but in this case, I knew the Holy Spirit kept me from replying. In the end, I didn't have to reply. The Holy Spirit not only worked in me but also through the woman's daughter to make her aware of her angry tone.

Many of us have experienced those moments when we may not have heard the Spirit say, "Stop!" but a verse comes to mind or a story from the Bible. Maybe we think of a psalm or a hymn. The Holy Spirit takes something we already know and pushes it to the front of our mind. That's guidance. That's the wonderful-but-mysterious way in which the Holy Spirit functions in those times we need direction.

Cec tells of an experience when he received an invitation to speak at a leadership conference. He had prepared his keynote speech, but the day before he left, he received a phone call from the conference leaders.

Among other things, the woman said, "There will be many nonbelievers present." After the call, Cec decided not to quote any biblical passages. He prayed for guidance and heard nothing.

A few minutes later he opened his Bible planning to turn to a passage in Ephesians, but the Bible opened and at the top of the page was Romans 9:6: "Not as though the word of God hath taken none effect" (KJV). Even though he realized that was not the con-textual meaning, he "heard" those words and sensed that he was to include the biblical references in his keynote message.

He obeyed, and no one objected. One man, who said he wasn't a Christian, thanked him for including references to his faith. "It's nice to hear people who speak from deep convictions."

※

Another thing to remember is that the Holy Spirit is peace. Sometimes the peace comes when the Spirit shows us how to escape or a way to avoid trouble. For example, a man contacted Cec to write a book about a world-famous celebrity. At first, Cec was interested, but as he prayed, "It just didn't feel right," he said. "I couldn't explain the reason, only the feeling, so I said no."

The spokesperson for the celebrity was angry and kept calling, trying to talk him into writing the book.

Cec didn't yield. A few days later, a news item accused the celebrity of unethical and immoral conduct.

※

Once Jesus assures the disciples that they won't be orphans and that the Holy Spirit will be with them, he tells them of his gift of peace.

"Peace I leave with you; my peace I give you. I do not give to you as the world gives" (John 14:27 [NIV]).

The promised peace overcomes fear and transcends doubts. Only God can give that kind of deep peace. The gift of peace is a special promise Jesus made to his followers and he reaffirms it in John 16:33. He points out that divine peace is different from the peace the world offers. The world offers a peace that comes if we avoid trouble or refuse to face unpleasant situations. The peace Jesus is talking about is more than that. Divine peace, translated from the Greek word *eirene,* never means the absence of trouble but always an inner calm despite the turmoil that rages around us. God's peace sustains us in the moment of our troubles and it's available to us at all times.

Inner peace is one of the great Christian virtues. In Philippians 4, Paul urges Christians to direct their thoughts on godly things, and if they do so, they'll have God's peace. "Don't fret or worry. Instead of worrying, pray. Let petitions and praises shape your worries into prayers, letting God know your concerns. Before you know it, a sense of God's wholeness, everything coming together for good, will come and settle you down. It's wonderful what happens when Christ displaces worry at the center of your life" (Philippians 4:8–9 [MSG]).

As you ponder your eventual liftoff, remember you're not alone and you don't have to figure out all the answers for yourself. The Holy Spirit is available for guidance. In fact, I think we grieve the Holy Spirit when we *don't* ask for guidance.

Departing Instructions

1. Call on God for his peace, no matter what your circumstances.
2. Ask for guidance. The Holy Spirit wants to lead you and often waits for you to ask.
3. If you don't ask for guidance, you fail God. Jesus sent the Holy Spirit to guide you all through this life.
4. Read Matthew 7:7–11. As you read, remind yourself Jesus gives this as a command and to help you know his will.

15

Head for the Final Destination

[Jesus said] "I have told you now before it happens, so that when it does happen you will believe."

JOHN 14:28–29 (NIV)

During my brief time in Heaven I learned many things. One of the most impressive is that there is no sorrow there. I knew that from reading the Bible, but I experienced it personally. It's one thing to read about what Heaven will be like and quite another to experience the sacredness and the perfection of that place. "There will be no more death or mourning or crying or pain, for the old order of things has passed away" (Revelation 21:4 [NIV]).

Another thing I learned is that I had no awareness of Earth while I was there. Some people don't like to hear that because they want to believe that we watch over those we leave behind. My answer is simple: If we had to witness their sorrows and observe their mistakes, we wouldn't be happy in Heaven.

And Heaven *is* perfect. It's the perfect destination to which Jesus is headed and it's the perfect destination for us.

Jesus had been in Heaven, come to Earth in human form, and now it was time for him to return to the place of utter perfection. But Jesus wasn't quite ready. He had to take care of his disciples and prepare them for his leaving. He has already spoken several times of leaving this world, but now he talks about more than just going away. He tells them his destination is Heaven, where he will be with the Father. Jesus was incarnated as a perfect human being and gave up all the perfection of Heaven to live on Earth among sinful people, but now he was going to be restored to his glory.

The process began when "Though he was God, he did not think of equality with God as something to cling to. Instead, he gave up his divine privileges; he took the humble position of a slave and was born as a human being" (Philippians 2:6–7 [NLT]). For us, the obvious beginning is in Bethlehem when Jesus was born to Mary.

Then Jesus reversed the process. At Calvary he suffered unbelievable physical torture, but he would return to his rightful place in Heaven alongside the Father.

If the disciples had been able to believe, and if they truly loved him, they would have been glad for Jesus. But they weren't ready to understand that.

Jesus wanted them to realize that although they would grieve his absence, he was in Heaven, a far, far better place. He would be in a place of perfection. He wanted them to know—just as he wants us to know today—they could be glad that those whom they love that are separated from Earth are alive in God's presence.

We feel the loss, of course, but even in our sorrow and loneliness, we rejoice because their troubles are over. As I speak with thousands of people whose loved ones have passed away in the years since I returned from Heaven, I ask if their departed loved ones were followers of Christ. When they reply yes, I offer my sincere condolence "for your temporary separation."

I often receive startled looks when I use the word *temporary*, but that's what it is. "The separation is real, but it is only temporary," I point out. "You will be reunited with them. There is coming a great reunion someday. They have entered, not into death, but into eternal blessing."

Jesus' death would release him from the human limitations of this world. He also wanted his disciples to see Heaven as a place of joy and peace. It's not that he didn't want them to feel their loss. That's only natural. But knowing Jesus' final destination could eliminate the pain.

I wonder if Jesus' words here are a gentle reminder that their anxiety is because they are centered on themselves. They seem unable to grasp the glory of Jesus' next step; they focus only on being alone and without their leader. Perhaps that's natural, but that's not what Jesus wants for them. He wants them not to be troubled about his death and not to mourn because he would no longer walk the dusty roads of Judea with them. He will be absent from them, but he will leave them an invaluable gift: his peace.

He wants them to rejoice that he is heading toward his final destination, the glorious place he left to come and live among them. And he's also preparing them so that when they move toward their final destinations—when they're only 90 minutes away from Heaven—they can rejoice and eagerly look forward to what's ahead.

Jesus knows what is ahead for them, just as he knows what's ahead for each of us. He never promises an easy, trouble-free life. He does promise peace in the midst of chaos and confusion.

That's an area where the Holy Spirit is *the expert.* No matter how troubled our hearts or how difficult our situation, the Spirit brings peace. This is one of the great characteristics of what it means to follow Jesus' departing instructions: We are not immune from grief, pain, rejection, or financial upheavals. Paul gives us the peace formula—and it is a divine formula: "Don't worry about anything; instead, pray about everything. Tell God what you need, and thank him for what he has done. Then you will experience God's peace, which exceeds anything we can understand. His peace will guard your hearts and minds as you live in Christ Jesus" (Philippians 4:6–7 [NLT]). Peter says it this way: "Give all your worries and cares to God, for he cares about you" (1 Peter 5:7 [NLT]).

In John 14:29, Jesus says, "I have told you now before it happens, so that when it does happen you will believe" (NIV). That's a powerful statement. By proclaiming his death before he's betrayed or beaten, Jesus shows that the soon-coming events won't surprise him or defeat him. His foreknowledge of events will become clear to them after the events take place. Jesus' quiet acceptance of what will transpire will lead to the deepening of their faith. They already believe—imperfectly perhaps—and this will help them to believe with a deeper, steadier, more intelligent faith.

For us, here's one thing I've learned about God's peace (and it's in the quotation from Philippians 4): Give thanks. That is, if we look backward and remind ourselves of what God has done for us in the past, we can handle what's ahead.

Along with reminding ourselves of the past, we can also remind ourselves of God's promises. They're all through the Bible, but here are a few:

- "Even though I walk through the valley of the shadow of death, I will fear no evil, for you are with me; your rod and your staff, they comfort me" (Psalm 23:4).
- "Fear not, for I have redeemed you; I have summoned you by name; you are mine" (Isaiah 43:1b [NIV]).
- "Don't love money; be satisfied with what you have. For God has said, 'I will never fail you. I will never abandon you'" (Hebrews 13:5 [NLT]).

Jesus' instructions to the disciples make it clear that the crisis is imminent. He says that Satan, the ruler of this world, "has no power over me" (John 14:30 [NLT]). He speaks of Satan's apparent control over the world and those who don't obey God, but for the disciples and for us today, that's a power Jesus will overthrow by his death and resurrection. And when he speaks of Satan coming, he means Judas will soon betray him.

The point to remember for us is that the devil has no real power over us. Neither does Pilate to whom Jesus will soon say, "You would have no power over me if it were not given to you from above" (John 19:11 [NIV]). Jesus faithfully follows the Father's saving plan to open the door of eternal life for believers. It also shows others in the world that the door is open for them— if they'll open their eyes.

Sometimes we need to remind ourselves of Jesus' promise while we live and await our own departing instructions. Some people constantly see evil forces, Satan, or demons attacking them—and I'm not arguing about that. Instead I want to emphasize that no matter how much evil comes against us or how difficult our troubles, because of Jesus we can overcome every temptation and hardship.

In an earlier time, Jesus rebuked the religious leaders and spoke of his own: "My sheep listen to my voice; I know them, and they follow me. I give them eternal life, and they will never perish. No one can snatch them away from me" (John 10:27–28 [NLT]).

Paul's magnificent chapter 8 of Romans says, "If God is for us, who can ever be against us?" (verse 31b [NLT]). He means "Who can prevail against us?" And he adds, "Can anything ever separate us from Christ's love?" (verse 35 [NLT]). The intended answer is no, and he lists a variety of terrible things that can occur in our lives:

"[W]e have trouble or calamity, or are persecuted, or hungry, or destitute, or in danger, or threatened with death" (Romans 8:35 [NLT]) and he says, "No, despite all these things, overwhelming victory is ours through Christ, who loved us" (verse 37 [NLT]).

We called this chapter "Head for the Final Destination" because you are the one who decides to get on board for Heaven. You're more than halfway through the book. If you haven't made your reservation, do it now. Jesus assures us of his peace and of the Holy Spirit's presence. He assures us that no one or no power is stronger than he is.

Why wouldn't you want to head for your heavenly destination?

Departing Instructions

1. Remind yourself that Heaven is a perfect place. When you reach there you will be made perfect and you can say, "God has been preparing me for this."
2. Make each day count as one more day of living service to the Savior.
3. Commit yourself to listen carefully to the Spirit's departing instructions.
4. "Whoever can be trusted with very little can also be trusted with much" (Luke 16:10 [NIV]). Commit yourself to live with this verse in your heart. As you live with these words, you remind yourself to be faithful in little things that lead you to be faithful in the big things.

16

Stay Connected
and Be Fruitful

*[Jesus said] "I am the true vine, and my Father is the gardener.
He cuts off every branch in me that bears no fruit, while every
branch that does bear fruit he prunes so that it will be even more
fruitful."*

JOHN 15:1–2 (NIV)

Hardships aren't punishments, but they are means of growth. Jesus uses the image of pruning or cutting away branches. Today, in a nonagrarian culture, he might have said, "I want you to mature in your Christian experience. You'll encounter hardships and problems, but stay connected. Call on me, and not only will you grow through the experience but you'll be able to share your experiences with others and help them through difficult places."

Here's one way each of us can be fruitful. "[God] comforts us in all our troubles, so that we can comfort those in any trouble with the comfort we ourselves have received from God" (2 Corinthians 1:4 [NIV]).

One spring during the years I worked in the television business, I became quite ill. Mostly it was fatigue, but I didn't slow down. I developed pneumonia and I still didn't slow down. Then I stopped. I was hit so hard I remained in bed for almost a month.

My strength slowly returned and so did my desire to return to some sense of normalcy. As the day came for my return to work I followed the same morning ritual I always had. One of the last things I usually did was to strap on my wristwatch before I walked out the door. As I put it on, I checked the time. I realized that neither hand was moving. I put the watch in my pocket and decided to take it to the jeweler during my lunch hour.

I went back to work and let the wall clock guide my morning. At noon I went to the watch repair shop.

I told the jeweler, "My watch has stopped. I'd like you to look at it but I assume the battery died and needs replacing."

"I'll take a look at it and be right back." He walked behind a large window. Wearing an eyepiece he strained to remove the back cover of the watch and gaze inside. Ever so slowly he looked up at me and his face formed a puzzled look.

Another minute later, he came to the front and held up my watch. "What did you say was wrong with your watch?"

"It's stopped. The battery must have run down while I was sick."

Smiling somewhat smugly he said, "Sir, this is a self-winding watch. It does not have a battery. Its power comes from the motion of your body. Wear it on your wrist and it will start to keep time again."

As embarrassing as that story is, it taught me an invaluable lesson. When I wore the watch it kept time. The connection to and the motion from my wrist caused it to function. When I laid my watch aside and didn't wear it, the watch no longer functioned.

If I had faithfully worn my watch, even when I was sick, it would have continued to keep time. It failed to function because I failed to be faithful.

Another time my computer refused to start. It had given me a little trouble the day before, but I thought everything was fine. I tried at least a dozen times to turn it on and it refused to boot up. I called two of my computer-savvy friends and followed what they suggested. Nothing worked.

In desperation, I called the help line of the computer manufacturer. The technician's first question was this: "Will you check to make sure you're plugged in?"

I looked under my desk. Apparently my PC cable was still in the electrical outlet, but barely and probably soon would fall to the floor. I pushed in the plug and immediately my computer booted up. Embarrassed, I apologized to the tech guy.

"It's the most common problem we get," he said and laughed.

As I thought about the incident with my computer, it seemed to me that's the way a lot of Christians try to live. They were once vitally connected to the Lord and the connection becomes loose or disconnected.

That's how I describe discipleship for modern audiences. Jesus used a different illustration but the principle is the same. Those who are connected to him, Jesus called his branches. He used the metaphor of the grapevine and said, "I am the true vine, and my Father is the gardener" (John 5:1 [NIV]). In the verses that follow, Jesus makes two major points. First, he warns against being unfruitful—not obeying his commands. "He cuts off every branch in me that bears no fruit" (verse 2a [NIV]). Second, "while every branch that does bear fruit he prunes so that it will be even more fruitful" (verse 2b [NIV]).

That has to be startling information to those disciples—not the pruning process, because they would have understood—but that he likens faithful discipleship to the vines being pruned by the gardener. He promises that those that don't bear fruit will be cast aside, but those who are already fruitful will be trimmed to make them even more fruitful.

That's a difficult concept for many people to grasp. Too often we think that when hardships, difficulties, or problems come our way, it's because God wants to punish us. Dear Christians often come up to me with sad faces. They usually want to talk privately, and they tell me of their ongoing pain or their tragic circumstances. When they finish they often have tears in their eyes. They ask, "What did I do to make God want to punish me this way?"

People who have debilitating diseases, financial disasters, addictions, job losses, whose loved ones have taken their own lives, or have faced other excruciating circumstances, always want to know why. They don't seem to realize that those problems can very well make us stronger and able to overcome bigger hardships that we must face later.

There is no promise (or bribe) for an easy life. Instead, Jesus promises that life won't be trouble free. If we truly believe the promise of Romans 8:28, it means that God promises everything to work for our good. "And we know that in all things God works for the good of those who love him, who have been called according to his purpose" (NIV). That's the part we all focus on and often people try to console us by saying, "Somewhere along the way you'll understand."

However, we don't have to wait until we reach some other

place along the way. Paul wrote this to the Romans, and after he says God promises to work things for our good, he concludes that the divine purpose for us is "to be conformed to the likeness of his Son" (Romans 8:29b).

This is to say that we can rejoice in God choosing us—but we also have to take in the entire concept. God chose us for a purpose. We are to be like Jesus Christ in this world. We'll never do it perfectly, of course, but we get better at being like Jesus Christ as we overcome temptations and win over serious battles.

This isn't the kind of material most people like to read, but it's something we need to know.

I've found much comfort in times of hardships (and we all have those bad times!) in reading Hebrews 12. In the eleventh chapter of the Book of Hebrews the writer provides a lengthy honor roll of those who acted in faith. The chapter ends with a list of the persecutions many faithful followers suffered: "[O]thers were tortured, refusing to turn from God in order to be set free. They placed their hope in a better life after the resurrection. Some were jeered at, and their backs were cut open with whips. Others were chained in prisons. Some died by stoning, some were sawed in half, and others were killed with the sword" (Hebrews 11:35b–37a [NLT]).

That's not the total list, but the writer goes on to say that those who suffered for their faith are like a large crowd of witnesses who surround us (see Hebrews 12:1). When I think of that image, it's like having a private cheering section. It's like the believers who have passed on sit in the cheering section as we fight our battles. They may not be present, but the record of those witnesses is found all through the Bible. Their achievements function as our cheering section that cries out, "You can do it! You can do it!"

The writer of Hebrews moves into an illustration of a race in which thousands watch us as we run. Nothing should distract us or make us turn off the path. It's interesting the way the writer puts it: "[S]ince we are surrounded by such a great cloud of witnesses, let us throw off everything that hinders and the sin that so easily entangles, and let us run with perseverance the race marked out for us" (Hebrews 12:1 [NIV]). The Greek word translated "patience, perseverance, or endurance," depending on the version, is *hupomone*. It's not the kind of patience that hangs on, grits its teeth, and accepts changes around the racer. *Hupomone* is a determination that pushes us to keep going on and that refuses to be sidelined. Obstacles don't stumble us and discouragements don't steal our anticipation of victory. It means we carry on until we reach our goal—until Jesus calls us to Heaven.

All the while we run the race, the writer points out that we need to keep our eyes on Jesus, "the champion who initiates and perfects our faith. Because of the joy awaiting him, he endured the cross, disregarding its shame" (Hebrews 12:2 [NLT]). Jesus is our example, not just because he's the Son of God, but because he ran the race, endured, and won. He endured the ignominy and the suffering. The writer also inserts, *disregarding its shame*. It could just as easily be translated (as it is in some versions) *despising* the shame.

I like the interpretation of these verses in *The Message*:

Do you not see what this means—all these pioneers who blazed the way, all these veterans cheering us on? It means we'd better get on with it. Strip down, start running—and never quit! No extra spiritual fat, no parasitic sins. Keep your eyes on Jesus, who both began and finished this race we're in. Study how he did it. Because

he never lost sight of where he was headed—that exhilarating fin-
ish in and with God—he could put up with anything along the
way: Cross, shame, whatever. And now he's there, *in the place of*
honor, right alongside God. When you find yourselves flagging in
your faith, go over that story again, item by item, that long litany
of hostility he plowed through. That will shoot adrenaline into
your souls! (Hebrews 12:1–3 [emphasis added]).

This section reminds us that we have the presence of Jesus in our lives. He is the companion along the way as we run the race. He's the goal of the race. The wonder of the Christian life is that as we race forward, the encouragement and the testimonies of the saints are urging us forward. And best of all, Jesus will meet us at the end.

That's not the end of the message. The writer shows us, the believers, that the suffering of others, and especially the sufferings of Jesus, are for a specific purpose in our life. He quotes from Proverbs 3:11–12 and writes, "My child, don't make light of the Lord's discipline, and don't give up when he corrects you. For the Lord disciplines those he loves, and he punishes each one he accepts as his child" (Hebrews 12:5–6 [NLT]).

When hardships or troubles come into our lives, instead of immediately crying out and wailing that God is against us, maybe those things happen because God loves us. He loves us enough that he tries to stop us from going astray or making a serious mistake—even if it hurts us. Maybe he loves us enough to toughen us so that we can face bigger and stronger obstacles in the times ahead.

Here's an example. There is a deep drainage ditch that surrounds South Park Baptist Church in Alvin, Texas, where I served at the time of my accident. Often it's no more than a gaping ditch with a trickle of water at the bottom. When a sudden south Texas rainstorm occurs, however, it can change into a raging torrent. The trench is separated from parking lots and sidewalks with large wooden rails for safety. I had never seen anyone down in that gully. Common sense would lead anyone to know to avoid that ditch—unless, of course, you were a nine-year-old boy.

One afternoon, Susan, a nurse who was one of the church members, rushed up to me at church and reported that she had just rescued my son Chris from that dangerous old ditch.

I raced over to see him. He looked like the proverbial drowned rat. Susan had already checked him over and insisted that nothing was hurt but his pride. I hugged him, happy that he hadn't been hurt. That night I punished him about as forcefully as I ever had.

Some could ask, "How does punishment interface with love?"

I punished him because I love him. I wanted him to remember his irresponsible, even defiant action. After being told never to get near that ditch, he had done so. It was not acceptable behavior and never would be.

I would even say it this way: I had to punish him because I love him. If I hadn't punished Chris, the message he received would be that I was indifferent to his actions or that I didn't care.

I also remember what S. Truett Cathy, founder of Chick-fil-A, said in a public speech. He told the story of the time he felt he had to punish one of his sons. He spanked the boy but before it was over, Truett himself cried more than the son. He was convinced he did the right thing in punishing the boy. It was also Truett's way of saying that he cared too much to allow his son to disobey and go in the wrong direction.

God goes on to make the point that we encounter problems but they're not punishment for our sins; they are instruments for our growth. "As you endure this divine discipline, remember that God is treating you as his own children. Who ever heard of a child who is never disciplined by its father? If God doesn't discipline you as he does all of his children, it means that you are illegitimate and are not really his children at all" (Hebrews 12:7–8 [NLT]).

From those verses I learn something important. Not only that God loves us, but that God disciplines us. We'll face hardships and setbacks in life, and all of them aren't the devil trying to destroy us. God wants to teach us.

Most of us don't learn too easily, and we seem to have to make some bad decisions that lead to mistakes and wrong actions. When we realize what a mess we've made, we cry out to God. We're forgiven, but that's only part of the lesson. We also learn. The greatest lessons of my life often followed heartbreak, a disastrous mistake, a terrible loss, or a seeming catastrophe.

We realize that the connection isn't tight. We're not cut off from God, but our cords seem to be barely attached to the power source. All of this is to say that if we're going to be fruitful and used by God, we have to live by being connected to the power source.

Perhaps even as you read these words, you realize that you are close to the edge of a precipice. Your connection to God feels weak. Your great suffering has caused you to waver in your faith. Don't lose heart. Instead, remind yourself that Jesus hasn't left you and he's running with you. If you've tripped and fallen down, he'll wait until you're ready to get back on the track. Out of your ordeal can emerge your deepest spiritual growth and most meaningful ministry.

Months after my accident I learned that sometimes the way to healing and health is through pain. Sometimes we have to walk through dark and lonely places.

For example, after the external fixator was removed from my left leg, doctors installed steel plates along the length of the femur to give my leg strength as I learned to walk again. Following months of therapy and rehab, I succeeded in walking again. Many people are amazed that I walk as well as I do today. It's a tribute to the work of a lot of doctors, nurses, and therapists.

Several years after the plates were installed my long-time orthopedic surgeon, Dr. Tom Greider, studied my X-rays when I went in for a checkup. "We need to go in there and get those plates off your femur," he said in a calm, matter-of-fact voice.

His words stunned me so I said, "If they're not bothering anything, just leave them in there. I certainly don't want another operation."

The good doctor explained that over a period of time, the bones grow dependent on the plates and they don't become as strong as they need to be.

"If I leave them in there, as you grow older that particular bone could grow brittle, especially near the end of the plates and become susceptible to breaking."

I reluctantly consented to the surgery.

Going back for another surgery reminded me that stress and

using our bones develops strength. Like most things, if they aren't used they atrophy, becoming brittle and weak. Spiritual atrophy is just like that. We need to practice our faith for it to become strong.

Jesus made it clear that part of our growing and bearing fruit also means being pruned. The biblical word is *paideia*, a word that means "teaching or instruction." Instead of grumbling about why life is so difficult for us, perhaps we need to ask, "God, what's going on that makes me need the discipline?" Or if we use Jesus' symbol of the vine, we can ask, "What's going on that makes me need to be pruned?"

Although God punishes evil, he also chastises and instructs those he loves. God disciplines believers when they go astray, but his wrath is on those who refuse to obey. This distinction is significant and shows that the purpose is different, even if the effects seem similar.

If we want to take the journey to Heaven, it involves our being disciplined and taught during our stages of preparation for liftoff. Even if we don't like the lessons, God says we need them and that all chastening or discipline is for our growth.

Several times, the Old Testament prophets denounced the people and pronounced judgment on Israel for its sin of not being fruitful. In the same way, Jesus says that the unfruitful branches are pruned off. Unless the disciples abide faithfully in Jesus they will be cast off as worthless and burned (John 15:2, 6).

It's one thing to be chosen, but the proof of being chosen shows itself in living a fruitful life. Some followers bear excellent fruit; others are useless and bear no fruit. Paul said it this way: "[O]n the judgment day, fire will reveal what kind of work each builder has done. The fire will show if a person's work has any value. If the work survives, that builder will receive a reward. But if the work is burned up, the builder will suffer great loss. The builder will be saved, but like someone barely escaping through a wall of flames" (1 Corinthians 3:13–15 [NLT]).

*

When Jesus mentioned no fruit, he may have been thinking of Judas; he may have been referring to the Jewish nation that had rejected him. Most likely, however, he meant the eleven men who were still with him and who would make disciples of their own. Some of those disciples would turn out to be professors of faith but not practicers. They would have all the right words, but none of the right deeds. They would be like a tree with all leaves and no fruit.

An example of that would be Demas, a disciple of Paul. Twice Paul mentions him as being one of the men who traveled with him (*see* Colossians 4:14 and Philemon 24). His final reference to that once-faithful disciple is sad. He writes to Timothy, "Do your best to come to me quickly, for Demas, because he loved this world, has deserted me and has gone to Thessalonica. . . . Only Luke is with me" (2 Timothy 4:9–11a [NIV]). Like many others who profess faith in Jesus Christ, Demas followed Paul's leadership. Obviously he saw wonderful things taking place and was on the front lines of the spiritual battlefield.

Then he turned back. His love for the world became more important to him than his love for Jesus Christ. There are many Demases in the world: They start well but get disconnected along the way.

The good news of this is that no matter how much we want to talk about our choice and our free will, the Bible makes it clear that God *chose* us—we've been personally selected by him and loved by him. Others have the opportunity to be part of the chosen, but we who have decided to follow Jesus realize the power of his words: "You did not choose me, but I chose you and appointed you to go and bear fruit—fruit that will last" (John 15:16 [NIV]). Although he spoke those words to the original disciples, the message is also for us today.

Jesus' words must have encouraged the disciples to know that he had chosen them. And in the days that followed and in the midst of their hardships and at those times when everything seemed dark, they could remind themselves, "God chose me. I am here today because God selected me for his service."

They didn't yet know the cost of that discipleship. But they would. When any of us agree to serve God, there is a price to pay. Not everyone wants to pay that price. Jesus made that clear.

I want to add this important caution. Sometimes people commit themselves to what we call full-time Christian service. They may think that's the only way to truly make a difference.

I think we limit the use of that phrase. Full-time Christian service truly applies to every person who is a follower of Christ—not just clergy or missionaries. Whatever your vocation, your calling is to full-time Christian service. The apostle Peter wrote, "But you are a chosen people, a royal priesthood, a holy nation, a people belonging to God" (1 Peter 2:9 [NIV]). We—all of us who believe—are people set apart by God for his service.

When many of us think about being followers, we tend to think of the benefits and the blessings that result from our relationship with God. That's not wrong, but if we read the words of Jesus in this chapter, he emphasizes fruitfulness. Perhaps that's why he spoke so much about the vine and the branches to the disciples. He wants to make it abundantly clear what he expects of them and of modern followers. Rewards and blessings come with responsibilities.

🖎

Be fruitful. That's the essence of Jesus' words. *Fruitful* certainly covers a wide area, but when Jesus spoke to the small band of his disciples he meant evangelism. He meant their way to be fruitful was to spread the good news to the world.

Until after the resurrection there is almost nothing about proclaiming the message of salvation or about reaching out to the whole world. There is no distinct command to spread the message. After the resurrection, the message is different.

- Matthew records Jesus as saying, "Therefore go and make disciples of all nations, baptizing them in the name of the Father and of the Son and of the Holy Spirit, and teaching them to obey everything I have commanded you" (Matthew 28:19–20 [NIV]).
- Mark's Gospel says, "Go into all the world and preach the good news to all creation" (Mark 16:15 [NIV]).
- Luke's Gospel has these words: "Then [Jesus] opened their minds so they could understand the Scriptures. He told them 'This is what is written: The Christ will suffer and rise from the dead on the third day, and repentance and forgiveness of sins will be preached in his name to all nations'" (Luke 24:45–47 [NIV]).
- In the upper room after the resurrection, Jesus says to the eleven, "Peace be with you! As the Father has sent me, I am sending you" (John 20:21 [NIV]).

- Although it's not a specific statement, Jesus' words to Thomas imply what he means: "Because you have seen me, you have believed; blessed are those who have not seen and yet have believed" (John 20:29 [NIV]).
- Acts 1 tells of Jesus' final appearance to his disciples and he says, "[Y]ou will be my witnesses in Jerusalem, and in Judea and Samaria, and to the ends of the Earth" (Acts 1:8 [NIV]).

As Christians today we tend to assume that bearing fruit means winning others to Jesus Christ. It's certainly not separate, but that's not what Jesus wants to teach as part of his final instructions. "If you obey me in everything, you will produce fruit." Those aren't his exact words but that's a summary. We will be fruitful if we remain faithful to him and obey him. We will be faithful when we rely on his help. Our fruitfulness shows in hundreds of ways, but it always begins with obedience to Christ's commands.

Stay connected. That's the command. Stay vitally connected.

Departing Instructions

1. Strive to obey Jesus Christ in every way because you have been chosen to live like a fruitful branch.
2. Accept that the problems that confront you are not accidents. They are part of God's plan to teach you and to make you stronger.
3. Yearn for the blessings that only God can give.
4. As you become more obedient, accept responsibility for your attitudes and your actions.

17

Hang In There

[Jesus said] "Remain in me, and I will remain in you. No branch can bear fruit by itself; it must remain in the vine. Neither can you bear fruit unless you remain in me."

JOHN 15:4 (NIV)

Music is one of my most vivid memories of Heaven. People often ask me if I heard any specific songs—songs that I recognized from here on Earth.

The answer is no, although some of it was similar to the music we sing. By that, I mean some of the heavenly music consisted of choruses praising God, like the ones that have become popular today.

But I also heard melodies like the great anthems and hymns that have inspired us here on Earth through the centuries. I still love those old songs, because each one conjures a memory from some church service or camp or revival or even a funeral.

I became a believer at age sixteen and one of the old songs we sang regularly in our church was "Abide with Me." I liked the tune and memorized the words purely from repetition, but I'm not sure I understood the meaning—at least not for many years.

Here's the first stanza:

Abide with me; fast falls the eventide;
The darkness deepens; Lord, with me abide;
When other helpers fail and comforts flee,
Help of the helpless, O abide with me.[2]

They're nice words but they didn't do anything to help me understand what it means to abide in Jesus. The few times any preachers or Sunday school teachers spoke on the topic, they seemed to hurry past the word *abide* and said it means "to stay" with him.

Why was it such a big deal if that's all it meant? Anyone should understand that. So maybe that wasn't all there was to it.

In past generations, Christians frequently wrote about abiding in Christ. It's an important concept. The Greek verb, *meno*, means "to remain" or "to stay," but the biblical concept implies a constant commitment and a vital, energetic connection with him.

This is where we see the significance of a disciplined spiritual life coming in, such as daily prayer and Bible reading.

Jesus said that unless disciples abide in him they would be cut off—and that means cut off from the close fellowship he wants with each of us. This is a stern but loving warning that the road to Heaven requires faithful obedience.

To abide in the biblical sense means we need to have a daily, immediate, and intimate contact with Jesus Christ. It's not something that merely happens, but it requires effort and discipline. I don't want to lay down laws and rules for abiding, but some of them seem fairly obvious.

2 Henry F. Lyte, 1847.

- If I love God, I'll read his book, the Bible.
- If I love God, I'll pray daily and fervently.
- If I love God, I'll remain faithful to his church.
- If I love God, I'll share my faith with others so that they may know him, too.
- If I love God, I'll examine my heart and seek to push away anything that divides us.

I'm again reminded of a song we used to sing often in my boyhood called "Nothing Between." And the chorus goes like this:

Nothing between my soul and the Savior,
So that His blessed face may be seen;
Nothing preventing the least of His favor,
Keep the way clear! Let nothing between.[3]

For me, that's the best way I know to think of abiding. I like to think of it as living a life so close to God that I'll never have any unconfessed sin in my life. It's like the modern saying, "Hang in there." It means not turning back and not giving up.

Jesus also talks about abiding in him as faithful obedience: "If you keep my commands, you will remain in my love, just as I have kept my Father's commands and remain in his love" (John 15:10 [TNIV]).

The point is that he shows us the source of blessing. If we want our lives to be blessed, strengthened, or directed, there's only one way for it to happen: We obey. He promises blessings only to those who are obedient.

3 Charles Albert Tindley, 1905.

Jesus says we have to decide to remain in him and not break off on our own and that we (the branch) cannot be fruitful without the vine (Jesus). Now, you may be thinking, branches can't simply decide to become independent grape producers. That's the problem, of course, with illustrations; they have limitations. But the point is that humans can rebel. We can break our intimate tie with Jesus and lose the source of our life and strength. And when we do that, we can't be fruitful.

This reminds me of a young man named Darrel. One day many years ago, Darrel walked across the church parking lot, and a couple of his friends in the youth group recognized him. They told him about our upcoming youth camp and encouraged him to attend. They brought Darrel over and introduced him to me.

"Darrel would like to go to camp," one of them said.

"Could he come with us?" asked another.

"Sure," I said, "if he wants to go and his parents will let him."

"My parents couldn't care less what I do. How much will it cost me?"

"Why don't you come inside to my office and we'll talk about it?" I said. I sensed that Darrel had little means of emotional or financial support. I offered him a scholarship, and he shyly accepted.

Youth camp was incredible that year. Darrel was a natural athlete. I often saw him wear other kids' clothes. Later, I learned that he had brought almost nothing to camp with him. In fact, he had little to bring. At the end of the week, he won the award of Camper of the Year, and before camp was over, Darrel asked Christ to become his Savior.

After we returned home, Darrel became increasingly involved

with the church youth group. He dated one of the church girls. But not long after that, word reached my office that he had been in a fight with some of the other kids and had begun to take advantage of some of our girls. I approached him about his behavior and he didn't deny any of the rumors. He just couldn't see why anything he did was wrong. After all, he'd been saved. He was going to Heaven. Why couldn't he live as he wanted until then?

We couldn't have been more redemptive toward him, non-judgmental, and supportive. In spite of our best efforts to speak the truth in love and to show him the way to be faithful, Darrel fell away.

Several times I talked to him, but it didn't seem to do any good. Darrel was clear about his stance: "Your religion has too many rules and requirements. I can't pull it off. I like being liked but I don't want to be told what to do, now or ever."

He refused to talk to me again.

Years later Darrel was arrested for illegal drug possession. My heart sank when I heard that. He didn't want discipline. He didn't want to be pruned. Like so many, he wanted cheap grace. He wanted eternal rewards, but he wanted no change of behavior, no discipline, and no sacrifice.

What do we need to do? Perhaps the best thing to do is to remind ourselves that the blessed life is a steady, grateful life and it means being faithful in God's service. Sometimes we may not like the task, but we can follow the example of Jesus. After much agonizing, he prayed for his Father to take away the cup (the suffering he would have to endure): "Take this cup away from Me; nevertheless, not what I will, but what You *will*" (Mark 14:36 [NKJV]).

That gives us the correct response to the things we find difficult or distasteful. We respond with, "Nevertheless," and obey.

I understand *nevertheless*. I travel a great deal, and I've had to learn that despite delayed flights, bad weather, and aching body, I have no excuse for not obeying. Sometimes I get weary talking to people, and I think I just can't talk to anyone else. I'm used up.

Just then someone says, "Mr. Piper, I need to talk to someone—someone who will listen."

Despite my weariness, I listen. I do it because that's the *nevertheless* principle at work. I have to decide that I will trust and obey. As the old hymn by John H. Sammis goes, "Trust and obey, for there's no other way to be happy in Jesus, but to trust and obey."

Jesus promises, "If you remain in me and my words remain in you, ask whatever you wish, and it will be given you" (John 15:7 [NIV]). With two conditions, Jesus promised his disciples to answer all prayers. First, they must abide in him by unwavering faith in him and with complete commitment to him. Second, his words (his teachings) must remain in them. As I understand this, he refers to a commitment of their heart and a commitment of their actions.

It's good to love Jesus, but that's not enough. Our love must result in action—the kind of action he commands. He wants our thoughts, purposes, and prayers shaped by complete dedication and loyalty.

It's a process.

We had an expression in the TV business for a program or a commercial that would run only once. We called it OTO, which meant one time only. Salvation is OTO; service to the Lord is continuous. Like marriage, serving Christ is a living thing. There is never a hump in life that we catapult over and it's all easy coasting after that.

For the past couple of years, I estimate that I've been on the road an average of 275 days a year. I call my wife every night at ten o'clock Central Standard Time whether I'm in Norway or Norfolk. It's still nice to talk to her at least once a day and to hear her voice. I don't always use these words, but my call is to say, "I care about what's happening in your life and I love you." Faith and faithfulness are words and action.

Jesus says that if the disciples fulfill these two conditions, not only will he answer prayer but also they will bear much fruit in their life of obedience and service.

✌

The responsibilities and expectations placed on us are on one side of daily life. The other side involves rewards and blessings of our relationship with Jesus.

Even though I was often surrounded by friends and family during my long road to recovery after my accident, there were times of deep and abject isolation. Physical therapy and rehabilitation can be a long, lonely road. Wonderful therapists were there to encourage and guide me, but ultimately I, as the patient, had to do the recovery work.

During such times, loneliness and isolation are often constant companions. This isn't just my own story, but I've heard countless others say the same thing.

Following a serious setback during my recovery, I stayed in an isolation room in St. Luke's Hospital in Houston for nearly three weeks. Because of a dangerous infection on one of the pinholes in my left leg, only nurses who wore masks, special garments, and shoe coverings were allowed into the room with me. Friends and family members could see me and talk to me through a glass window in an outer room.

I lay flat on my back, one leg in a cast, the other sheathed in steel, and a left arm with rods penetrating it. Massive doses of antibiotics coursed through my veins. Despite all of that, calmness came over me during those days. I truly felt the presence of God in that room. It could have been only God enabling me to abide in peace.

I had no distractions, no outside cares, and no preoccupations. I felt as though Jesus kept me company in the most tender of senses. When I drifted into sleep, he stood beside me. When I awakened he was there. I felt his presence and knew that he truly stayed with me every moment.

During my years of recovery there was an ebb and flow to my sense of closeness to God. Of course, God never changed, but occasionally I drifted a little. My sense of being cut off from others because of my injuries and emotions forced me to cling to the Lord as never before. Another old gospel hymn comes to mind and says it all, "Where Could I Go but to the Lord?"

❦

We also need to remind ourselves of the positive effect we have on others by abiding in Jesus Christ. Too often we put the emphasis on the benefits we receive—and that's true—but to abide means that we bear fruit and influence others.

Here's one way to explain how I see this matter of fruitfulness. This is the fourth book that Cecil Murphey and I have written together. The series began with *90 Minutes in Heaven*. God blessed our efforts and our writings have become bestsellers. But it's more than the books selling well. It also means that our efforts of living as close to Christ as we know how influences others and challenges them to turn more fully to the same Savior.

We consider the books and tapes we produce as ministry tools. Each one is prayerfully designed and carefully prepared to meet needs. The motto of Don Piper Ministries is "Hope and healing for a new generation." Our daily goal is to point people to Heaven through Jesus Christ and to prepare them for meaningful lives until they go there. That's what this book is about: Jesus' departing instructions for those who remain on Earth while we prepare for our divine liftoff.

As I think about my preparation for final liftoff, I review my life and sometimes I smile. One of the last things I ever thought I would be doing at this time in my life is being an itinerant evangelist. I thought I would be a local church pastor until Jesus called me home. But I've learned to abide in Jesus Christ, and preaching around the world is what I do.

Immediately I think of a woman to whom I talked recently. She told me that her husband had died. His sudden and unexpected death led to a disastrous breakdown of her life.

The painful process took her a long time to work through— months and months of just hanging on to God. But her experience resulted in a new occupation. She is now a professional grief counselor.

Someone commended her for her sensitive work and said, "You're a natural. This is your gift."

She laughed and said, "I would never have thought of being a grief counselor. My life had to fall apart before I saw that I could do this special ministry. I can help others in their grief, because I grieved for such a long time."

🖋

One of my favorite stories comes from a young female marine who attended one of my meetings. Let's call her Sherry because I don't want to use her real name.

Sherry was deployed to Iraq with her platoon that included Dorothy, a deeply committed Christian. Several times Dorothy invited Sherry and the other marines to join her in her tent for Bible study. Sherry and the rest constantly ridiculed Dorothy, making fun of her faith and flaunting their promiscuous lifestyles. Because of that mocking, others denied their faith and even lived promiscuously. During the entire deployment they persisted in making fun of Dorothy, but the woman didn't falter.

After they returned stateside, Sherry considered going to a Bible study with Dorothy. That night, just as Sherry decided to say yes to the Bible study invitation, another marine came into the barracks on her way to a party. She convinced Sherry to forego the Bible study and party instead.

While Sherry contemplated her decision yet again, she received word from her commanding officer that Dorothy had died in an accident. Embarrassed by her ridicule of her now-departed friend and heartbroken over her continued rejection of a faith she had once followed, she refused to attend the party. Instead, she went to an evening service at a church where I preached about Heaven and finding a new normal.

After that service, which took place near Camp Lejeune, North Carolina, Sherry stood at the book-signing table. She cried as she told me her story. Then she stopped and her face lit up.

"I know God has forgiven me. And I've found my new normal."

"What does God want you to do now?" I asked.

"Dorothy never gave up on me even though my fellow platoon members and I were so cruel to her. Her last act on Earth was to invite me to church. From this moment forward, I know what I must do—"

I smiled when she finished her statement.

"I'm going to take her place."

✥

I also think about the inner-city teacher who had been raped, her throat cut, and her body left for dead. A man walking his dog came along, found her, and called 911. She recovered. She told me that she has a divine call to help her students escape the crime and degradation with which they are confronted every day.

Then there's Salome Thomas-El, who grew up in the projects of Philadelphia. His father left, and his mother raised all eight children. Salome became a believer, was recognized as a gifted student, and he planned to go into sports broadcasting with a job offer from ESPN.

As he prayed for guidance about his career choice, a former teacher challenged him to teach in the inner city. She told him, "You're a natural teacher and you can make a tremendous difference in the inner city. You can give these kids hope and show them the way out of the ghetto through education."

Salome tells his story in *I Choose to Stay: A Black Teacher Refuses to Desert the Inner City.*[4] He has won a variety of awards,

---

4 Salome Thomas-El with Cecil Murphey, *I Choose to Stay: A Black Teacher Refuses to Desert the Inner City.* (New York: Kensington, 2004).

including the Best Philadelphian of 2006. He sees it as his life calling to remain in the inner city and to raise his students above poverty and hopelessness.

After telling these stories, I'm convinced that God isn't as much interested in our abilities as he is our availability. We become available as we abide with him. That's part of our preparation for living until we leave this Earth.

✗

Sometimes we find ourselves attracted to people for various reasons. But I've learned that people who live close to God have a kind of invisible aura around them. They don't have to tell us they are holy; they don't have to talk or do anything to convince us. We know because something shines through their inner being and we sense that they have a special connection with Jesus Christ.

I'd like to tell you about one more person: Gaye Eichler has devoted her life to the Lord's work. She was a faithful church member and a talented church musician. Life took some cruel turns for Gaye, but she never turned her back on what she could do for Jesus. Instead she has devoted herself to making a difference in the spiritual lives of single adults all over the state of Texas.

Through her work at the Baptist General Convention of Texas, Gaye has organized conferences, retreats, and other events, bathing them in prayer, and is committed to minister to those who are single by choice and those whose relationships have come apart. Seldom have I ever known anyone who has more tirelessly fought for resources to meet the spiritual and emotional needs of single adults.

Gaye never planned to be a single adult, but she did plan to care for those who are. Her name is legendary in single-adult circles. I worked with her on several single-adult projects, and she exudes confidence and encourages others to work hard for the same cause. She has inspired me many times. Her warm smile and spectacular sense of humor are something I love being around. Although she's only a few years older than I am, I used to tell her, "I want to be like you when I grow up."

She's a little woman with a big heart for single adults. I've been around her enough to know that she has a special connection with Jesus. She does her work with humility, humor, and guts. There's no doubt in my mind she *abides* with the Lord.

If I could only accomplish one thing with this book, it would be to point everyone to the One who coordinates all departures. His instruction begins with a single word: *Abide.* It's a way of saying, "Be ready for me so that when I'm ready for you, nothing will hold you back."

Departing Instructions

1. Abide. That is Jesus' command to you. Be faithful. Stay true.
2. Prayerfully offer yourself. If you abide in Jesus Christ, it means you are willing for him to use your life in any way he sees fit.
3. Ask yourself: "Am I being as faithful as I know how?" Unless your answer is yes, go to question #4.
4. What changes do you need to make to be more faithful in abiding in Jesus?

18

Use Your Gifts Faithfully

[Jesus said] "Remain in me, and I will remain in you. For a branch cannot produce fruit if it is severed from the vine, and you cannot be fruitful unless you remain in me. Yes, I am the vine; you are the branches. Those who remain in me, and I in them, will produce much fruit. For apart from me you can do nothing. . . . But if you remain in me and my words remain in you, you may ask for anything you want, and it will be granted!"

JOHN 15:4–5, 7 (NLT)

The Israelites had one early, major victory over their enemies. In that momentous battle, they didn't lose a single soldier, and they totally destroyed the city of Jericho. But that victory also led to Israel's temporary defeat. That's a powerful story recorded in the sixth chapter of the Book of Joshua.

It goes like this: In their confidence of God being with them, Joshua sent spies to scout out Ai, the next place they had to conquer. The spies came back and said it would be an easy victory, and it was a small town. Instead of sending out all the soldiers, they told their leader, "Send two or three thousand men to take it and do not weary all the people, for only a few men are there"

(Joshua 7:3 [NIV]). Instead of praying for guidance, Joshua and his people acted presumptuously.

That day three thousand soldiers went out to destroy Ai. Instead, the people of the small town defeated them. Thirty-six Israelites died. After the embarrassing defeat, "Then Joshua tore his clothes and fell facedown to the ground before the ark of the LORD, remaining there till evening. The elders of Israel did the same" (verse 6).

Joshua cries out and blames God for the loss. He asks why God had brought them there if his purpose was to destroy them. He asked why the Israelites had not stayed on the other side of Jordan. He goes on and on in his groaning. Finally he stops feeling sorry for himself, and God gets a chance to talk. He tells Joshua to get off the ground and to stand up. "What are you doing down on your face? Israel has sinned" (verses 10–11a).

If Joshua and the people had asked God for help, they would have known about the sin. God had instructed them that they were to take nothing from the city of Jericho. "The city and all that is in it are to be devoted to the LORD" (Joshua 6:17). However, a man named Achan had taken gold and clothing.

The leaders didn't pray for help. They assumed God would guide them into victory. Or perhaps, like a lot of moderns, the attitude is one of, "Okay, God, you can sit this out. I can handle it."

But they couldn't.

Neither can we.

🖋

It amazes me that people can get in religious gatherings and talk about their dependence on God, but when they go to business gatherings the emphasis seems to be on what they can accomplish on their own.

We all have gifts and abilities, but sometimes we forget that those talents are God-given. We have them to use in serving him and in helping others. Depending on God doesn't mean that we can't function unless we set aside a time of protracted prayer or go through a lengthy religious ritual. It does mean we remind ourselves that we do what we can because God gives us the ability.

Cec has a motto on his bookplates that reads, "Everything I am and everything I have are gifts of God." Those are good words to remind all of us that all talent is God-given. If we remember that the Holy Spirit empowers us to achieve, we are abiding in Christ.

Many people don't see the importance of God in their lives. Or perhaps I should put it this way: They don't see any difference between themselves and nonbelievers.

In religious circles, the cliché is "It's all about him," meaning it's all about God. One of my friends said recently, "I cringe when I hear that phrase. The people who repeat those words usually mean, 'It's all about me.' "

At first I didn't understand what he meant, but as he explained, his meaning became clear. He said, "If I have to *tell* you it's all about God, then I must be doing a poor job of demonstrating it. If I demonstrate my dependence on Jesus Christ, you'll know."

"How will I know?"

"Because Jesus Christ will be such a strong force in my life," he said, "my motivations will slip out no matter what I say or do."

As I considered his words I thought of people who came to me for counseling when I was a pastor. One thing I noticed was that when a man kept telling me how much he loved his wife, he alerted my suspicious mind. If he loves her so much, I'd wonder, why does he keep telling me? Who is he trying to convince?

I also thought about a prominent Christian writer in the early 1980s. He had written two books that were honest, wonderful, and sold in the millions, and I was one of his fans. In his third book, he wrote about his family. I noticed that at least five times he stated how much he loved his wife and how much he depended on her. Did he have to say it five times?

About two years after that book came out, the writer and his wife divorced.

Yes, I think I got it. At first, I had resisted my friend's words because I thought he was trying to say that we shouldn't talk about our faith or about God at work in our lives.

"That's not what I mean," he said. "If God is in control of your life, you'll talk about your faith and his help, but the words will flow naturally. You won't have to force me to believe that you believe."

🖋

I write this because of the powerful language Jesus uses in chapter 15. He emphasizes that without him we can accomplish nothing. He uses the image of a grapevine and branches. Jesus pictures himself as the true vine and we are branches. He talks to the disciples about remaining in him. He explains the consequences if they don't and the results if they do.

Here are a few of the statements Jesus makes in John 15 (TNIV).

- "Remain in me, as I also remain in you. No branch can bear fruit by itself; it must remain in the vine" (verse 4a).
- "Neither can you bear fruit unless you remain in me" (verse 4b).

- "If you remain in me and I in you, you will bear much fruit" (verse 5a).
- "[A]part from me you can do nothing" (verse 5b [TNIV]).
- "If you do not remain in me, you are like a branch that is thrown away and withers" (verse 6a).
- "If you remain in me and my words remain in you, ask whatever you wish, and it will be done for you" (verse 7).

While thinking about this chapter, I kept going back to verse 5: "Apart from me you can do nothing." I never used to think too much about such statements, but since I began to travel and speak in late 2004, those words have come to have powerful meaning to me. I don't like to complain about my pain and the results of my accident, but the reminder is with me every waking moment. Some days I have to call on God for physical strength just to help me get out of bed.

"Without you, Lord, I can't do it," I've said many times.

That's true for me but that's actually true for all of us. We need to depend on divine help every step of the path each day. But too many of us go through our tasks as if we could do everything by ourselves. We live in a culture that puts so much emphasis on self-achievement.

I once saw the sermon title on a sign in front of a prominent Atlanta church: "You can be all you want to be." I didn't hear the message, but the title sounded like the old human-potential movement twenty years ago that constantly emphasized that we had no limitations.

Well, we do have limits; all of us have them. We need the Lord's help to move beyond what we can do for ourselves.

Jesus spent a lot of time on the vine-and-branches image.

213

That means the message was something of great importance to him that he needed the disciples to understand. It also means it's something we need to understand.

What does it mean for us that we can do nothing without him? In one sense, it's an exaggeration. We can do many things ourselves. We don't pray to be able to stand or sit or eat or walk. We don't have to pray to do the routine things such as drive a car, wash dishes, or change clothes.

It may help if we think of the statement as referring to motivation and purpose. Jesus used the image of the vine and the branches to show that the branches depend *totally* on the vine for nourishment so they can bear fruit. If anyone cuts off those branches, they become dead wood. They're useless.

For us, it means that our motivation to work and to serve others needs to come from Jesus Christ. It's not that we can't do good deeds on our own, because we can. But to do them properly, we need to be energized and motivated by Christ. It means we desire to follow and serve him.

Another thing this says to me is that we should work for God's glory and do it without expecting or demanding credit or appreciation for what we do. If we work for Jesus and we sense we've pleased him, isn't that enough?

Cec struggled over this principle when he became a ghostwriter. A publisher asked him to write books for celebrities but his name would not appear on the books (hence the term *ghost*). Until the 1990s that was the acceptable practice among most publishers.

At first, Cec anguished over that issue. "If I write it, people ought to know," he said. But as he continued to pray, he faced the significant question: *Can I write and not care who gets credit?* He finally decided that he could do that as his service to God. He wrote a number of books for famous and infamous people without getting any credit until the policy in publishing houses began to change.

To give of ourselves without caring who gets credit—isn't that how the Lord wants us to work? We do what we can do with the gifts and abilities we have. If we do such things from the right motivation, we honor God.

In the Sermon on the Mount, Jesus says, "Be careful not to do your 'acts of righteousness' in front of others, to be seen by them. If you do, you will have no reward from your Father in Heaven" (Matthew 6:1 [TNIV]).

He goes on to say the same thing about prayer and about fasting. If we do such things to call attention to ourselves, we have our reward now. If we do things for the glory and praise of God, the day will come when God will reward us.

I don't like using the word *reward,* because it sounds as if we have to earn everything. That's not correct. When we abide in Jesus Christ—when we recognize our talents come from above—we take the first step toward future reward. The second step is faithfulness—using those abilities to enjoy our lives and to enrich others. From that service we receive the intrinsic rewards. We know we're being fruitful for God. Even though others may not know, God sees everything.

I can't define the prizes and honors but I'm sure of one thing: God is just and faithful. If we honor him with our talents and gifts, God recompenses us accordingly. It's not how much we do (or don't do), but it's based on our faithfulness with what we have.

For instance, Jesus once commended a poor woman who dropped two small coins in the collection box at the temple (*see*

Mark 12:41–44). Some scholars translate it as two mites but the coin was called a *lepton*, and it was the smallest coin used.

Jesus said that her tiny contribution was greater than the others because they tossed in what they could easily spare; she flung in everything she had.

The principle applies to our abilities as well. On the great day when we appear before Jesus Christ, we'll learn what he thinks about the way we've lived. In 2 Corinthians 5:10, we read: "For we must all stand before Christ to be judged. We will each receive what we deserve for the good or evil we have done in this earthly body" (NLT).

"Remain with me," Jesus said. That means to serve him until we depart from this life. And he reminds us that we need him. When he says that without him we can't do anything, he means that our actions count when they're based on recognizing him as the giver and the rewarder.

Departing Instructions

1. Examine your heart. Keep your motives as pure as possible.
2. Serve God with your abilities but remind yourself that God is the one who has given you those talents.
3. Each day, say to yourself, "I can do nothing significant without God's help." As you habitually repeat those words, you remind yourself of the source of your ability.
4. Thank God for the talents you have. They are divine gifts and they aren't just for you, but they are so you can be of more service to God.

19

Love Others as Jesus Loves You

[Jesus said] "This is my commandment: Love each other in the same way I have loved you. There is no greater love than to lay down one's life for one's friends. You are my friends if you do what I command. I no longer call you slaves, because a master doesn't confide in his slaves. Now you are my friends, since I have told you everything the Father told me. . . . This is my command: Love each other."

JOHN 15:12–15, 17 (NLT)

Years ago when I did a lot of talent work on television, it seemed as if everywhere I went people thought they knew me. Sometimes a cluster of four commercials would run on a TV station break, and I would be seen on three of the four ads. I was a spokesman for banks, furniture stores, car dealerships, utility companies, and others. I even did a spot dressed as a semi truck driver encouraging viewers to "learn to drive the big rigs." In short, I was on TV a lot.

One of the interesting by-products of that career was that when people saw me in public they often treated me as if I were one of their lifelong buddies. It was sometimes embarrassing to have strangers slap me on the back and call me by my first name, and it took some getting used to.

One of the reasons this was unsettling is because I have always placed extremely high importance on authentic friendship. Friends like Cec, Todd, Darrell, David, Mark, Sonny, and Cliff are gifts from God and they enrich my life. They know me and I know them. I'm blessed to have so many wonderful men and women who consider me a friend. It is very humbling and most cherished, but *friend* is a term I try to use carefully.

I wonder how many times parishioners have said to me, "You're my best friend." I don't take those words lightly. They usually came from a troubled teen whom I had helped or a man who struggled to readjust after a divorce. Sometimes it came after I had spent a lot of time in the home of someone who had been gravely ill.

For anyone to call me a friend—and to mean it as more than a casual way to refer to an acquaintance—is special and poignant.

When I read the words of Jesus on his way to the Garden of Gethsemane, he makes a statement to the disciples that I hope changed their lives. "You are my friends if you do what I command. I no longer call you servants, because a servant does not know his master's business. Instead, I have called you friends, for everything that I learned from my Father I have made known to you" (John 15:14–15 [NIV]).

The word *servant* is misleading. The Greek word *doulos* means "slave." The words were almost interchangeable because a servant couldn't just quit. The rich either "owned" them because they paid for them or they were what we later called *indentured servants—*

people who were, in effect, slaves for a period of time, usually seven years in the Jewish culture.

To be called a slave of God is, in itself, a strong and meaningful term. It speaks of our deep commitment and our irrevocable relationship. Understandably, the word *slave* strikes terror in people's hearts today because of the justifiably negative connotation the term has earned over time. The biblical concept of slave was different from the brutal treatment experienced by Africans captured, put in chains, and brought to America or Europe.

In Deuteronomy 34:5, the word *servant* is used of Moses and later of Joshua in Joshua 24:29. Psalm 89:20 reads, "I have found David my servant; with my sacred oil I have anointed him" (NIV). In several of his letters, Paul starts with the expression, "Paul, a servant of God" (as in Titus 1:1). The Book of James begins, "James, a servant of God and of the Lord Jesus Christ" (verse 1:1).

As shown in the Old Testament, there were some cruel slave owners, but it was generally a relationship of respect. Someone said a slave was a "living tool and wise people take excellent care of their tools."

Paul writes to the Christians at Colossae, "Masters, provide your slaves with what is right and fair, because you know that you also have a Master in Heaven" (Colossians 4:1 [NIV]).

Slaves were a significant part of the economy in centuries past. The law of the slave in the Old Testament states that individuals could sell themselves to labor for someone for six years. At the beginning of the seventh year they were set free. "But if your servant says to you, 'I do not want to leave you,' because he loves you and your family and is well off with you, then take an awl and push it through his ear lobe into the door, and he will become your servant for life. Do the same for your maidservant" (Deuteronomy 15:16–17 [NIV]).

The passage in Deuteronomy refers to someone who becomes a slave out of necessity but later becomes a lifelong servant out of devotion. Some have compared that to the way it works with believers. In our early days of Christianity, we obey out of duty— we do what's required of us. As we mature, we voluntarily obey out of our love for Jesus Christ and in appreciation of what he has done for us. As we grow, we realize that God truly works in us and does everything for our growth and blessing. As we recognize that reality, we become willing and perpetual love slaves. We know that Jesus will take care of us.

We can become both a love slave and a friend. The slave emphasizes duty to Jesus; friendship emphasizes relationship to Jesus.

This passage reflects our commitment and our love for God. We willingly give ourselves to serve him for as long as we live, and we do so because we grasp the relationship between intimate friends. That's what it means when we give ourselves to Jesus Christ. The commitment is one of choice and not of obligation.

In the Old Testament those whose lives pleased him, God calls his servants or slaves, but he doesn't call them friends. The Old Testament contains only one instance when God calls a human being a friend. In Isaiah 41:8, the prophet writes: "But you, O Israel, my servant . . . you descendants of Abraham my friend" (NIV).

This shows that friend isn't a word that Yahweh or Jesus uses lightly. So when he uses the word with his disciples, it is a big deal.

As Jesus takes his eleven disciples into a deeper relationship it is also an invitation to us. He wants our friendship and freely offers his. But it's not an association that everyone can claim. Jesus makes it clear that friendship is more than becoming a believer. "My command is this: Love each other as I have loved you. Greater love has no one than this, that he lay down his life for his friends" (John 15:12–13 [NIV]). After he spoke those words he went on to call them friends. Jesus then adds, "You are my friends if you do what I command" (verse 14).

When Jesus changed the depth of his relationship with the disciples from slaves to friends, I'm not sure they grasped that immediately—perhaps not until after they received the Holy Spirit.

What must it have been like to see Jesus as Lord, Savior, and God and have him say, "But you're now my friend"? What is it like for us to consider that the Creator of the universe would condescend to us and offer us such closeness? To offer us salvation is amazing; to go beyond that and offer us intimacy can stagger us. *God wants my friendship?* That association signals a unique connection. It is a union with the divine that's beyond anything in this world.

Whenever the eleven grasped the friendship, it certainly transformed their relationship with him. It was no longer a matter of underlings serving a superior. It became a friend who makes himself vulnerable to others and invites them into his world to cooperate with him in his mission.

Jesus offers an intimacy that is so powerful that, as the Book of Acts unfolds, we realize those disciples willingly give their lives for him or for others.

But friendship isn't automatic and it's not carelessly offered. Jesus laid out the condition of friendship with him: The disciples had to truly love each other. But he isn't limiting his message to the disciples in the upper room with him; it is meant for us, too. We are to love each other as Jesus loves us.

It's impossible to love with the degree that Jesus loved, and we understand that. But his command means that we freely become servants to others' needs.

Too many today are afraid of being "used," and yet friendship means giving ourselves unreservedly to others. Some might take advantage of us, which is the risk we face if we truly give ourselves to serve and encourage others. But loving others doesn't depend on their worth; it depends on our willingness.

Think of Jesus giving himself to Judas. That one-time disciple had every opportunity as the others, but he chose not to follow. Judas could have been counted among Jesus' friends.

It's easy to love our friends and to care deeply about them, but Jesus meant more. He says that the greatest love any of us can have is to lay down our lives—to willingly die—for others.

In 1981, a powerful film called *Chariots of Fire* about the gold-medal Olympian Eric Liddell touched many hearts. He won the 1924 gold medal in the four-hundred-meter race. Liddell was a runner—and a fast one—but he was more than that: He was a seriously committed Christian.

Two years after the film came out, Cec visited Edinburgh and met Eric's sister, Jenny Summerville. They talked about the film and the books that had been written about her brother, but she said that none of them had told the best part of the story.

Here's what she told him: In 1941, when the British government urged all their citizens to leave China, Eric Liddell chose to stay after the Japanese invasion. He sent his wife, Florence, and their two children to Canada. He willingly identified with the Chinese people despite the suffering that he knew he would have to endure. After World War II, Liddell's sister heard from people who had been in the Japanese prison camp with her brother. He remained the faithful minister to them. Many times he shared his meager rations with those he felt needed the food most.

No matter how oppressive the situation, Liddell urged others to forgive the Japanese and all their enemies. Eric Liddell gave his life for those he loved—even his enemies.

He died of malnutrition shortly before the liberation of China. His sister believed he died because he shared his meager rations with others.

Probably none of us will ever face anything like Eric Liddell, but he followed the example set by Jesus and the early disciples. He was willing to die for his faith.

Let's be clear that Jesus doesn't mean we have to become martyrs or make heroic sacrifices. He doesn't ask us to give others permission to treat us rudely and harshly. He means we show the open heart and the ready hand whenever we're aware of others who need help we can give.

He intends us to love others so much we would be willing to give our lives for them. If we are willing to give our lives, it implies we'd willingly give anything less. And "anything less" means being inconvenienced for them, praying for them, spending time with them, encouraging them, and even rebuking them when we think they're wrong. The kind of friendship Jesus offers is serious and implies a complete commitment of ourselves.

The apostle John understood the message. He writes, "This is how we know what love is: Jesus Christ laid down his life for us. And we ought to lay down our lives for one another" (1 John 3:16 [TNIV]). The verses that follow show the practical application of laying down our lives: "If any one of you has material possessions and sees a brother or sister in need but has no pity on them, how can the love of God be in you? Dear children, let us not love with words or tongue but with actions and in truth" (verses 17–18).

I once heard a preacher say, "People can die for their faith in times of intense persecution. But most of the time, it's harder to live for their faith." That preacher might have been right.

To live as Jesus' friend isn't mindlessly following rules. We need to remember that our relationship with others is an advertisement to the world about our friendship with Jesus. In order to have the privilege of being called Jesus' friend we need to assume the responsibility that friendship entails.

When Jesus tells his disciples they are no longer slaves but friends they had little sense of the commitment and intimacy that Jesus wants. Shortly afterward, they will run away, and Peter, the one who perceived him as the Savior, will deny him three times.

The disciples give little evidence of deserving Jesus' love, but from his example we learn that we love not only those who deserve our commitment but we also love those who don't deserve it.

One of the many messages Jesus shared was that we need to forgive and accept those who are unworthy of being loved.

Twice in chapter 15, Jesus commands the disciples to love one another. When he said (in verse 17), "Love each other," he uses the present imperative tense of the Greek, which makes it more than a one-time event. The command could be easily translated into English as, "Love and continue to love one another."

And, just as amazing, Jesus didn't add any qualifiers to that command. He didn't say, "Seek out those who are worthy." He advocates a prodigious, abundant giving of ourselves to anyone who needs us. Again, the disciple John explained this in his first letter. "We know what real love is because Jesus gave up his life for us. So we also ought to give up our lives for our brothers and sisters" (1 John 3:16 [NLT]).

Those words are vague so he follows up the statement with specific ways that we express our love: "If someone has enough money to live well and sees a brother or sister in need but shows no compassion—how can God's love be in that person? Dear children, let us not merely say that we love each other; let us show the truth by our actions" (verses 17–18).

🖋

The friendship of Jesus means a great deal to me, and I never want to take that relationship for granted.

Hundreds of times since *90 Minutes in Heaven* was released, I would be ready to speak in a church service when a music minister, a soloist, or a musician, would look at me and wink or nod before he or she began to perform a particular song. I knew what was coming whether the person conducted a choir, sang a solo, played an offertory, or led in a hymn. The occasion varied but the song didn't. It is the great hymn "What a Friend We Have in Jesus."

They tried to get my attention because they thought they knew the significance that song plays in my life.

Those who have read *90 Minutes in Heaven* know that "What a Friend" was the song Pastor Dick Onarecker was singing over my dead body under a tarp in the wreckage of my car when suddenly I returned to Earth and began to sing with him.

Yes, it was a powerful experience for me to return to this world with that hymn in my ears and on my lips. What many don't realize is that the song had great significance in my life long before Dick selected it to sing to a dead man.

As a young Christian who had spent his childhood traveling the world with my U.S. Army family, I seldom had time to make friends. Before I could get really close, Dad would be transferred. I became a Christian not many years after my dad retired and we settled in one place.

Only then did I begin to love singing that song. I loved it for the most personal of reasons: *I needed a friend.* I had always wanted a friend who would never move away. Jesus became that friend. Dick could never have known that day when he selected to sing "What a Friend We Have in Jesus" how much it would mean to me.

Of course, the song has taken on additional significance to many as the song I came back to Earth singing, but for me, "What a Friend We Have in Jesus" is not a hymn anymore. It is truth. I am *his* friend. But even more important is that Jesus is my friend. And he'll never move away.

As you prepare to meet your best friend in person, be ready. Practice loving others here on Earth, and one day you'll do it perfectly in Heaven.

Departing Instructions

1. You have started your Christian life as a love slave of Jesus Christ, but strive to take the big step and become his friend.
2. You are already his friend if you do as he commands. Commit to obey him in even the smallest things.

3. As you live on Earth, determine to live your life so that others will recognize you as Jesus' friend because of your actions and attitudes.

4. As you move toward your day of departure, make each day one of a growing, living commitment. Pray this way: "Jesus, you are my friend. Help me each day to love you more fully so that others will recognize me as your friend."

20

Remember You Are Chosen

[Jesus said] "I no longer call you servants, because a servant does not know his master's business. Instead, I have called you friends, for everything that I learned from my Father I have made known to you."

JOHN 15:15 (NIV)

Long before Jesus became the Savior, he was the Teacher. He taught by example, but he also imparted knowledge by his words. He led the first disciples as rapidly as they were able to absorb it. Sometimes he rebuked them as part of the teaching.

Earlier Jesus tried to explain that he had to go to Jerusalem and that "[h]e would be killed, but on the third day he would be raised from the dead" (Matthew 16:21 [NLT]).

Peter didn't like those words and "began to reprimand him for saying such things" (verse 22). "Jesus turned to Peter and said, 'Get away from me, Satan! . . . You are seeing things merely from a human point of view, not from God's'" (verse 23).

When James and John want top positions in the kingdom Jesus seems to shake his head because they didn't grasp it. "You don't know what you are asking!" (Mark 10:38 [NLT]). Another time the disciples asked, "Who is greatest in the Kingdom of Heaven?"

(Matthew 18:1 [NLT]). Instead of a direct rebuke, "Jesus called a little child to him and put the child among them. Then he said, 'I tell you the truth, unless you turn from your sins and become like little children, you will never get into the Kingdom of Heaven. So anyone who becomes as humble as this little child is the greatest in the Kingdom of Heaven'" (verses 2–4).

These were examples of teaching, of enlightenment, and they needed to pay attention.

$$\mathcal{K}$$

Who doesn't like being chosen? Remember the times as children in school when we played games at recess? Some of us had our names called early and some were chosen at the end. Regardless of whether we were first or tenth, it always felt good to rush toward the team we would play for.

It's not exactly like that in the Christian life, but it's still a matter of being chosen—and we don't have to fret about first, fifth, or being the last one. Being chosen by Jesus isn't something about which we boast, but it's something we ponder for encouragement and for inner assurance. His choosing us is unmistakable: "I have chosen you," he says in John 15:19 (NIV).

We can respond with a sense of comfort and excitement because of this. Comfort because we know God loves us and because we know him, we follow him. We can feel that release of joy and peace because we not only know we're chosen but we know we were selected to serve Jesus Christ and obey his will.

We can feel excitement because this knowledge gives us courage to go forward in life without fear. Our life has meaning. Too often people overlook that powerful fact.

I think of my late neighbor, George Rooney, forced to retire at age seventy. After that, he walked around, looking defeated and tired and showed no interest in anything. "I feel useless," he said to one of his friends. Less than two months later, I saw him at a restaurant and he radiated exuberance. He seemed like a new person.

George excitedly told me about his work with Meals On Wheels—he coordinated delivering meals to disabled individuals. "When a driver doesn't show up, I take care of it." He was also the program director for the senior's group in our church.

He served in a number of voluntary capacities until he died of a heart attack at eighty-nine. Although we had moved and I had lost contact, I met one of his friends in the grocery store. "George's best years were after he retired," she said. "Until only days before he died he was busy helping others."

As I thought about the seventy-year-old George and the man who died nearly twenty years later, I think I understand the difference. He had a purpose. He had a purpose in living, but more than just living, he felt that God could use him to encourage and help others.

George exemplifies the principle. He had a reason to live joyfully. His friend said that at his eightieth birthday party, George told everyone, "God chose me to do this. I used to earn a living, now I'm living a purpose."

Like George, when we realize we've been chosen by God, especially when we have a sense of purpose along with being chosen, we can accomplish many significant things through our efforts and our connection with Jesus Christ.

Often we don't understand that God loves us as we are; he just wants to change us by giving us a reason to enjoy this life. This is a new concept for many. It's not that we've never heard that Jesus loves us. But to *hear* the words and to *believe* the words aren't the same thing. When we're convinced that God created us individually and put us on Earth at exactly this time for a task that only we can fulfill, and he did it because he loves us, we can see ourselves differently. We live differently.

The great George Whitefield said, "We are immortal until our work on Earth is done." Too often we focus on the idea of living until we complete our purposes. I think the real focus is that we are loved by God and because of that caring love, we can fulfill whatever he has called us to do.

Paul says "Even before he made the world, God loved us and chose us in Christ to be holy and without fault in his eyes" (Ephesians 1:4 [NLT]). God formulated a plan *before the creation of the world* took place. As part of that plan, he showed his love by choosing us.

I don't understand how that works and I doubt that anyone else does either. I do know that once I became a believer, I found great comfort and encouragement as I realized God *chose me*. I'm here on Earth on divine assignment.

To be on divine assignment, as I put it, doesn't mean everything is easy. Paul's assignment took him into dangerous places. He wrote to the Corinthians, "I know I sound like a madman, but I have . . . been put in prison more often, been whipped times without number, and faced death again and again" (2 Corinthians 11:23 [NLT]). And that's not just the testimony of a famous man. Any of us who realize that God has chosen us and that we have a task to accomplish for him, face difficulties—at times almost unbelievable.

As many people know, I died January 18, 1989, and remained dead until Dick Onarecker prayed me back to Earth. After thirty-four surgeries, I'm still alive, still active, and still doing what I feel God has called me to accomplish. I'll continue doing exactly this until God takes me home—permanently.

I don't talk much about this, but I have never had a day without pain since my accident. Some days I hurt less than others, but the physical pain constantly strikes me. I could have gone on disability, but that wasn't God's purpose. I persevere and will continue to do so, despite the physical pain, until my Heavenly Father is ready for me.

Cec Murphey, my co-writer, understands this concept. One of the most dramatic examples in his life occurred when he was a missionary in Kenya, East Africa. He had been in the country less than three months when he was beaten by a teacher and half a dozen teenage boys. They planned to kill him and poured kerosene all over his body. When they realized that no one had a match, they panicked and ran away. The lack of a match saved his life. It took time for Cec to recover and one of his first thoughts was to return to the United States. Another missionary even suggested he leave. But upon praying about it, he realized he couldn't leave.

"God called me here. If God called me, he's responsible to take care of me."

Cec and his family stayed nearly six years. As he looks back on that incident, he still says that he remained because he knew he had been called (or I could substitute the word *chosen*). To know that God was with him in those terrible moments gave him the determination to stay and serve.

That's how this concept works. Jesus spent a lot of time with his eleven followers. He wanted them to know that he loved them and that he had work for them to do, and that he had a special place in Heaven for them. If we read through these five chapters (John 13–17) of final instructions, we're ready to read the Acts of the Apostles. All through the book they do mighty deeds— sometimes miracles that are almost impossible for nonbelievers to accept. But that's only part of the story.

- In chapter 4, the Jewish leaders beat them.
- In chapter 7, the leaders stone Stephen, a powerful young Christian.
- In chapter 8, persecution breaks out in Jerusalem and believers (except the apostles) flee the area.
- In chapter 8, Saul (later called Paul) has a commission to force Christians to depart from the faith and he persecutes them, and even kills them.
- Peter is imprisoned in chapter 10.
- The apostle James suffers a painful death in chapter 12.
- Paul gets stoned and is left for dead in chapter 14.
- In chapter 16, Paul and Silas are beaten and imprisoned.

The story goes on and on and doesn't end with the final chapter of Acts. For most of the first three centuries, Christians faced death and every form of persecution. Hebrews 11 records the story of those who believed God and suffered for their faith. The writer refers to their exploits and moves on to write, "Others were tortured and refused to be released. . . . Some faced jeers and flogging, while still others were chained and put in prison. They were stoned; they were sawed in two; they were put to death by the sword. They went about in sheepskins and goatskins, destitute, persecuted and mistreated. . . . They wandered in deserts and mountains, and in caves and holes in the ground" (Hebrews 11:35–38 [NIV]). What could inspire such loyalty to Jesus Christ? It had to be something powerful and sustaining during the darkest moments.

- They knew they belonged to God.
- They knew they had been chosen.
- They knew God had a purpose for them.

They were chosen to bear fruit by being faithful. The marvelous comfort God offers us is powerful because we know we are on his side. Or better, we know God is on our side. That was the message Jesus wanted his disciples to grasp.

Departing Instructions

1. Remember that God loves you and that love will never decrease.
2. Also remember that God chose you—and the reason you were chosen is to serve in ways no one else can serve. Whether it's a big public role or one hidden in the shadows, Jesus' parting instruction is for you to be faithful.
3. You have an important purpose in life. It's a purpose, a task, a calling, a job—no matter what you call it. Open yourself to God and ask him to equip you to fulfill that purpose.
4. When you face your dark moments and encounter obstacles, remind yourself: "Jesus loves me and wants my life to glorify him."

21

Choose the Hard Road

[Jesus said] "If the world hates you, remember that it hated me first. The world would love you as one of its own if you belonged to it, but you are no longer part of the world. I chose you to come out of the world, so it hates you. Do you remember what I told you? 'A slave is not greater than the master.' Since they persecuted me, naturally they will persecute you. And if they had listened to me, they would listen to you. They will do all this to you because of me, for they have rejected the One who sent me."

JOHN 15:18–21 (NLT)

During the time I was a minister of education, I arrived at the Sunday evening service a few minutes late one week. As I entered the back of the auditorium an usher beckoned me over. I knew him well. He was a devoted and diligent usher. Since the service had already begun, he leaned over so he could whisper into my ear. He pointed to a group of young people and mentioned one particular young man, "See that boy over there?"

I nodded.

"Can you believe he just walked into church tonight looking like that?"

I knew immediately what the elderly usher was referring to;

not the boy's scruffy jeans, not his sandals, not his T-shirt with holes. It was the boy's orange baseball cap.

"Yes, sir, I see it," I replied.

"Do you think I should ask him to leave?"

"Why would you want to do that?"

"Because he's wearing a hat in church. My mother would have dragged me out by my ear if I ever did such a thing."

"Mine, too," I agreed. He looked a little pleased with himself, so I asked, "But is your mother here tonight?" I asked.

He looked at me a little disconcerted and said, "Why, no, she's been in Heaven for years."

"Then let's not worry about it too much."

He started to protest. "It just doesn't seem right."

"Have you ever seen that young man before?"

"No, I haven't," he said.

"Then he's a guest."

"Sure, I guess he must be."

"In that case, my brother, let's just welcome him. Perhaps he needs us. Maybe he'll turn to Jesus Christ tonight. Don't worry about the cap. God can take care of that."

He stared at me as if he wasn't sure what to do.

"Let's just love the boy, hat and all. That young fellow came to God's house tonight. How many young people are out there who didn't show up with or without a hat?"

The usher tried to smile but he failed because just then a few tears slid down his cheek.

I understood the usher. My Grandma Kulbeth would have never dreamed of going to church without a fancy hat, high-heeled shoes, and white gloves. If you saw her on Sunday morning you knew she was headed to God's house, the church. "Christians should act and look like Christians," she would say.

That reminds me of a time a few years ago when an older minister and I stood next to the coffee table at a large convention. A number of people passed. Some wore suits; others passed by in jeans or cutoffs. Both of us, of course, had grown used to seeing such a difference in clothing.

"You know, I remember when Christians looked different," he said. He had grown up in a denomination where the women wore their hair in buns or braids and their clothing had to fully cover their arms and legs. No man would ever attend a worship service in anything but his best clothes and wouldn't think of wearing jewelry or having pierced ears.

"I'm not saying we ought to go back to telling people what they should wear," he said, "but wouldn't it be nice if we could distinguish Christians in public by the way they dressed?"

"Like priests' collars and the nuns' habits?" I asked. "Should we wear them?"

He laughed and said he didn't mean we should. "But so many Christians look and behave like everyone else. What's to distinguish us?"

I didn't think he was expecting an answer, so I didn't reply, but I've thought about his question many times. What does distinguish us from others?

The New Testament refers to our attitude and our behavior and maybe that's all we have to show who we are and to whom we belong.

At the time Jesus spoke to his disciples, his followers were hated and often persecuted. To proclaim their faith in Jesus could result in death. Jesus warned them of the terrible persecution they would face.

Most of us don't face such overt persecution, but we face opposition in many ways (*see* John 15:18–16:11). I've heard the saying, "The world suspects nonconformity and often hates it."

If we follow Jesus Christ along that heavenly road, we will act differently because we *are* different. We've been changed from the inside and not everyone appreciates or respects our difference.

As followers of Jesus we need to act like Christians—to display "right behavior." To many people, right behavior means little more than courtesy toward others. To the original disciples of Jesus, it meant they faced physical torture or death for their acknowledgment of Jesus.

For us, while we may not face physical torture or death because of our love for Jesus, others may misunderstand us. People—even other Christians—may rebuke us because we're focused on living the right way.

I have a friend who believes strongly that physical exercise is part of his right behavior. He runs four to six miles every day and has been doing that for thirty years. A few people have criticized him.

"Ease up," someone said.

"Don't take that exercise so seriously."

That's a form of persecution, although I doubt most people would call it that. I also know a church that asked one family to leave the church where they had been faithful members for twelve years. The parents disapproved of some of the social activities of other teens and spoke up often. "We don't need your negative voice around here," the minister of youth told them.

Here's another instance: A Christian student is taunted by her friends because she has committed herself to remain pure until marriage. Her classmates make fun of her and call her names.

Each of the people in these instances feels persecuted for doing what he or she believes is right.

Jesus said, "If the world hates you, keep in mind that it hated me first" (John 15:18 [NIV]). With those words, Jesus' tone gets darker than it has previously been in his departing instructions. He's called the disciples friends and spoke of love, and now he gives them the other side of the picture. He is saying, "If you travel the road of faith, you won't have an easy journey."

It's a message to us, too. It's a great privilege to be a disciple and a friend, even though that relationship puts demands on us. Jesus goes on to say that such a life brings hostility toward us from the unbelieving world.

Jesus had certainly encountered hostility and hatred. Several times the Jewish leaders tried to capture him, to stone him. For example, "Again they tried to seize [Jesus], but he escaped their grasp" (John 10:39 [NIV]). The disciples have certainly been aware of the desire of the Jewish leaders to get rid of the Lord. He outsmarted them at every turn. They tried to trap him with words, but he was always ahead of them. The more he triumphed, the more intensely they hated him.

Jesus wants the disciples to know that he now faces death as the outcome of his good works and his teaching. Those who serve him should expect to receive the same hatred and ill-treatment: "If you belonged to the world, it would love you as its own. As it is, you do not belong to the world, but I have chosen you out of the world. That is why the world hates you" (John 15:19 [NIV]).

By following Jesus, they have broken with the hostile forces around them. Because they have come out of the world and into the fellowship of believers, the people of the world will hate them. They've disowned the world and as a result they will feel the hatred.

Someone once said the reason people hate real Christians is because their lives function like mirrors. When people look at them they see themselves. They see their own failure, shame, and guilt. And it's not because of the words the believers speak; it's because of the lives they live.

As Jesus talks about the dark side of the future, it's as if he said to them, "I'm going to suffer and I'll die. Do you think that just because I'm gone, the persecution and hatred will end?" He quotes a proverb that the servant isn't greater than his master, and that implies they can't expect better treatment than he received. Jesus warns them that they will also share the scorn and bad treatment—persecution from those who reject his message and loyal response from those who receive it: "If they obeyed my teaching, they will obey yours also" (John 15:20b [NIV]).

He explains why the people of the world will reject him: because they don't know the Father who sent Jesus and who rightly claims the obedience of the disciples. "They will treat you this way because of my name, for they do not know the One who sent me" (verse 21).

Jesus makes a strong point that the people can't plead ignorance as an excuse for unbelief and hostility to Christ. The Jews of his day failed to obey Moses and the prophets. They had heard God's words read regularly but they refused to obey them. An earlier segment recorded in John's Gospel refers to Jesus as light and the Gospel writer says, "Light has come into the world, but people loved darkness instead of light because their deeds were evil. All those who do evil hate the light, and will not come into the light for fear that their deeds will be exposed. But those who live by the truth come into the light" (John 3:19–21a [TNIV]).

Jesus focuses on the great sin of those who reject the opportunity to believe in him. They would have no guilt if he hadn't come with the Gospel and offered salvation. But because he came, preached, and did works of divine power, he takes away their excuse and that leaves them guilty of sin in rejecting the message that Jesus brought from God.

They can't say, "I love God, but I hate Jesus." The Father sent Jesus, and to reject Jesus is to reject God as well.

There is no middle ground. We stand on one side or the other. We also need to remember that for years after the resurrection, the followers of Jesus endured persecution and were hated by their own people and by those who didn't want to know the truth. They were hunted and tortured if they stayed true to their faith. No Christian could ever say, "I didn't understand that life would be this way." Jesus had warned them. The first disciples also warned their followers.

Paul writes of his own persecution many times and says, "In fact, everyone who wants to live a godly life in Christ Jesus will be persecuted" (2 Timothy 3:12 [NIV]). Jesus had previously warned that people in their own family would hate them and betray them (*see* Mark 13:9–13, Matthew 10:17–29, and Luke 12:49, 51–53).

Jesus says that two identifying marks of a true Christian are love for others and persecution for their faith. If a follower of Christ does not love others can he or she be an authentic follower? That's a serious question for us to ponder.

Likewise, if persecution is a mark of Christians, what does it mean if we're *always* liked, admired, and appreciated? Haven't we missed something?

As we examine our own hearts we have to ask ourselves: Have we ever suffered, endured ridicule, discrimination, or physical pain because of our faith in Christ? Jesus unequivocally states that for Christians who are living faithful lives before the world, persecution is inevitable. I agree.

Even though we don't suffer the kind of persecution many early believers did, we still don't have an easy road to travel. If we stand for what we believe, we'll have those who oppose us.

For instance, Cec remembers when he taught sixth grade in the public schools. The school decided to hold a carnival for navy relief. (The naval base was about ten miles away, and many of the students came from military families.)

When he was not present, another sixth-grade teacher named Jeanette volunteered Cec to run a gambling booth and to be in charge of a kind of lottery program. When he heard about it, he said he did not believe in gambling and didn't think it would be consistent with his lifestyle.

Jeanette became angry and used some rather foul language. She challenged his position and pointed out that navy relief would benefit even if the games were rigged. But Cec stuck to his beliefs. "I'm a Christian, and I don't feel this is right."

This really angered the other teacher. "What do you think I am? A heathen?"

Cec didn't answer her, but it didn't matter: Jeanette never spoke to him for the rest of the school year. She also gossiped about him to other teachers, saying that he was narrow, difficult to get along with, and really was too religious to talk to.

Here's another example: A woman named Judith was castigated by her boss because she refused to work one Sunday morning. "That is my time to go to church." She agreed to work any other time or any other day, but her boss still fired her.

Were both of those forms of persecution? I think so. It's unfortunate, but it happens. In other countries, people are still being killed for their faith; here we're merely ridiculed or ignored.

✍

If we stand for what we believe, we can expect others to disagree. Some people who call themselves Christians show their fervor and dedication every time they come to church; but they don't show it well when they go to the workplace.

Perhaps they're afraid; perhaps they feel they have to be perfect. One man said he swore at work so he'd fit in with the others. I wish he had decided to be an example and a witness of Christianity in action.

Recently I spoke with a woman who felt that if she spoke up, she'd be ridiculed. She began to work at a job at the beginning of the Christmas season. A few days later, one woman said to her, "You don't really believe that virgin birth story, do you?"

Before she could reply, her phone rang and she didn't have to answer. After that she made sure she never said anything about being a Christian.

I'm reminded of Paul's words to Timothy. He wrote about the many persecutions he endured but said, "Yet the Lord rescued me from all of them. In fact, everyone who wants to live a godly life in Christ Jesus will be persecuted" (2 Timothy 3:11b–12 [TNIV]).

Sometimes the persecution comes because of godly living. Sometimes it comes because we live a life that honors God and shames those who don't.

Although Paul warns about persecution, isn't it possible that persecution may mean we're living by Jesus' departing instructions?

Departing Instructions

1. Make it your lifestyle to live so that others will know you belong to God and serve him.
2. Ask yourself, "What do I need to do to live in the light—in holy light—so that I honor Jesus Christ in everything I do?"
3. Stand firm. Sometimes others won't understand or will speak against you. If you feel you are right, let the persecution become your badge of honor for your faithfulness.
4. Love those who oppose you. They're people who need to be loved just like you.

22

Learn from the Holy Spirit

[Jesus said] "There is so much more I want to tell you, but you can't bear it now. When the Spirit of truth comes, he will guide you into all truth. He will not speak of his own but will tell you what he has heard. He will tell you about the future. He will bring me glory by telling you whatever he receives from me. All that belongs to the Father is mine; this is why I said, 'The Spirit will tell you whatever he receives from me.'"

JOHN 16:12–15 (NLT)

Before I entered seminary, I believed I had a good understanding of theology; I knew the answers to many spiritual questions. Seminary was primarily extra training I had to go through. I knew I'd learn, but I was sure I had already grasped most of it.

Seminary surprised me: As I went through my classes, I realized that there were more than several things I hadn't understood. On a few issues I had been dead wrong. My three years of study opened my eyes to many truths I hadn't thought about.

Years later, when I died in an automobile accident, I went to Heaven for at least 90 minutes. That event changed my perspective on many things. I saw life differently. In our book *Heaven Is Real*, I started to share insights I had gained from that brief visit.

I won't repeat stories from our earlier books, but I want to say this much: I've learned more from my own experience than I have from anything else. The difficulties, tragedies, and losses of life and the ways they change us are not taught in books or on some ivy-covered campus.

Maybe that's why our experiences are so important. I had read about Heaven in the Bible, heard sermons on it, read books and articles on the subject. But when I experienced it, everything in my life changed. Heaven ceased to be a *possibility* for me and became my *reality*. Although this is difficult to explain, Heaven is now my reality, not the life I now live on Earth.

I live in Texas and I travel all over this country and many others. But because I have known the reality of Heaven—however briefly—it has changed me. My life here seems temporal—and it is. I don't mean that I hate my life, because I don't. But I live with a different attitude today than I did before my accident in 1989.

Life is temporary and transient. Intellectually, I knew that before my accident—as we all do—but now it is an emotional understanding as well. Traveling to Heaven revolutionized my perspective. I feel as though I now live closer to the heavenly reality.

Because I lost my life once, I live this "bonus part" differently. I know how quickly life on Earth can end. I'm aware of the fragility of our earthly existence. I realize how impermanent this life is, but I know how permanent Heaven is.

Experience makes a significant difference: We can study and know about something; yet when we experience it, the meaning is even more powerful.

Because I had seen pictures, videos, and movies about the scope and grandeur of the Grand Canyon, I so wanted to see it for myself. I could look at pictures of the Grand Canyon, explain its measurements, and expound on the scientific data. But until I took my family to see it a few years ago and stood there in person and experienced the magnitude of its natural beauty, I didn't really *know* the place. To behold its glory firsthand is to really know why the canyon is grand.

It's the same with Heaven. I am truly blessed to have had the opportunity to be at the gates of Heaven. It was an incredible gift that profoundly impacted my life then and continues to impact me just as strongly today. I've sometimes questioned why that experience happened to me. And then I think how wonderful it would be if everyone had the same perspective that I do—certain knowledge of Heaven. But sometimes we're not meant to know.

⚘

Think about what Jesus is telling his disciples in John 16:12–15 (NLT). During his years with them, he had taught them and prepared them. He explained his relationship with the Father. As eyewitnesses, they had seen his power at work in meeting human needs. But he tells them there is more that they don't yet know. "There is so much more I want to tell you, but you can't bear it now" (verse 12 [NLT]).

In this same passage, Jesus refers to the Holy Spirit as the Spirit of truth (John 16:13). One great purpose of the Spirit is to reveal to us divine truth. We call that revelation. The implication here is that divine revelation is progressive. We don't get it all in one large hunk. It's something we grasp slowly. As we understand a principle, we're ready for more. But the Spirit reveals only as much as we're able to comprehend right then. This also reminds us that there is never an end to the revelation and understanding of God. The problem comes when people feel they know everything and refuse to examine long-held beliefs.

Like me before seminary, the original disciples might have thought they had everything worked out and understood it all. They didn't, of course, and they never would grasp everything. As they moved forward in their relationship with God, they would continue to learn. And as they learned, they shared their insights with others.

Here's an example from the Bible. Peter preached to the Jews. That was his commission, but he didn't understand that the gospel was for all people and not meant to be restricted only to the Jews. God had to speak to him in a vision or dream (*see* Acts 10:9–23). Peter had the experience but he still didn't understand what it meant. Only after he went to the home of a Gentile named Cornelius and personally witnessed the power of the Holy Spirit work in him could he say, "I see very clearly that God shows no favoritism. In every nation he accepts those who fear him and do what is right" (Acts 10:34–35 [NLT]). Later he went to Jerusalem and had to convince the other church leaders that God loves Gentiles as much as Jews.

That still wasn't the end of learning the lesson for Peter. Later, Peter pulled back from the Gentiles. Paul says, "Before certain men came from James, [Peter] used to eat with the Gentiles. But when they arrived, he began to draw back and separate himself from the Gentiles because he was afraid of those who belonged to the circumcision group. The other Jews joined him in his hypocrisy, so that by their hypocrisy even Barnabas was led astray" (Galatians 2:12–13 [NIV]). Peter still hadn't fully comprehended the fact that the word was for all people.

Such passages from the Bible encourage me. If Peter didn't get everything straight in one spiritual dose, it means he was like the rest of us. Sometimes we have to get the message pounded into our heads several times before we really get it.

Jesus makes it clear that the disciples haven't gotten everything from him yet. "I have much more to say to you, more than you can now bear. But when he, the Spirit of truth, comes, he will guide you into all truth" (John 16:12–13 [NIV]).

As I read these statements, I'm reminded again that as we move toward Heaven, we never stop learning. Or at least, Jesus Christ always has things to teach us.

If we're disciples, it means being open to truth. Too many people want lists of rules to follow. They like regulations because they like to look at themselves and say, "See, I haven't lied or stolen today, so I must be pretty good."

But Jesus doesn't make the way easy. He points out that the Holy Spirit will guide us "into all truth" (verse 13). We never reach the place of knowing everything, but the Holy Spirit will direct us away from error and lead us into a greater illumination.

During his three and a half years of being with the disciples, Jesus was unable to teach them the entire lifetime of information they needed. He could teach them only what they could accept at that stage of their spiritual growth. The Spirit of truth, Jesus promises, will carry his work forward because the Spirit speaks only what he hears from the Father. He imparts to each disciple all the truth they need to know *right then*. Whatever they need to know about the unknown future he will make known to them.

The Spirit will never disown or repudiate Jesus' teaching. Instead, he will always glorify Jesus by witnessing to him and carrying forward his ministry. Verse 13 says that whatever the Spirit hears—from the Father—he will declare to them.

"All that belongs to the Father is mine. That is why I said the Spirit will take from what is mine and make it known to you" (verse 15). This provides two ideas: First, the Son shares the Father's purpose and truth. Second, when the Spirit teaches what the Father wants known, he is at the same time teaching and explaining what Jesus has taught. He continues in a fuller, more advanced and outreaching form the work and teaching of Jesus the Son.

Here's something I learned in seminary and now I pass it on to you: In the Bible, when something is mentioned twice, it's important and three times means that it's exceptionally significant. That means that four times must be a most powerful truth God wants us to absorb. *Four* times Jesus promises the Holy Spirit (*see* 14:16–17, 26; 15:26; 16:13–15). Jesus must have meant this to be an all-important lesson for them.

¥

Before and after my accident, I sought the insight that only the Holy Spirit can give. Since the accident, I've become better conditioned to be more attentive when I seek. While I was flat on my back for months with little or no diversions, I learned to focus and to take pleasure in several eternal lessons in my life before and after January 18, 1989:

- I have learned that in the darkest hours, God is often the closest to me.

- I have learned that the things I worry and fret over the most are usually the things that never come to pass.
- I have learned that although they are not always the answers we expect, God answers our prayers.
- I have learned that listening to God is a discipline. He speaks, but I have to learn to listen.
- I have learned that God is still producing miracles.
- I have learned to value the power of a personal testimony as I watch people respond to my simple words. It truly is amazing grace for me to see God change lives.
- I have learned that all humans seek hope. Whether they're aware of it or not, they long for a better life now and an eternal life when this one is over.

As you contemplate your departing instructions, remind yourself that you don't know everything, but you know enough to be obedient and open to the truth the Holy Spirit shows you.

Departing Instructions

1. As you prepare yourself for your eternal destiny, pray to understand more about Jesus Christ, yourself, and what it means to live a God-honoring life.
2. Open yourself so that you will learn to recognize God at work in your life by experience. That is, God will lead you and you'll be aware of it.
3. Choose to live in such a way that the Holy Spirit can constantly reveal more truth to you so that you can live more faithfully.

4. Ask God to make you totally teachable.
5. Pray, "Holy Spirit, help me to grasp each new lesson the first time I hear it. Don't make me have to learn and relearn the same lessons."

23

Prepare for the Joy Ahead

*[Jesus said] "In a little while you will see me no more, and then
after a little while you will see me." Some of his disciples said to one
another, "What does he mean by saying, 'In a little while you will
see me no more, and then after a little while you will see me.'...
They kept asking, "What does he mean by 'a little while'? We don't
understand what he is saying." Jesus saw that they wanted to ask
him about this, so he said to them, "Are you asking one another
what I meant when I said, 'In a little while you will see me no more,
and then after a little while you will see me'? I tell you the truth, you
will weep and mourn while the world rejoices. You will grieve, but
your grief will turn to joy. A woman giving birth to a child has pain
because her time has come; but when her baby is born she forgets
the anguish because of her joy that a child is born into the world."*

JOHN 16:16–21 (NIV)

As I've already said, people often tell me about the death of a
loved one. I usually answer, "I'm sorry for your temporary loss."
Most of the time, a startled look appears on their faces.

"It is only for a brief time, you know," I add. "Soon you'll be
reunited."

We talk a little more and they seem to understand. But that
understanding doesn't take away the immediate pain. They feel

their loss—and that's natural. They hurt and they miss that person whether it's a spouse, a child, a parent, or a friend. We all experience similar emotions at the death of someone we love.

Jesus understood human emotion and foresaw that his disciples would feel sorrow and a strong loss after he left, but he reassures them that after the sadness will come joy.

For those of us who believe, his death and resurrection illustrate the point Jesus made. The disciples will feel sorrow when he dies; they will rejoice when he lives again.

The death and resurrection are the essence of the Christian faith. Death alone isn't enough; being raised from the dead was the divine proof of God at work. It also reminds us that one day we will die—hence the departing instructions—but to leave is only part of it. That's the time of impermanent loss. After the sadness, after our departure, comes the joy inexpressible, the fulfillment of everything Jesus promised.

The pain is now, and the pain doesn't last; the joy lies ahead, and the joy is eternal. And sometimes I think that the more difficult our life here, the greater our joy there.

Jesus knew that and tried to instruct the eleven men. He didn't want them to think that life is easy and be disappointed when things became difficult. By warning them, even if they weren't able to hear it then, they could go through the hardships, persecutions, and even hatred. They could endure because they knew that existence on this Earth isn't the final state of life. This is the preparatory stage for a life of great joy.

Because of that, he could say to them, "I tell you the truth, you will weep and mourn while the world rejoices. You will grieve, but your grief will turn to joy" (John 16:20 [NIV]).

He illustrated his point by using the example of a woman who gives birth. She experiences pain in the delivery process, but "when her baby is born she forgets the anguish because of her joy that a child is born into the world" (verse 21).

I understand that metaphor. We had a lovely daughter named Nicole, and then Eva became pregnant with our twin sons, but this time her pregnancy was fraught with difficulties. Two previous pregnancies had already ended in a miscarriage and a tubular pregnancy that could have claimed her life. When she experienced problems that go-around we were filled with dread.

Five months into her pregnancy with Chris and Joe, the obstetrician worried that Eva wouldn't carry to term, so he put her on complete bedrest until the due date. That meant four months of lying in bed. She was unable to work or do simple things like walk around the house. Her feet swelled badly and we had to help her just to stand up. She hardly slept. The physical hardship was immense, but even more difficult was the mental anguish. We didn't know if the twins would survive, and we were especially frightened because of our past experiences.

The day of the birth arrived and soon we held our newborn sons, with big sister, Nicole, looking on. We felt we were the happiest family on Earth.

Just as in the illustration Jesus gave, once the twins were born, Eva forgot the months of pain and forced rest.

✒

Jesus promises a joy that can't be taken away. In that image of a pregnant woman in labor, he points out that after the delivery of her baby, she forgets her pain. The promise to us is that the joy of

Heaven will be so wonderful that we'll forget the pain, sorrow, and adversity along the way.

The Lord gives us one example to show the change between a woman's pain and her joy. We have daily examples of sadness when a loved one is afflicted with Alzheimer's or any form of dementia or a godly friend slowly dies of amyotrophic lateral sclerosis (Lou Gehrig's disease). Many times at funerals I've heard ministers or friends speak of the release of pain, freedom from a devastating disease. And they go on to talk about the reunion.

I think of many of what we sometimes call the revival hymns— those still-loved songs. They tell of hardships, disappointments, and difficulties. No matter how many stanzas, the last one would usually center on Heaven. It wasn't enough to trust Jesus on Earth and to work for his kingdom. That was all preparation for the great reunion in Heaven.

Here are a few:

- "When clothed in His brightness, transported I rise / To meet him in the clouds of the sky, / His perfect salvation, His wonderful love, / I'll shout with the millions on high."[5]
- "Man may trouble and distress me, 'twill but drive to Thy breast; / Life with trials hard may press me, Heav'n will being me sweeter rest."[6]

---

5 From "He Hideth My Soul" by Frances J. Crosby; music by William J. Kirkpatrick, 1890.

6 From "Jesus, I My Cross Have Taken" by Henry F. Lyte; by Mozart, 1833.

- "I shall go there to dwell in that City, I know, / Since Jesus came into my heart; / And I'm happy, so happy, as onward I go, / Since Jesus came into my heart."[7]
- "Then He'll call me some day to my home far away, / Where his glory forever I'll share."[8]

This is the theme of one of Jesus' major departing instructions: It won't be easy now, but turn your back on the pain of today and face the joy of tomorrow. He doesn't intend us to deny the hardship, but he wants us to see that, as necessary as it is, great joy will follow.

As much as he can, Jesus prepares the disciples to mourn. And they will, but he also wants them to grasp that mourning isn't the end of the journey. Joy will replace their sorrow. They will soon face the moment when it looks as if there were nothing but sadness and darkness in the world. Jesus says that those who hate him will rejoice while the disciples weep. That's the transitory stage.

The day will also come when the situation is reversed. The world's shallow joy turns to sorrow; the disciples' apparent sorrow turns to joy. It was true for them. It is just as true for Christians today.

The joy of the world is based on outside sources: a raise in pay, a pleasant experience, or feelings of love for another person. The Christian joy goes beyond circumstances. We can do what Paul urges: "Rejoice in the Lord always. I will say it again: Rejoice!" (Philippians 4:4 [NIV]).

7 From "Since Jesus Came into My Heart" by Rufus H. McDaniel; music by Charles H. Gabriel, 1914.

8 From "The Old Rugged Cross" by George Bennard, 1913.

We need to remind ourselves that the deep, inner joy we have from God cannot be taken away. We may feel loss. We may weep and feel moments of discouragement, but it never leads us to despair. Even in the midst of our deepest pain, joy is present and ready to bubble up.

The apostles will learn that lesson quickly. From the day of Pentecost, Christians experience immense joy and praise, despite the hardships and the persecutions. For example, after God healed the lame man by using Peter on the day of Pentecost, the Sanhedrin (the Jewish legislature) called the apostles in, questioned them, and "commanded them not to speak or teach at all in the name of Jesus" (Acts 4:18 [NIV]).

And how did the apostles respond? "But Peter and John replied, 'Judge for yourselves whether it is right in God's sight to obey you rather than God. For we cannot help speaking about what we have seen and heard'" (Acts 4:19–20 [NIV]).

The account ends with the rulers threatening them, but the threats have no effect on the disciples. They are spiritually empowered and they aren't afraid of the threats. Why should they be? They knew the source of their strength; they knew the deep joy of serving Jesus Christ.

The best example of Christian joy in action I can think of occurs in Acts 16. We read that Paul and Silas were brought before the magistrates, "and the magistrates ordered them to be stripped and beaten. After they had been severely flogged, they were thrown into prison" (Acts 16:22b–23a [NIV]).

Here's how their response differed from that of the other prisoners: Instead of crying out in pain and groaning—and being severely flogged must have been extremely painful—we read,

PREPARE FOR THE JOY AHEAD

"About midnight Paul and Silas were praying and singing hymns to God, and the other prisoners were listening to them" (verse 25).

During difficult periods, it may seem as if sorrow is all-powerful and it may be—temporarily. We may need to remind ourselves that God is sovereign and everything is ultimately under his control. He knows our hardships, sorrows, sadness, and mourning—and he cares.

But that's not all: Jesus promised the Holy Spirit's presence. We may not always be aware of the Spirit, but he guides us and encourages us (*see* John 16:17–24).

One of the greatest promises to us in our times of pain and agony reads likes this: "'I will never fail you. I will never abandon you.' So we can say with confidence, 'The Lord is my helper, so I will have no fear. What can mere people do to me?'" (Hebrews 13:5b–6 [NLT]).

True Christian joy is in the presence of Jesus Christ. When we focus on him, the pain that went before is forgotten just like the illustration Jesus gave.

Jesus promises that "In that day you will no longer ask me anything" (John 16:23 [NIV]). They won't need to ask because they will see the risen Christ and receive the gift of lasting joy. They will also have a fuller understanding of what life through faith in Jesus means. Guided by the Spirit, they won't have to ask but they'll know how to live faithful and loyal lives. Jesus goes on to repeat that if they ask in his name, they will receive anything they ask.

Because of my trip to Heaven, I have a fuller grasp of what Jesus meant. I experienced such utter joy and inner peace that nothing can destroy it. No matter what disasters hit, no matter how tired or pain-filled my body, I can look beyond to that day when I will take up permanent residence in Heaven. Until then, everything here on Earth is transitory.

When I offer my sympathy to people for their loss, it's also a word to me. I want to return to Heaven. I'm ready and eager. When God is ready for me, I'll joyfully go back. I know—through personal experience—what lies ahead. Nothing, absolutely nothing can destroy that joy and anticipation. You can be as eager as I am.

Departing Instructions

1. Take it as a fact of life that you will face hardships.
2. Remind yourself that those hardships and problems are temporary but your relationship with Jesus Christ is permanent.
3. Focus your attention on this: Jesus promises joy—permanent joy—that the world and circumstances can't take away.
4. Ask God to give you the strength to overcome every temptation and to win over every trial as you wait for your liftoff to Heaven.

24

Remain Teachable

[Jesus said] "I have spoken of these matters in figures of speech, but soon I will stop speaking figuratively and will tell you plainly all about the Father. Then you will ask in my name. I'm not saying I will ask the Father on your behalf, for the Father himself loves you dearly because you love me and believe that I came from God. Yes, I came from the Father into the world, and now I will leave the world and return to the Father." Then his disciples said, "At last you are speaking plainly and not figuratively. Now we understand that you know everything, and there's no need to question you. From this we believe that you came from God."

JOHN 16:25–30 (NLT)

KSLA-TV, Channel 12, is the CBS television network affiliate in Shreveport, Louisiana. After my graduation from Louisiana State University (LSU) in 1973, I held a degree in broadcasting and was hired to work at Channel 12. During a period of eleven years I rose in responsibility from sales-service director to national sales manager.

One day while I chatted with John Hitt, who was then the chief engineer of the TV station, he remarked that they were about to replace the Norelco studio cameras with newer models. Mr. Hitt asked if I knew of any college or university that might benefit from receiving those old cameras as donations.

Immediately my mind flashed back to my student days using the TV studios at LSU where the equipment was functional but antiquated. At LSU we had many black-and-white cameras that, by contemporary standards, were dinosaurs.

After our conversation, I phoned Dr. John Pennybacker, who had been one of my favorite professors, and discussed the possibility of a donation with him. He was excited and said that the university would be delighted to have the cameras. We made a date for delivery and Dr. Pennybacker asked if I would escort the shipment personally. I was delighted to oblige him.

I arrived on the LSU campus with the equipment and was immediately welcomed by Dr. Pennybacker. After offering his sincere thanks he said, "We're going to lunch together. I'm taking you to the faculty club."

When I was a student I had passed the club on campus daily. For us students, the faculty club was almost like the holy of holies. We could only dream of what went on inside that building. While we dined on food of questionable desirability in the cafeterias, we sometimes speculated that the faculty ate gourmet meals in their own club. Now I was about to find out.

We walked across the beautiful campus of LSU, which is covered with stately elms and broad magnolias. Dr. Pennybacker and I entered the club, where we checked and stowed our coats and briefcases. A waiter escorted us to a large table. I had expected a quiet table for two, but he took me to one with seven other professors. Most were involved in some way either with journalism or broadcasting.

With obvious pride in his voice, Dr. Pennybacker introduced

me to each professor. Feeling utterly overwhelmed at this point, I seated myself and, to my surprise, they directed a barrage of questions to me about the state of the media in the United States. Those educators couldn't seem to get enough information from someone who actually worked "in the trenches."

It was such a spirited luncheon. Several times I looked up to see students in dinner jackets and bow ties as they poured tea or served plates of Creole food.

Finally, I mentioned about how happy my TV station was to be able to make a donation to LSU and how honored I was to be back home.

I turned to Dr. Pennybacker and said, "Thanks for the good work you do here, Dr. Pennybacker."

He placed his hand on my shoulder and said, "You're welcome, Don, and just call me Jack."

From then on, I did. Our relationship had changed. We were no longer student and professor. We were colleagues.

When I was in college and seminary, all of us called our professors by the title of doctor or professor. I wouldn't have considered addressing any of them by their first names. It just wasn't done. Aside from it being common practice, I held them in high respect and a few of them in awe. They were the experts—the professors—and we were the learners—the students.

The day comes, however, when students graduate. Once they graduate, the relationship changes. It's not that students no longer respect the professors, but the dynamics of the relationship change. No longer is there a clear demarcation of one being inferior to the other; they have become peers. It may not be whether they use a first name or no longer defer to the person as professor, but the relationship becomes different. And both of them know it.

This helps me understand the change between Jesus and the disciples. He led them forward and took them from being servants (or slaves) and said that they had become his friends—not a term he would have used lightly. He takes them even further. Besides being friends, they are collegial in the sense that they can now speak on the same level.

After that he makes a promise (and it's a repeat of something he said earlier): He says that when we truly know and serve God, we are able to go to him and ask for anything in Jesus' name and he will give it to us.

Sometimes we don't even need to use words. There were times in the hospital when I was in such pain that I could barely verbalize my feeling or desires. Occasionally, I would wake myself screaming, groaning, and moaning. In those times of excruciating pain, I was reminded that the Bible says God hears our prayers and answers them even when we cannot speak the words. The Spirit intercedes for us "with groans that words cannot express" (Romans 8:26 [NIV]).

It's like mothers and their children. I've been in a room with several mothers and one infant in another room will cry. The mother of that infant will recognize the cry of her child. More than that, just from the tone of the unhappy voice, she'll know exactly what her child needs. As a male, I don't understand how that powerful relationship works, but I know it does.

I also know that God is aware of our groans and cries even when we can't verbalize them.

God hears us, not only our words but what's inside our hearts, and he answers prayer. Jesus reassures the disciples that when they ask things in prayer in his name, the Father will answer them. The Son won't be indifferent to their petition—and he never is—because the Father loves them and is eager to help them. And the Son won't need to urge the Father to answer. The Father loves them; he knows that they have loved Jesus and the Father will be ready to grant their requests, bless their lives, and support them in their lives of obedience and witness to the Son.

The same holds true for us. But I do want to point out a few things. Jesus tells them to ask "in my name" (John 16:26 [NLT]), and so do John 14:13–14 as well as John 15:16. However, it's not a mere formula to tack on "In Jesus' name" to conclude a prayer.

As I've pointed out earlier, to ask in his name carries a strong note of guidance. The point is that when we use Jesus' name, we need to think carefully about what we ask. Without going into heavy theological jargon, it means that we are able to ask with the authority of Jesus—as if Jesus himself were asking. That lays a serious burden on us to ask compassionately and for the things that honor God.

If we pray in Jesus' name in the true biblical manner, God has promised to answer. But it's also more than simply praying the words. We also need to live consistently with the things for which we ask.

Just as Jesus changes the status of the eleven men from disciples to friends, he also changes the manner of petitioning God. As they live the life, God honors their requests and grants what they ask.

As wonderful as that promise is, what really impresses me is that Jesus tells the disciples that their relationship has reached a new level because now he will speak plainly and directly to them.

"Though I have been speaking figuratively, a time is coming when I will no longer use this kind of language but will tell you plainly about my Father" (John 16:25 [NIV]).

The Greek term translated *figuratively* is a word used for Jesus' parables but it means "sayings that aren't easy to understand." Or it can be a statement that the casual listener doesn't grasp because it demands thought before the meaning becomes clear. It's like a riddle—as if Jesus says, "So far I've been giving you clues and hints to push you to think about what I meant. Now I'm ready to speak plainly to you."

Jesus says he has been speaking to them in figurative language and he doesn't mean he deliberately tries to keep them from understanding. He means that to help them at this stage of their spiritual growth he has used such illustrations, just as he did about the woman giving birth. Even with the illustrations, they haven't fully grasped his meaning. But now he will speak plainly and they will fully understand.

How wonderful to hear and comprehend the promises of Jesus. How amazing to hear God speak directly. Sadly, many people—including believers—don't feel that God is speaking to them and working in their lives. But God speaks to us and moves in our lives in proportion to our ability to grasp his words and actions at that moment. As we mature spiritually (and God wants us to mature), we discover a closer walk with the Lord. We find a deeper understanding of God's divine direction.

Scholars, preachers, and teachers have said this more eloquently than I can, but I know God speaks to us today and wants to communicate with us.

For example:

- We read a statement in the Bible, sometimes one that we've read many times, and it suddenly comes alive for us. That's God communicating.

- We pray and listen for God to respond to us. We may not hear an audible voice, but God speaks to our thoughts. That is, we hear an answer inside our minds.
- We talk with a friend, a pastor, perhaps even a therapist or a stranger, and the person (often unknowingly) says something that strikes us as exactly what we need to hear. That's another way God speaks to us.
- We don't want to overlook circumstances. Sometimes God orchestrates events so that the situation becomes so obvious all we need to do is to take one step forward (or perhaps a few steps backward). "The steps of a good man are ordered by the LORD, And He delights in his way" (Psalm 37:23 [NKJV]).

As we think carefully about the things we ask God to do for us, sometimes it's good to pause and ask ourselves, "Is my walk with God any closer or my fellowship any deeper now than it was a year ago? Five years ago? When I first became a believer?"

To give ourselves an objective answer probably isn't possible. But inwardly, *we know*. If we've grown warmer in our relationship, we know; we also know if we've grown more distant.

We may not be able to measure our own spiritual progress accurately, but we certainly have a sense of whether we've moved forward or we're stuck where we were ten years earlier.

In John 16:28, Jesus points toward his preexistence by saying, "I came from the Father and entered the world; now I am leaving the world and going back to the Father" (NIV).

Apparently the disciples get it this time. He isn't saying

something new; he says it differently. They respond with, "Now you are speaking clearly and without figures of speech. Now we can see that you know all things. . . . This makes us believe that you came from God" (verses 29–30).

As they speak those words—confident that they are strong and ready for what lies ahead—Jesus speaks again. He commends them and says, "You believe at last!" (verse 31).

But he goes on to say the time will come—and has already arrived—when they will be scattered to their own homes. He means they'll run away—and "You will leave me all alone. Yet I am not alone, for my Father is with me" (verse 32).

Jesus knows that when he is arrested, their faith and courage will be tested. He warns them that they'll run away in fear and confusion. He predicts their future failure. He doesn't do that to unnerve them or to take away their steadfastness or inner peace. In fact, it's exactly the opposite. Because he knows what will happen, he tells them and they will understand that he has foreseen their failures, that he loves them in spite of their actions and lack of steadfastness, and that he will remain faithful to them.

Just as I had to try to successfully endure the incredible pain I experienced after the accident so that I could help others to endure theirs, perhaps the disciples have to fail so they can understand the meaning of Jesus' words to be used mightily by God in the coming days. When he speaks of the changed relationship, he also explains what will happen.

Even though they say they understand, Jesus knows differently. It's the same today. We yearn for a closer relationship, and it is available. But along the way, sometimes we stumble. We don't always live up to the truth that we hold dear. In those times when we falter, we also realize something: We know the truth, but we haven't fully experienced it.

A minister once said it this way, "We know beyond our grasp." He meant that we know many truths but until we fully experience them, they're not ours. My trip to Heaven made me very much aware of that. My ordeal on Earth prepared me to meet needs in a special way—special in the sense that I would never have been able to help them before the accident.

Each of this life's experiences is a potentially teachable moment. Our task is to listen closely and obey God's voice.

Departing Instructions

1. Make yourself teachable. Be like young Samuel who cried out, "Speak, for your servant is listening" (1 Samuel 3:10b [NIV]).
2. Commit yourself to become teachable so that your knowledge of the truth and your grasp of the truth are equal.
3. Don't fail. But if you do fail, remember that God is eager to forgive you.

25

Know the True God

[Jesus] looked toward Heaven and prayed: "Father, the time has come. Glorify your Son, that your Son may glorify you. For you granted him authority over all people that he might give eternal life to all those you have given him. Now this is eternal life: that they may know you, the only true God, and Jesus Christ, whom you have sent. I have brought you glory on Earth by completing the work you gave me to do. And now, Father, glorify me in your presence with the glory I had with you before the world began."

JOHN 17:1–5 (NIV)

The most powerful part of Jesus' departing instructions takes place in John chapter 17. The entire chapter is a prayer that we can break into three parts. First, Jesus prays for himself (verses 1–5). He follows that with petitions for his disciples (verses 6–19). The third portion of his prayer is for those who will believe through the witness of him given by the disciples (verses 20–26).

This is the climax of his teaching. These will be his final words before he is betrayed and arrested. In the few verses in which he prays for himself, we glimpse the heart of our Savior. It's like listening in on a personal, private prayer by Jesus, but it's written for us to listen in.

What makes this prayer different is that the speaker isn't a needy soul, petitioning the all-powerful One, but is the perfect, sinless Jesus. He knows that in his relationship with the Father he is always heard.

Some refer to this as Jesus' high-priestly prayer because of its direct-address form. He doesn't refer to the Spirit—it's a direct Son-to-Father prayer. The account starts out, "He looked toward Heaven and prayed" (John 17:1 [NIV]). From there on we have the words of prayer recorded. Jesus recognizes God's transcendence and greatness and calls him Father.

Once more Jesus says that the time of his death has come. He accepts his death as the Father's will, but he prays that in death and resurrection the Father will glorify the Son, giving him victory over Satan and the world and exalting him to close fellowship with the Father. In that redeeming death and triumphant resurrection, the Son will bring honor and praise to the Father by fulfilling the divine will.

When Jesus became a total human being, he received power over humanity: "For you granted him authority over all people that he might give eternal life to all those you have given him" (verse 2). He follows that with an often-quoted statement, "Now this is eternal life: that they may know you, the only true God, and Jesus Christ, whom you have sent" (verse 3).

What is eternal life? John's Gospel uses the phrase repeatedly, but hasn't defined it until this point. Jesus gives the one definition: Eternal life is to know the Father as the one and only true God and to know Jesus Christ as the Son whom the Father sent to carry out the divine purpose.

We tend to think of eternal life as a life that has no ending.

That's certainly true, but for Jesus, the life without ending is ours when we know God. One way to think of it is that the moment we belong to God, he endows us with life without end.

To "know" God isn't merely to know about him. It isn't just to acknowledge him. To know the Father and the Son is to be bound to God in a close and blessed fellowship in which we continuously receive the gift of life as well as the power to live as God wants us to live.

From time to time I get disparaging e-mails from folks who say my books and theology are mean-spirited and exclusionary. They say, in so many words, that they believe living a good life, having a belief in a moral system, or following some kind of a supreme being should be good enough to earn them a ticket to Heaven. "Anyone who claims that only Jesus saves and provides access to Heaven is inconsiderate, even hateful," was the way one e-mail read.

I'm sorry if they read me that way. I have strong beliefs and I want to speak them with as much love and compassion as I can. People don't have to agree with me or follow what I say. But I want to go back to the words of Jesus himself, which I've quoted earlier in this book. Jesus said, "I am the way and the truth and the life. No one comes to the Father except through me" (John 14:6 [NIV]). Because I serve a loving God I can also state that he absolutely doesn't want anyone to miss Heaven.

The Old Testament used the word *know* as a way to speak of sexual knowledge (*see* Genesis 4:1 [KJV]). The idea is that one man and one woman joined in marriage become one in the sight of God. But *to know* God is a deeper intimacy. It is the most intimate human relationship possible. The incredible prospect of actually knowing the Creator of the universe is almost beyond comprehension. But God desires to know us and to be known or experienced by us.

Since God's creation of humanity it has been his desire to have close fellowship with us. That desire has seemed to guide his dealing with us in spite of our continual rebellion against him. Christ represents God the Father's supreme effort to reconcile us to himself. At this very moment he is still reaching out to you and to me.

✎

Eternal life is to know God through Jesus Christ—to experience him—and to live in grateful faith and loyal obedience. True believers find great joy during this earthly life and in the coming age. Because I've experienced both, I can assure everyone that the greatest joys on Earth—as real and as wonderful as they are—are nothing in comparison to the perfection of joy in Heaven.

I can testify to this in spite of the fact that I have felt immense happiness since I was prayed back: the college graduations of all my children; the marriages of my children; the birth of my granddaughter, Carlee; wonderful additional years of marriage to Eva; meeting thousands of souls with whom I will spend eternity.

But before we reach our permanent home in Heaven, we must die.

We have nothing to fear from death. I'm not in the least bit suicidal and I am in no great hurry to leave this Earth. But truly, I have absolutely no fear of death or dying because I'm positive about what will happen to me after this existence on Earth. I have nothing to fear from the last judgment mentioned in the Bible. Why should I? I've already entered into eternal life. I've already begun to experience the blessedness of citizenship in a kingdom that has no end.

During his years on Earth, Jesus faithfully carried out the Father's will. In his great high-priestly prayer, he says, "I have brought you glory on Earth by completing the work you gave me to do" (John 17:4 [NIV]). By doing what the Father sent him to accomplish, he has led others to believe; and in their faith they bring honor and praise to the Father. Jesus exhibited in his earthly life the pattern we should all follow for ours.

The great moment is almost here for Jesus. The Son prays that he may enjoy the same glory he formerly had with the Father before he came to Earth in human form. "And now, Father, glorify me in your presence with the glory I had with you before the world began" (verse 5).

In the verses that follow, Jesus says clearly (in verse 9), at that moment, he's not praying for the world. Instead he is pleading for strength and resilience for those who have followed him. He concentrates on the relationship between the disciples and himself. They have special need of his prayer. They will need divine help to go through the next few days until they experience victory at the empty tomb on Sunday.

Beyond that, he knows they will remain in a hostile world. Jesus' enemies can no longer attack him directly, but they can and will attack him by opposing his disciples. His followers will be left to witness to him in the face of the world's stubborn unbelief. He asks the Father to protect them (verse 11).

Obviously, they will need divine protection. The Father who chose them and gave them to Jesus as his disciples will surely keep them from following the evil life. He will lead them from failure to forgiveness, from defeat to determination.

Jesus also prays for their unity—that they may be one, just as truly one as the Father and the Son are one. The unity was vital for them, and it's as vital for us today. Being one isn't just becoming a church member (although that's a good decision), but it's being actively involved in the lives of others, of caring and showing your compassion for the hurting. It's also receiving encouragement and consolation from others when we're down.

Because Jesus is going to the Father, and will not live in daily, visible companionship with the disciples, they will need special care. He prays this so the disciples will be aware of his special concern for them.

I find great encouragement from these words. Think of it this way: We are as important as those eleven men for whom Jesus prayed. His prayer for them sets the tone for God's dealings with the disciples of the disciples, down through all generations.

"I am praying not only for these disciples but also for all who will ever believe in me through their message" (verse 20 [NLT]). That's our connection with Peter, James, John, and the others.

As we read Jesus' departing instructions to them, the words are for us as well. One day each of us will depart and, if we absorb these words, we're readying ourselves for our personal liftoff.

If we know the true God of Heaven and seek unity with other believers, we're absorbing our personal departing instructions.

Departing Instructions

1. Know Jesus. You will never know him fully in this life, because it's an ongoing task, but you can mature in your relationship with him.
2. Draw closer to Jesus. As you move closer to your day of departure, ask your Heavenly Father to help you know him

in the most intimate way possible. None of us knows our departure time—and for some it comes unexpectedly—but if we're moving forward, we're always ready for the final, departing step.

3. Share Jesus. To know him isn't only to enjoy him, but it is to share our joy and expectations with others who also need him.

26

Know God's Name

[Jesus said] "I have manifested Your name to the men whom You have given Me out of the world."

JOHN 17:6 (NKJV)

It's easy to pass over something significant Jesus means when he prayed, "I have manifested Your name." Most of the modern translations read something like this: "I have revealed you." The more literal Greek is "I have revealed *your name*." For us these two translations may seem similar, but the first disciples likely would have grasped the difference.

As I pointed out earlier, in the Bible a name is more than what people call someone. It refers to the character and the nature of a person.

Here Jesus clearly states that he had made God's name known to those people. Any good Jew would immediately have realized what he meant. A number of verses in the Old Testament have a somewhat similar wording.

- "Those who know your name trust in you" (Psalm 9:10 [TNIV]).

- "Some nations boast of their chariots and horses, but we boast in the name of the Lord our God" (Psalm 20:7 [NLT]).
- "I will declare your name to my people" (Psalm 22:22 [TNIV]).
- "But I will reveal my name to my people, and they will come to know its power" (Isaiah 52:6 [NLT]).

When Jesus prays, "I have manifested (or made known) your name," his words mean that he has enabled his chosen few to grasp the true nature of God. But it's more than that.

There is something powerful in that statement that we tend to overlook as Christians and that is that he made known the *sacred or covenant name of God*. It is not a name that unbelievers and Gentiles used. It was a name reserved only for God's people, and it was also to remind them of his covenant with them and his faithfulness. That name is a word that no one knows how to pronounce because no one has spoken it for several centuries.

After the return from exile in Babylon in about 586 B.C.E., the Jews considered the personal name of God too sacred to be uttered by sinful, human lips. There was a single exception when the high priest spoke the name one time each year. Until the destruction of the Jerusalem Temple in 70 C.E., on the Day of Atonement, the high priest went into the sacred part of the Temple, called the Holy of Holies. While there, he spoke *the* name.

For the past two thousand years, no Orthodox Jew has spoken the sacred name, even though it appears often in the Old Testament. When Jews came across the special name they substituted *Adonai*, the common Hebrew word for "Lord." In English translations, Lord—written with a large capital followed by three smaller capitals—is used for the sacred name. The name was so sacred that ordinary people weren't supposed to know it.

Part of the reason no one has spoken the sacred name is because we're not sure how to say it. Part of the problem of pronunciation is that the Hebrew Bible was written only with consonants to save space on the scrolls. For the sacred name of God, we find four consonants, referred to as the Tetragrammaton. The letters are YHWH. (Y and W are interchangeable and so are V and W.) For many years, scholars assumed the pronunciation was *Jehovah* (JHVH) and many of our older hymns reflect that, such as, "Guide Me, O Thou Great Jehovah." Most scholars today agree that the name should probably be pronounced *Yahweh*.

Although scholars aren't sure how to translate YHWH, we do know the name is based on the verb that means "to be." We get a hint of the meaning of the sacred name in Exodus 3. God appeared to Moses through the burning bush and commanded him to rescue Israel from their suffering. Moses offers excuses for not going and he talks to God.

Here's the conversation:

Moses said, "Suppose I go to the Israelites and say to them, 'The God of your fathers has sent me to you,' and they ask me, 'What is his name?' Then what shall I tell them?" (Exodus 3:13 [NIV]).

Here's God's answer to Moses: "I am who I am" (verse 14).

So perhaps YHWH means "I will be what I will be." I've always said the best meaning I can think of is to say it this way: I am the one who is, who was, and who always will be.

The exact meaning of the sacred name may still be a mystery, but the point I want to make is that Jesus revealed God's character to his band of followers. It's as if he says in his prayer to the Father, "I have told them your name—a name so sacred that people do not speak it." And it is more than knowing the meaning of the name; it's also about a relationship.

By keeping the name YHWH mysterious and sacred it also made the character of God mysterious and beyond human understanding. God was remote. God was "up there" someplace. In so much of the Old Testament God is portrayed as all-powerful, majestic, and totally different from human beings. Several times God is referred to as a father in the Old Testament, but most of the time *father* is used in a more general sense, especially to the nation of Israel and not to individuals.

When Jesus revealed God's name, he brought the Sovereign Ruler of the Universe into a relationship with ordinary people.

One thing the disciples should have picked up—and certainly the early Christian readers of John's Gospel would have grasped: Jesus is stating that he is God. Not just any God, but the God of the Old Testament, the God who revealed himself to Israel.

Several times in the Gospel of John, Jesus says, "I am." John's Gospel records his saying that with these words in verse 6:35: "I am (*ego eimi*) the bread of life." He uses the same two words in other verses in John (for example, 6:41; 8:12; 9:5; 10:7, 9, 11, 14; 11:25; 14:6; 15:1, 5). In each instance, he emphasizes who *he is*. Jesus uses the same words in John 8:58, when he says, "Before Abraham was born, I am! (*ego eimi*)" (NIV). Early Christians would have connected that Greek construction, *ego eimi,* with Exodus 3:14. In that verse, Moses begs God to declare his name. He asks who he should say that God is to the Egyptians and Israelites. God answers, *"ego eimi ho on"* ("I am the one who is").

Jesus' use of *ego eimi* was surely deliberate. He gives himself the same name that Yahweh used in the Old Testament for himself. This name and expression underline Jesus' statements in John's Gospel.

In the New Testament, Jesus brings the tenderness and warmth of God and makes us see the Father who is beside us, who loves us, and embraces us. Jesus reveals what we call the imminent God—the one who is near us. Later, in the Garden of Gethsemane, Jesus will pray, "*Abba*, Father, . . . everything is possible for you" (Mark 14:36 [NIV]). *Abba* is Aramaic, the form of Hebrew spoken in Jesus' day, and it referred to the Father but it was a more familiar term, more like our English *daddy*. It was a word reserved only for the use of family members.

Cec Murphey tells the story about his then-young daughter, Wanda, who heard adults calling him by his first name so she began to do the same thing.

He didn't scold her. Instead, he placed her on his lap and said, "You know, all those people around us have to call me by my first name, but you have a special name. It's a name only you and your brother and sister can call me. It's 'Daddy.'"

He explained it was a special name and no one except his three children had the right to use it. For the next hour she ran around telling her brother, sister, and anyone who would listen, "I can call him Daddy but everyone else has to call him Cec or Cecil."

That's how it is with *Abba*. It's a special name only for the family of God, in the same way the sacred name of Yahweh is also a special, restricted name. To the Jews, Yahweh referred to the all-powerful, invisible king and mighty warrior. To Jesus, he is Daddy.

Both views are orthodox, and most of us not only see God as the great Creator and One who delivers us from our troubles, but we also think of the compassionate, tender God embodied in Jesus Christ.

Paul uses the intimate form, *Abba*, twice in his letters:

1. "For those who are led by the Spirit of God are the children of God. The Spirit you received does not make you slaves, so that you live in fear again; rather, the Spirit you received brought about your adoption to sonship. And by him we cry, '*Abba*, Father'" (Romans 8:14–15 [TNIV]).
2. "Because you are his sons, God sent the Spirit of his Son into our hearts, the Spirit who calls out, '*Abba*, Father.' So you are no longer slaves, but God's children; and since you are his children, he has made you also heirs" (Galatians 4:6–7 [TNIV]).

Jesus taught them the loving and intimate character of God. Now he is not some all-powerful being who wants to punish everyone and should be feared. He is like a loving parent.

As I wrote those words, I thought of a man named Tom whom I met years ago. He was well-educated and tended to look down upon people who weren't as smart as he was. He hadn't been around the church much, but he came to a morning service one day.

The preacher was beloved and had a deep understanding of the Scripture, but he wasn't "book smart" and occasionally made grammatical blunders when he spoke. That preacher's lack of polish would ordinarily have turned Tom off and caused him to walk out, but something held him at church that day. The preacher spoke about God as a loving Father. He started with the parable about the prodigal son and preached about the loving father who never gave up on his wandering, wasteful son.

As Tom listened to that sermon, he was deeply touched. He had never perceived of God as a tender, caring parent. His own father was an abusive alcoholic. Never had he associated words such as love and compassion with the word *father*.

The more the preacher talked about the fatherhood of God, the more deeply the words touched Tom, who later told me, "I became a Christian that day because I wanted to be embraced by a loving, caring Father."

♦

When Jesus said he revealed God's name to his disciples, early Christians would have smiled. Yes, they knew. In the midst of their hardships they could remind themselves that God in Christ was with them. "Because he himself suffered when he was tempted, he is able to help those who are being tempted" (Hebrews 2:18 [NIV]).

Jesus made known the name and character of God, but he lived in such a way that they could see God in him.

We don't know the circumstances, but Jesus asked his followers who people said he was and received various answers.

"Then he asked them, 'But who do you say I am?' Simon Peter answered, 'You are the Messiah [the Christ], the Son of the Living God.' Jesus replied, 'You are blessed, Simon, son of John, because my Father in Heaven has revealed this to you. You did not learn this from any human being'" (Matthew 16:15–17 [NLT]).

How *did* Peter know who he was? God revealed that to an open-minded Peter. But I think there's something important to note here. Peter saw Jesus—the real Jesus. He had already walked with him a long time, possibly as long as three years. He had observed his leader, watched the way he behaved. *Peter knew.*

Peter knew because he followed a man who knew the name of God—a man who lived the character of God.

Is it any different today? Earlier Jesus said that others would know that we are his disciples if we love each other (*see* John 13:34–35). It's no secret or mystery: If we live the words we teach and sing about, others know.

Several times in my life, hurting people have called me in the middle of the night. Sometimes it was because I was their pastor. But just as many times, the person on the phone said, "You're the first one I thought to call. I knew you would understand."

If we know the name of God—that is, if we live as those who yearn for God's loving character to show through us—we know. And so do others.

As our own departing instructions, we need to embrace the name and the character of God. That's the best way others will know that we're among those who are waiting for the final blast off.

Departing Instructions

1. Know God's name and character so well that you behave like his child.
2. Pray that you will honor God's name in all your activities with others.
3. Seek to become more and more like Jesus. "Christ suffered for you, leaving you an example, that you should follow in his steps" (1 Peter 2:21 [NIV]).

✿

27

Honor God in Everything You Do

[Jesus prayed] "As you sent me into the world, I have sent them into the world."

JOHN 17:18 (NIV)

I don't remember his name but I remember his words. He was the administrative assistant to the president of a small Christian Bible college. I sat across from his desk and we talked about serving God. He told me that he had graduated from the college three years earlier and had worked for the president ever since.

He was a dynamic type of person and quite articulate. At one point I said, "I suppose one day you're going into the ministry."

"I am in ministry," he said.

"I mean, full-time Christian ministry." (I was young when I said that.)

"This is full-time, Christian ministry," he replied and wrapped his arms around his typewriter (which was before computers were commonly used in offices). "This is my ministry and my calling."

I must have looked puzzled because then he added, "God sent me to this office. This is where I can most effectively serve him."

He was right, and I admired him for his dedication. That also opened my eyes; he had a broader view of commitment and service than I did. Too often, we imply (even if we don't mean to) that the *real* call for service is to be a pastor, a Christian education leader, or a missionary. But the truth is God calls each of us into service in a variety of ways.

We don't see the emphasis on ministry in the Old Testament; there is no focus on professional prophets and preachers. Instead we see ordinary people, raised up, called, and sent by God. Joseph was a bragging, seventeen-year-old son of a rich man; Gideon was an illegitimate son and from a small clan; David was a shepherd and so was King Saul. The prophet Amos was a fruit farmer. There we see God calling ordinary people to do extraordinary things. It wasn't because of their training or because they had "Reverend" in front of their names.

The emphasis changed with the spreading of the Gospel.

In John 17:18 Jesus said, "As you sent me into the world, I have sent them into the world" (NIV). After his resurrection, he met with the same disciples and said similar words, "As the Father has sent me, I am sending you" (John 20:21 [NIV]).

Jesus is sending the disciples out into the world. He intends that his immediate band of followers will become apostles. The Greek word *apostolos* means "one sent out with a commission," much like an ambassador today.

In fact, we all function like ambassadors. Paul gives us this message when he writes to the Corinthians: "And he has committed to us the message of reconciliation. We are therefore Christ's ambassadors, as though God were making his appeal through us.

We implore you on Christ's behalf: Be reconciled to God" (2 Corinthians 5:19b–20 [NIV]).

Because the New Testament emphasizes the spread of the message of salvation from Jerusalem to the ends of the Earth, the writers emphasize preaching and teaching the Word of God. But nowhere is it meant to say that others have a lower or less acceptable role.

In 1 Corinthians chapters 12 and 14 Paul writes about spiritual gifts and ministries. He lists the various gifts as healing, speaking in unknown languages, interpreting messages, but he does so because that's what he was asked about. He wasn't asked, for instance, about serving in the weaver's guild so he doesn't comment on that. But that doesn't mean being a weaver cannot be an act of service.

Paul does, however, give the principles of conduct that apply to every phase of life. Chapters 12 and 14 refer to the gifts, but at the end of chapter 12 he tells them to desire spiritual gifts and adds, "And now I will show you the most excellent way" (1 Corinthians 12:31b [NIV]). He then moves into chapter 13, and it's what we often call the love chapter. His point is that it's all right to want spiritual abilities—and he even says to desire them—but the best way is to let those gifts flow from an attitude of love for people.

I've gone into a lot of detail on this but I want to make it clear that God chose us and sends us out in special service. That special service is that we should love and obey him no matter what the job or the task. It doesn't matter whether we work for a megacorporation, an accounting firm, or what many refer to as "Christian ministry." God fits us for the tasks to which he has called us. It doesn't matter what we do to earn a living.

When he writes to the Colossians and the Ephesians he mentions other situations. One of them is the relationship between slaves and their owners: "Slaves, obey your earthly masters in everything you do. Try to please them all the time, not just when they are watching you. Serve them sincerely because of your reverent fear of the Lord. Work willingly at whatever you do, as though you were working for the Lord rather than for people" (Colossians 3:22–23 [NLT]).

This tells us that a job doesn't define who we are. It's the way we behave when we do our jobs. Until that great call to Heaven, our task is to be faithful in our jobs, regardless of what they are.

Our job titles aren't as important as how well we do our jobs. Recently, my wife and I ate lunch at the chain called Jason's Deli. A tall, skinny man, perhaps twenty years old, bussed tables. I have never seen anyone move as quickly as he did. We were there for about three-quarters of an hour, and that man never slowed down.

As I watched him, I thought that's the way God wants us to work for the kingdom. We have daily tasks to do and our responsibility is to honor him by our diligence and commitment.

Departing Instructions

1. You have been sent. Regardless of the kind of job you have, be the best at it that you can.
2. Seek direction. Ask God to show you how to be more faithful and to do your task better.
3. Thank God for the gifts you have received so you can fulfill your job—whatever it is.
4. Be joyful in your work. If necessary, remind yourself that you are in your particular field of employment or you're a homemaker because that is what God has called you to do. Do it well.

28

Be One with Others

[Jesus prayed] "I have revealed you to those whom you gave me out of the world. They were yours; you gave them to me and they have obeyed your word. . . . Sanctify them by the truth; your word is truth. . . . My prayer is not for them alone. I pray also for those who will believe in me through their message, that all of them may be one, Father, just as you are in me and I am in you. May they also be in us so that the world may believe that you have sent me."

JOHN 17:6, 17, 20–21 (NIV)

W e might call it the final prayer. It's no accident that the last words of Jesus' parting instructions are a prayer. Remarkably, he makes most of the petitions on behalf of his followers—those whom he now calls his friends.

Jesus doesn't ask only for these eleven men. He also prays for the unity of all his disciples. "My prayer is not for them alone. I pray also for those who will believe in me through their message, that all of them may be one" (John 17:20–21 [NIV]). Those words show Jesus' assumption and confidence that his small band of followers will do their task and that others will believe because of them. The "others" are us, all believers, including us twenty-first-century Christians.

If we look at the entire prayer, Jesus prayed first for himself as he faced the cross. He then pleaded for his disciples and for God's keeping power for them. From there he entreats his Father for those who in distant times and far-off lands may also enter into the Christian oneness.

At the time of this prayer, he has few followers and faces his own betrayal, beating, and death. Yet his confidence is unshaken as he prays confidently for those who will come to faith. He looked forward to those who will believe in him through the witness of the first disciples.

Jesus knew the eleven men and their weaknesses. He had already foretold their running away in fear. He knew they didn't fully understand him or his departing instructions. Yet he prayed for those same men with complete assurance that they would spread the good news throughout the world. Jesus didn't lose faith in those eleven; he doesn't lose faith in us who are here two thousand years later.

As the witness spread and the church grows, it would be increasingly difficult for followers to be one in spirit and mutual love. So he pleaded for the unity of the entire church in John 17:21, and not for a formal connection but for a vital unity as real and close as that which exists between the Father and the Son—a mutual indwelling in which each lives in the other and the both are one. His plea for oneness among believers is defined in the following words: "[J]ust as you are in me and I am in you. May they also be in us so that the world may believe that you have sent me" (verse 21).

That unity would convince the world that the Father sent Jesus and that something of the divine glory that the Son had already given them would shine in rich splendor (verse 22).

Jesus prayed for the church—the universal church of all times—which means people. It includes us today. The unity for which he cried out wasn't one of organization or a sense of religious unity. He asked for a unity of personal relationships. He embodied that with his Father by his love and unswerving obedience. It was an invisible accord of love—of human caring for each other—based on the relationship of heart with heart.

This accord isn't a human possibility; it comes only by the divine presence working within the church. When they—when we—find such perfect unity, with Christ in them and the Father in Christ, the world will truly know that the Father has sent his Son to be the Savior of the world.

Whether we realize it or not, in Heaven there *is* unanimity and accord. Denominations and theological differences will be wiped away. So why don't we prepare for that eternal harmony now?

I've seen glimpses of this internal unity. For example, in 2006, during an ecumenical service in Gladewater, Texas, several churches came together to sponsor an area-wide rally where I was the featured speaker. Represented were the United Methodists, Assemblies of God, Christian Church, Disciples, Baptists, Presbyterians, and a host of other congregations that combined to organize a service bringing hope to that east Texas hamlet. The evening was a testimony to what the people of God can do when they work together in unity of spirit.

Unity: That is the key.

Perfect unity won't take place here—we all know that—but part of our instructions before departing are to work toward that vital unity—the sense of family unity.

Cec served as a missionary in Kenya and was still there when England granted the country independence. There could have been bitter fighting (as happened forty years later), but former British prisoner Jomo Kenyatta became their leader, and he used one word to rally the people together. The word was *harambee*. It's a Swahili word that means "to come together, pull together, or work together." It signifies unity.

Jesus prays for a vital unity among believers as real and as close as that which exists between the Father and the Son—a mutual indwelling in which each lives in the other and both are one. For us, the unity isn't perfect; it can't be perfect with weak, fallible disciples. But whenever we focus together in a spirit that exemplifies Jesus' irrefutable love, we manifest the unity for which the Lord prayed. At times that unity may be only a handful and at other moments thousands.

It's easy to point to what we don't show the world, but whenever and wherever we unite to express our mutuality, we show our unity. Then—and only then—will the world be able to believe that the Father has sent Jesus and that the Gospel is true.

I sincerely believe that as much as our individual testimonies have meaning, even stronger is the united witness of what we'll do for Jesus Christ.

Here's an example of that unity. Mike Wolff started an organization called the Carpenters Helpers (www.thecarpentershelpers .org) in Littleton, Colorado, in 2005. He wanted to unite Christians to reach out to help the poor and the elderly. Mike chose a retirement mobile home community near his church.

The resident manager was skeptical and asked if the residents would have to listen to a lot of preaching. Mike assured the woman that if people asked why they were there it would be explained to them, but regardless, they came to help. Despite her initial reservations, and after some persuading, she gave permission.

Mike started with five other men from a Bible study group, and today volunteers come from numerous para-church ministries, congregations, and a private Christian school in the area. Their current goal is to install water-saving toilets donated by the Denver Water Board under a pilot program to monitor community water saving. At the time of this writing, they are trying to take out old models and install 255 new units within ninety days. Some of the local residents have even volunteered to work side by side with the ministry to help see to the completion of this sizable project.

Whenever the management sends out letters of compliance or any of the people have problems with their mobile homes and can't afford to fix them or don't know how, Mike and the Carpenters Helpers come.

That's only a small part of what they do, but that's Christian unity in action. When the Carpenters Helpers or other groups reach out to the needy without payment or expectation, that's when we show our unity and our connection to Jesus Christ. And when we show that love for each other we are showing the world the glory of God.

✑

There are two things I want to point out here about discipleship that leads to that vital harmony. First, it is based on the realization that Jesus came from God. That is the Incarnation of Jesus. He left the glory of Heaven to be born and to live as a human being. The early Christians believed—as we do today—that they were ambassadors and that other people heard God's voice and saw God's deeds through their lives perhaps even more than through their message.

Second, true discipleship involves obedience. I've said that several times in this book, and that's an extremely important thing for us to remember. Full and total obedience is the ultimate proof of our faith. True disciples keep God's Word and have accepted the mastery of Jesus. So long as we wish to do what we like, we can't be disciples, because we have to submit.

In his prayer for his disciples, Jesus offers them two things. The first is joy, because they had been chosen and loved.

The second is a word to bring home one significant fact: Believers are different. They are not like the world, because at their best, their values and standards don't flow with the culture around them.

Paul writes to the Philippians:

Dear brothers and sisters, pattern your lives after mine, and learn from those who follow our example. For I have told you often before, and I say it again with tears in my eyes, that there are many whose conduct shows they are really enemies of the cross of Christ. They are headed for destruction. . . . But we are citizens of Heaven, where the Lord Jesus Christ lives. And we are eagerly waiting for him to return as our Savior. He will take our weak mortal bodies and change them into glorious bodies like his own (Philippians 3:17–21a [NLT]).

Jesus promises, "All I have is yours, and all you have is mine. And glory has come to me through them" (John 17:10 [NIV]). The first part is natural and easy to understand. After all, we know that all things belong to God. The second part is astonishing: "All you have is mine." This is one of the great statements of Jesus' oneness with the Father.

Jesus prayed for harmony among his followers. Today we're aware that where there is exclusiveness or divisions, it hurts the cause of Christianity.

When I was called to serve as pastor of Murphy Road Baptist Church in Plano, Texas, the Lord laid it on my heart that the then-rural area would benefit greatly from an area-wide revival. I was encouraged when a well-known evangelist agreed to lead the meeting. I determined to get as many local pastors as I could to cooperate in this community-wide event. Some pastors were cordial but noncommittal. Others remained standoffish. Even though I proposed that the revival be held in a neutral site, it appeared that some churches were distinctly afraid other churches might receive members at their expense. It was one of the most discouraging occurrences of my ministry. I left there four years later never seeing my vision come to pass.

On the other hand, I love the attitude of my late friend Claude Huskey. He was the pastor of a small, independent church in Rockford, Illinois. He met another pastor who said he planned to start a church on the same road but about three miles away. "Come and do it. There are enough people for both of us," Claude said. "You do what you can do and I'll do what I can and maybe we'll meet somewhere in the middle of the road."

He didn't see the other's work as competition. They were both after the same things, so why fight each other? That's an example of the kind of unity that honors Jesus Christ.

Part of preparing for liftoff is to see each believer as significant and as important to God as we are. We also see everyone—of any faith—significant and loved by God. When we live in harmony with others, we're living the message that Jesus gave just before his betrayal.

Departing Instructions

1. Serve God with enthusiasm. Make him the center of your life.
2. Seek unity. Unity doesn't mean we must all believe exactly alike. Unity overcomes minor differences and focuses on major agreements.
3. Commit yourself to work for unity among all believers. Remind yourself that Jesus prayed for you and others to become one.
4. Prepare *now* for the unity that comes at the end of this life. If you can pull together with other believers, you are following the departing instructions.

29

Final Preparations for Liftoff

Within the past decade the topic of Heaven has become significant to most people. It wasn't always that way. When Cec and I wrote *90 Minutes in Heaven, Daily Devotions Inspired by 90 Minutes in Heaven,* and *Heaven Is Real,* we had no idea how voraciously people would desire to know about Heaven.

Yet we should have realized that Heaven has always been a topic that people care about. In the early church, they often sang and wrote of the last days on Earth and their journey to their final home.

As I pointed out earlier, many of our beloved hymns end with a stanza about Heaven. Even the best-loved, "Amazing Grace," first published in 1779, commonly has these words printed as the final stanza:

> *When we've been there ten thousand years,*
> *Bright shining as the sun,*
> *We've no less days to sing God's praise*
> *Than when we first begun.*

Composers of such hymns hadn't been to Heaven but they wanted to be ready. It's as if they saw Heaven as the ultimate goal of our existence and didn't see their songs as complete without reminding singers of that fact.

That's one of the reasons for this book: I want to help others be ready to cross that final life bridge and be ready to enter the gates of blessedness. And I want to illuminate and celebrate the words Jesus left for us as he took his leave from Earth. I'm thankful that he didn't leave us unprepared or uninformed.

Because he gave us explicit departing instructions, I urge you to get ready, because each of us must face that final liftoff into Heaven.

Leaving isn't a choice; the destination is.

Earlier I said that I had made a decision when I was in my teens. We can call my experience by any number of names from *being born again, born anew, becoming a new creation in Christ, becoming a follower of Christ, converted,* or *being saved.* The terminology isn't important, but it means to commit ourselves to follow Jesus Christ. That commitment results in a heavenly reservation. That's all it takes—reserving *your space* in God's eternal Heaven.

Jesus promised a room or a place for each of us. As I think about that, I'm reminded that my son Chris and I spend hundreds of nights each year in hotel rooms as I travel and speak. We've jokingly talked about writing a book on the wide variety of accommodations we have experienced. But one thing is consistent. When we arrive, we approach the front desk, give our names and tell them we have reservations. They promptly check their records, acknowledge that they have been expecting us, and give us our room keys. Our names are on their books and our rooms are waiting.

As I've previously pointed out, Heaven is a prepared place for prepared people. No one wanders into Heaven accidentally. None of us gets inside unless our names are already written in the Book of Life.

Regardless of the many jokes we hear about arguing with St. Peter to convince him to let us through the gate into Heaven, we won't get inside unless our names already appear in the Book of Life.

The good news is that Jesus offers the invitation to everyone. It's simply a matter of admitting our need for help—our need for divine help. When we acknowledge that we can't save ourselves (and most of us can hardly even improve ourselves), that's when we're ready to make our reservation.

And the message isn't just about our eternal destiny. The message is also that we can enjoy a full, rich life *right now.* Our life now can be significant, joy filled, and purpose driven. Because we know the ultimate end, we can live more successfully in the interim. No matter what troubles strike or how difficult our situations, if we're believers, God helps us in our daily struggles. He gives us the assurance that our eternal future is settled.

What kind of life are we living today?

In the national cemetery in Vicksburg, Mississippi, the tombstone of my great-great-great-grandfather Israel Piper stands as a silent sentinel to an all-too-brief life. He and hundreds of others gave their lives at that pivotal Civil War battle. Like the thousands of grave markers at Vicksburg, the information chiseled on the stone is spare, but revealing: It contains the name, rank, state he represented, and finally his dates of birth and death. Often overlooked is a symbol—not even a word, but only a mark of punctuation. It's a dash.

The humble dash that separates the date of birth from the date of death constitutes the only remaining record of the life my grandfather lived. That dash signifies all he was and all he did while he was here on Earth.

What does the dash signify in your life? What is your life between birth and your liftoff?

God wants each of us to enjoy our life, because our destination is clear and the end is wonderful, no matter how many bridges we must cross. God desires that we might have a better life now and an eternal life ahead.

I want to quote two promises Jesus made originally to his early disciples, but they were intended for all believers throughout history:

- "My purpose is to give them a rich and satisfying life" (John 10:10b [NLT]).
- "I am leaving you with a gift—peace of mind and heart. And the peace I give is a gift the world cannot give. So don't be troubled or afraid" (John 14:27 [NLT]).

If Heaven is your heart's desire, consider these important departing instructions:

First, the Bible says that no one is good enough and that every one of us fails. That's why we call ourselves sinners. The word *sin* is from a Greek archery term, *hamartia,* which means "to miss the mark"—to miss hitting the center of the target. In the third chapter of Romans, the apostle Paul quotes liberally from Psalm 14 to make it clear that no one is worthy or good enough to gain access to God's eternal presence (*see* Romans 3:10–18, and especially verse 23).

Second, once we realize we can't get to Heaven on our own, we turn to the One who makes entrance possible. Jesus said, "Come to me, all you who are weary and burdened, and I will give you rest" (Matthew 11:28 [NIV]).

Third, we need to believe that Jesus told us the truth. We need to be able to say, "I believe." Paul wrote, "the gift of God is eternal life in Christ Jesus our Lord" (Romans 6:23b [NIV]). To the Ephesians he wrote that we are saved or set apart for Heaven through our faith: "[A]nd this not from yourselves, it is the gift of God—not by works, so that no one can boast" (Ephesians 2:8b–9 [NIV]).

It's that simple. I made the decision when I was young and that decision changed my life: At that moment I knew where I was headed.

I didn't live every moment from age sixteen to until I was hit by a truck at age thirty-eight thinking about eternity. I tried to focus on living a life that honored the God I had promised to serve. In fact, I was actually on my way to church to lead a Bible study when the accident occurred. But I lived what most people could call a normal life. It wasn't perfect, but I wanted God to be my focus.

I also want to point out that many people fail—even good, sincere, and dedicated Christians. That's why the Bible constantly offers forgiveness. God is eager to forgive us when we fail at any point along the way and wants to pick us up and point us in the right direction.

Heaven *is* real. I know because I've experienced that reality. Someday I will cross the final bridge and I'll meet those same people again at the gate. And they'll be joined by others whom I have loved and lost for just a little while, others who have passed on since I was there last. They'll usher me into the presence of Jesus Christ. The words I yearn to hear Jesus say, are, "Well done, good and faithful servant."

I want everyone to be ready. I want everyone to cross that final bridge with the assurance of a reserved space in Heaven.

🖋

In this troubled world we need peace. Those who doubt their eternal destination have no peace now and certainly have no peace eternally. Jesus offers peace: "Let not your heart be troubled" (John 14:1 [NKJV]). That's peace. It comes only through Christ.

Ultimately, when this life is over—and it will be over one day—we want a heavenly destination. The Bible uses many words to describe Heaven, and they all represent something tangible, even concrete: a country, a city, a kingdom, a paradise, a house. Heaven is not a myth, it's not a maybe. It's a real place, a more real place than the one you're in right now.

So here is the clear plan for knowing Jesus and joining him in Heaven. Follow Jesus. Go to the place. Receive peace.

🖋

When I sign books, I write, "See you at the gate" above my signature. That's been the focus of my life in the years since my brief trip to Heaven.

If you are searching, may you make the right choice. Whether you die by disease or accident won't be your decision. You can, however, choose to be ready.

If you haven't done so, please make your reservation.

If you do, someday, I hope to meet *you* at the gate.